VISUAL AND OTHER PLEASURES

Theories of Representation and Difference
General Editor, Teresa de Lauretis

Visual and Other Pleasures

Laura Mulvey

Indiana University Press
Bloomington and Indianapolis

Manufactured in Hong Kong

Library of Congress Cataloging-in-Publication Data
Mulvey, Laura.
Visual and other pleasures/by Laura Mulvey.
p.   cm.
Articles originally written between 1971 and 1986.
ISBN 0–253–36226–1.   ISBN 0–253–20494–1 (pbk.)
1. Women in motion pictures.   2. Motion pictures—Political
aspects.   3. Feminism.   I. Title.
PN1995.9.W6M84   1989
791.43'09'093520—dc 19   88–9627

1 2 3 4 5   93 92 91 90 89

Contents

List of Plates

Introduction

The articles and essays published here were not originally intended to last. I often sacrificed well-balanced argument, research and refinements of style to the immediate interests of the formative context of the moment, the demands of polemic, or the economy of an idea or the shape and pattern of a line of thought. Until recently there seemed no point in collecting my articles together; on the contrary, to publish them between two covers seemed to contradict my perception of my writing as essentially and necessarily ephemeral. But, for the following reasons, I changed my mind.

The articles were written between 1971 and 1986, a fifteen-year period that saw the Women's Movement broaden out from a political organisation into a more general framework of feminism. They were written to articulate rather than to originate, to catch something of the interests and ideas that were already around in the air, within the changing context that the Women's Movement and its aftermath provided. Because context and moment were important in their inception, these articles have retained a link with their historical moment and context that, I hope, gives them a documentary quality. The 'documents' are separate and discrete but when placed in sequence, certain themes and strands begin to form patterns or even story lines. They chart the early development of a debate that was generated in the first place by politics, that broadened out into aesthetics and that has finally come to influence some spheres of academic thought. This debate, primarily about women and representation, has been responsive to theoretical trends and developments, but has also inflected them. In this book, the early pieces are, to me, like stepping-stones, spontaneous and tentative, generated purely and simply by the energy of the Women's Movement. By the end of the book, the pieces are written within an acknowledged intellectual milieu, feminist theory, as though the stones had gradually filled out into something more to form, not a mainland perhaps, but at least quite a substantial island.

The book is called *Visual and Other Pleasures* in order to cite my most influential essay, that has seemed, over the last decade, to take on a life of its own. This book provides an opportunity to re-place the essay by publishing it within the historical context provided by the chronology of my other writings. Written in 1973, polemically and without regard for context or nuances of argument, published in 1975, after many references and quotations in the following years, it has acquired a balloon-like, free-floating quality. I hope that publishing it here will not explode it, but bring it back to earth.

There is also a personal narrative running through the book, the story of a long and painful struggle with writing. It was the Women's Movement that made it possible for me to begin to be able to write. In spite of my class, family and education (bourgeois intelligentsia, university education and women writers and intellectuals in my background) and a long-standing addiction to reading, the idea of putting my own words on a page produced enormous resistance that at times almost amounted to phobia. The Women's Movement put expression and language on the political agenda; what to say and how to say it faced one with the question of the politics of authorship. Suddenly a perspective on the world had unfolded that gave women a position to speak from, and things that had to be said not from choice but from political necessity. And the politics of the personal insisted that material was there for anyone to draw on, allotted by history and ideology, by oppression and exploitation, not subject to specialisation, expertise or education. From very early days, the question of control over language and its production was taken on as a political issue. Women's exclusion from the *public* voice and the language of culture and politics was challenged, not by strategies for inclusion in patriarchal discourse, but by an oblique movement into an autonomy that refused given ideas of creativity.

The 'politics of authorship' was particularly important. At that time, the Women's Movement insisted on unsigned, collaborative writing, as a political gesture of principle against the ownership and authority implied by signature; and as a way of setting up conditions which would allow women to feel collective strength and begin to build new means of expression, founded on the personal and informal, but transforming them. There was a sense of collective excitement and charged purpose; a liberation from the reductive 'I' and the heavy burden of self-expression that goes with it. There was also an intuitive pleasure in an aesthetic grounded on heterogeneity and anonymity, even if at that point it amounted to little more than each group producing in turn an issue of our journal. Although only the first piece in this collection was written in these circumstances, it was a moment of transformation for me. I could begin to write, a little, but my difficulty in using the first person persisted for some time. Paradoxically, it was the success of the 'Visual Pleasure' article, and the critical debate that developed in its wake, that forced me to take stock retrospectively of what I had written and diminished my sense of being 'spoken by and through' a historical and political moment. In 'Afterthoughts on Visual Pleasure', published in 1980, it was no longer possible to avoid the first person altogether. But all the articles and essays collected here were written, to a greater or lesser extent, with a sense of enablement through historical circumstances rather than innate, individual ability.

During the 1970s there was a strong reciprocal influence between my writing and the films I directed with Peter Wollen. We started to work on films together in 1974, when we were both abroad, outside our separate political contexts, and both wanted to forge an alliance between the radical tradition of the avant-garde and the feminist politicisation of images and representation. From my point of view, each of the films we made in the 1970s responded to and extended the problems I was trying to pose in my writing. In the films, theory and politics could be juxtaposed with narrative and visual poetics, reaching out beyond the limits of the written word and its precision to something that had not yet found a precise means of verbal articulation. The films could confront questions of film criticism with film itself, debate images with counter-images, intellectual strategies with visual play.

Our first film, *Penthesilea*, made in 1974, has certain links with my article 'Fears, Fantasies and the Male Unconscious (Allen Jones)'. Both the Amazon myth and Allen Jones's collection of pin-ups tell a story of male castration anxiety, how it can be projected on to the female image and produces a fascination with phallic femininity. *Riddles of the Sphinx* was an attempt to break away from the polemical and iconoclastic spirit of 'Visual Pleasure and Narrative Cinema', and struggled to find ways of looking at film and pleasure in the cinema that would challenge an assertion of the male gaze in or through the camera's work. It was also an attempt to take an initial step into positive cinema, to move beyond the negative aesthetics of counter-cinema to find new images and new formal means of representation for women's feelings and experiences. This was, perhaps, a high moment of Utopian optimism, when a new cinema seemed possible. *Amy!* was influenced by 'Afterthoughts on Visual Pleasure', dealing specifically with the narrative spheres allotted to female protagonists, and the fate of a heroine who adopts an active relation to narrative space and resists the intimidating look of the camera in its role as sculptor of passive femininity. By 1980 the atmosphere was changing politically and aesthetically under the pressures that I discuss in *Changes*. During the 1970s, it had seemed necessary to undergo a rite of passage, to travel through the scorched earth of counter-cinema, to come out the other side. The 1980s produced new political and production circumstances, before, in a sense, we were ready for the end of the journey. *Frida Kahlo and Tina Modotti* recorded and documented the Whitechapel exhibition and catalogue, quite simply. *Crystal Gazing* was made in 1981 in reaction to the onset of Thatcherism and prefigures many of the political and aesthetic problems discussed in *Changes*. *The Bad Sister* recapitulates many earlier preoccupations (particularly *Riddles of the Sphinx* and *Amy!*) in the new production context of video and Channel 4.

The iconography of the Sphinx and her riddles draws together a series of motifs that have to do with femininity and curiosity. Curiosity describes a desire to know something secret so strongly that it is experienced like a drive. It is a source of danger and pleasure and knowledge. Its pleasure is derived from the fulfilment of a desire to know, either by seeing with one's own eyes or through the intellectual exercise of puzzle or riddle solving. The detective, investigative, pattern of narrative, that I discuss in Chapter 15, is motivated by the pleasure of curiosity. Like voyeurism, curiosity is active and thus, in Freud's terms, masculine, but it can confuse the binary male/female, active/passive opposition that I associate with visual pleasure in Chapters 3 and 4. In the myths of Eve and Pandora, curiosity lay behind the first woman's desire to penetrate a forbidden secret that precipitated the fall of man. These myths associate female curiosity with an active narrative function. But, iconographically, the female form can connote enigma and the enigma of the feminine under patriarchy.

Feminist critics (I can here cite Teresa de Lauretis's citation of Shoshana Felman in *Alice Doesn't*) have frequently discussed Freud's description of femininity as a riddle and, for Teresa de Lauretis, the feminine enigma is: 'the desire that will generate a narrative, the story of femininity, or how a [female] child with bisexual disposition becomes a little girl and then a woman.'[1] This allocation of enigma in terms of male/female difference confirms the active masculine nature of the narrative drive. The feminine represents a boundary, a space to be traversed, similar to the *limen* inhabited by the Sphinx 'frontier between the desert and the city, threshold to the inner recesses of the cave or maze'. (This argument adds another dimension to my use of the concept of liminality in Chapter 14.) Joseph Rykwert notes this elusive but suggestive cluster of motifs when he associates the Sphinx with the riddling guardian of the city gate: 'whoever it was that wanted to pass the monster had to find his way through a maze, or show his knowledge of a maze like pattern by drawing it. Frequently, the purpose of initiation ceremonies is to provide the postulant with the knowledge of how to cope with such immediate and unfamiliar matters as the mysterious nature of the other sex, and its negative characteristics by a symbolic device.'[2] Once again, transition through a space or through a rite of passage, the sphinx riddles and mazes are associated with the enigma of sexual difference.

For patriarchal mythology, feminine beauty or sexual allure can constitute a further aspect to the enigma. For the Symbolists, film-noir, and (as I argue in Chapter 7) for Godard, female beauty is a mask that conceals deceit and danger. This theme doubles in the Pandora myth with that of her curiosity. Fashioned by the gods to be given to man in exchange for fire, Pandora's beauty concealed 'that which was sheer guile not to be withstood by men'. Her mythology is embellished by her iconographical attribute, the box from which she released trouble into the world. Dora and Erwin Panofsky comment: 'In nearly all European languages the phrases "Pandora's box", "boite de Pandore", "caja de Pandora", "Pandoras ask", "doos van Pandora", "Buchse der Pandora", came to be accepted as idiomatic, denoting any source of multiple disaster . . . and furnishing the titles for many a play or novel centered around an attractive but destructive specimen of femininity.'[3] The Panofskys show that a substitution in the Renaissance caused Pandora's box to shrink from a very large jar or urn in the ancient myth to a small box that she could carry in her hand. Freud would probably have solved this iconographical problem in a similar manner to his interpretation of the jewel box in Dora's dream.[4]

The box, and its motif of inside/outside, echoes the motif of Pandora's exterior beauty/interior duplicity. In women's art, this split is acknowledged but transformed out of its misogynist origins. The exterior mask of constructed beauty represents for, say, Frida Kahlo or for Mary Kelly (in *Corpus*) a defence against the outside world and the male gaze. It conceals interior suffering, either physical suffering associated above all with child-bearing and the disorders of the womb or the suffering of the mind associated with woman's place in the emotional and sexual sphere celebrated by the melodrama. The inside/outside opposition is central to the themes of melodrama that I discuss in Section III. The interior space of the home and the interiority of emotion provide a narrative scenario for a female protagonist with minimal outlets for exterior cathartic action. Female protagonists that are outside the melodrama genre and are central to narrative action and plot development bring back the motif of riddles and curiosity.[5] The narrative conventions of popular culture can adapt to heroines who are spies, investigators, or detectives. In Bette Gordon's movie *Variety*, the heroine enacts the tautology posed by feminine curiosity: she spies on a man who is sexually interested in her, to find, in the last resort that it is her own sexuality, the mystery of feminine sexuality, that is the true subject of her curiosity.

It is tempting to argue that curiosity is the opposite of fetishism and that it is as particularly (but not exclusively) feminine as fetishism is masculine. The fetishist becomes fixated on an object in order to avoid knowledge, he has to abandon the desire to know the true nature of sexual difference in order to avoid castration anxiety. He has to block sexual curiosity or curiosity about female sexuality. The fetish is stable, an object, an artefact. It avoids the restless probing of curiosity to see what lies behind a mystery. I have come to consider that curiosity, as a drive, can offer some partial solution to the problem to the polarised distribution of drives in spectacle. Masculine castration anxiety (discussed in Chapters 2 and 3) inflects scopophilic pleasure towards misogyny. It activates the fetishistic aspects of voyeuristic pleasure, in which the female form has the allure and threat of Pandora.

The image of woman as spectacle and fetish sets in motion another chain of metonymies, linking together various sites in which femininity is produced in advanced capitalist society: woman as consumed and woman as consumer of commodities, women exchanged in image and women transforming themselves into image through commodity consumption. But feminist aesthetic theory became, itself, fascinated by the image and by analysing the image, turning away from the problems of the real, influenced both by the impact of semiotics on contemporary culture and the revulsion against realism that characterised the late 1960s and 1970s. Experience and understanding of the world become more and more filtered through its reflection, as though the curse of The Lady of Shallot had descended on our society. The feminist emphasis on image, discourse and representation (that I will argue was a necessary extension of feminist politics) seems both to have been strategically correct and still necessary today, but also pre-figures the present power of the image, and its tendency to take off into pure self-referentiality and play, losing touch with historical reality. In terms of my own history, I sometimes feel that the excitement, novelty and sheer difficulty of semiotic and psychoanalytic theory overwhelmed other political concerns and commitments. The priority was to establish the psyche's political reality and its manifestation in image and representation. Looking back from the late 1980s, it seems as though deeply important changes were engulfing society while I was looking elsewhere, at the cinema or at the unconscious.

The story of the fate of the body in feminism illustrates both the importance of theory and a tendency for theory to retreat into its own world. The Women's Movement of the early 1970s insisted on the political significance of certain spheres of apparently non-political experience. The key instance of this, which generated campaigns, actions, and then debates and theories, like the spokes leading out from the central point in a wheel, was the woman's body. In the politics of the early Women's Movement, the body was a site of political struggle. Campaigns for women's right to control reproduction and motherhood were accompanied by, for instance, the Miss World demonstration and the 'this ad exploits women' campaigns. And it gradually became clear that the question of the woman's body had a significance that crossed the frontiers of the physical, organised by the discourses of the law and medicine, into the realm of representation. Women's struggle to gain rights over their bodies could not be divorced from questions of image and representation. The mythology of the feminine under patriarchy set up a series of problems in which the woman became a phantasm and a symptom. These problems called out for the vocabulary and the concepts of psychoanalysis. Analysis of the representation of femininity in popular culture had to become an analysis of collective fantasy under patriarchal culture.

Before I became absorbed in the Women's Movement, I had spent almost a decade absorbed in Hollywood cinema. Although this great, previously unquestioned and unanalysed love was put in crisis by the impact on feminism on my thought in the early 1970s, it also had an enormous influence on the development of my critical work and ideas and the debate within film culture with which I became preoccupied over the next fifteen years or so. Watched through eyes that were affected by the changing climate of consciousness, the movies lost their magic. In my case, the old economy of fascination became displaced, rather than dispersed, into a fascination with the mechanics of cinematic pleasure and voyeurism. At the same time, Hollywood provided a mass of source material that broadened out the 'images of woman' question into new terrains, including popular mythology and collective fantasy. This new, politicised economy of fascination needed new concepts and a new vocabulary in order to analyse and understand these shadowy areas. And once the body as site of struggle moved beyond the immediate social and legal issues to include sexuality and its representations, the belief that women's reality could adequately counter male fantasy was not enough. Social and cultural relations had to be analysed in terms that could deal with fantasy as a force and the materiality of desire. Psychoanalytic theory opened up the possibility of understanding the mechanics of popular mythology and its raw materials: images of sexual difference, instincts and their vicissitudes, primal fantasy. Structuralism and semiotics opened up the possibility of understanding the way images work as signs and symptoms, patterns of rhetoric, narrative and narration. A previously invisible world whose images, sensations and inklings had previously evaded one's grasp materialised with the language that could name its objects, like the appearance of invisible ink in front of a flame.

With the help of these theoretical tools, feminist theory took an initial stand. This is reflected in the shift between the Miss World demonstration (which was inspired by the belief that women's reality could be liberated from an alienating masquerade) and my article on the visual language used by Allen Jones as reference and source material. I argued, with the help of psychoanalytic theory, that the sexualised image of woman says little or nothing about women's reality, but is symptomatic of male fantasy and anxiety that are projected on to the female image. In this sense the image of woman that had circulated as a signifier of sexuality could be detached from reality, from referring to actual women, and become attached to a new referent, the male unconscious. The direction of the gaze shifted, satisfyingly, from woman as spectacle to the psyche that had need of such a spectacle. Psychoanalytic theory provided this investigative gaze with the ability to see through the surface of cultural phenomena as though with intellectual X-ray eyes. The images and received ideas of run of the mill sexism were transformed into a series of clues for deciphering a nether world, seething with displaced drives and misrecognised desire.

Work on feminism and psychoanalysis and, for that matter, work on the feminist avant-garde, arguably represent a Utopian dimension in feminist theory and aesthetics. However, the Utopian impulse to create 'something new', specific to the problems of women and out of the experience of oppression, came up against an extreme wariness about building on foundations that were not strictly correct in theoretical terms. This oscillation took over both theory and practice. It was never resolved during the seventies, a time of confidence and optimism that could probably have confronted the need for political fantasy and poetics more directly. To my mind, the problem of the mythology of motherhood has been central to this oscillation and our wariness could be linked to a fear of regression and fear of loss of language that is associated with the pre-Oedipal in psychoanalytic theory. I would also argue that these anxieties were fed by the swing in our theoretical interest towards our newly discovered fascination with mechanisms of signification. The impetus towards thinking 'something new' was replaced by a dependence on the authority of the word. Perhaps also in the case of avant-garde aesthetics, a preoccupation with theory of the production of meaning, important as one strategy among others, can risk collapse into tautology.

Members of a political movement can come to feel as though their struggle is making history, steering the course of the future along the lines of their own political desire. Intellectuals can suffer from the same illusion. There is a sense that transcendent analysis and total understanding lie within reach. The difficulty is to stay in touch with the contingencies of history, which might demand different strategies without compromising principle. Political desire, even as expressed through a progressive movement, needs to be constantly examined and re-examined. For instance, the Women's Movement's demands for women's rights in the labour market and consequent challenge to women's allotted place in the home are absolutely correct. But the demands of feminism also prefigure the changes brought about by the malign chaos of free-market forces and a social structure in decay; women participate more in the labour force, the nuclear family structure is under strain and sex roles become more flexible. This does not imply that feminism should alter its politics; rather, that it should constantly theorise the relation between political aspiration and social change and stay one step, at least, ahead of the game. In the 1970s there was still an illusion of political optimism, a belief that history could still progress towards a better world. Now we see forces of epochal change unleashed by widespread conservatism in the name of market forces, without commitment to an attempt to control or understand history. Perhaps one could say that the contingencies of history have now become all too visible, leaving theorists and intellectuals disorientated. But the forces of history can be affected, inflected deflected, and there is no need for the great post-industrial shake-up to happen precipitously, with the minimum of human or humane control. Theory that has developed around the psyche and representation, under the influence of feminism, should not stand back from the social and economic. As images proliferate like a vast screen papering over the signs of decay, curiosity backed by psychoanalytic theory and semiotics need to be juxtaposed and interwoven with economics and politics.

Parallels are often drawn, nowadays, between the transition from the 1920s to the 1930s and from the 1970s to the 1980s. In the context of the themes of this book, especially the problem of how to profit from the lessons of hindsight without succumbing to the temptation to reject experiment as mistaken, or concern with images as unserious, or the discoveries of psychoanalysis as irrelevant to history, it seems appropriate to cite those difficult transitions. Over the last two decades, radical art movements have looked back to the traditions of, for instance, Brecht, the Surrealists, the Soviet avant-garde, to rediscover and redeploy avant-garde strategies and aesthetic theories that had become lost or buried in the intervening three decades. It also seems appropriate to look back to the lost tradition of Marxist psychoanalysis that failed to survive the traumatic events of Fascism in the 1930s, the war in the 1940s and the cold war in the 1950s. The juxtaposition 'politics and psychoanalysis' must now be added to the juxtapositions 'art and politics' and 'psychoanalysis and representation'. Feminism gave these juxtapositions new relevance in the 1970s and it is still central today.

LAURA MULVEY

Notes

1. Teresa de Lauretis, *Alice Doesn't* (London: Macmillan, 1984).
2. Joseph Rykwert, *The Idea of a Town* (London: Faber & Faber, 1976).
3. Dora and Erwin Panofsky, *Pandora's Box. The Changing Aspects of a Mythical Symbol* (London: Routledge & Kegan Paul, 1956).
4. Sigmund Freud, 'A Case of Hysteria' *The Standard Edition* (London: The Hogarth Press, 1953).
5. Folk tale heroines who control narrative through wit and riddle-solving ability should also be mentioned here. See, for instance, 'The Peasant's Clever Daughter', *The Complete Grimm's Fairy Tales* (London: Routledge & Kegan Paul, 1975).

Acknowledgements

The author and publishers would like to make the following acknowledgements:

'The Spectacle is Vulnerable' is reprinted from *Shrew*, December 1970.

'Fears, Fantasies and the Male Unconscious' (February 1973) and 'Fassbinder and Sirk' (September 1974) are reprinted from *Spare Rib*.

'Notes on Sirk and Melodrama' is reprinted from *Movie*, Winter 1977–8.

'Afterthoughts on "Visual Pleasure and Narrative Cinema" inspired by *Duel in the Sun*' is reprinted from *Framework*, Summer 1981.

'Dialogue with Spectatorship' is reprinted from *Creative Camera*, Summer 1983.

'Magnificent Obsession' is reprinted from the catalogue of the exhibition held at the ARC Gallery, Toronto, and the Optica Gallery, Montreal, 1985.

'Impending Time' is reprinted from the catalogue of the exhibition held at the Riverside Studios, London, and the Kettle's Yard Gallery, Cambridge, 1986.

'Images of Women, Images of Sexuality' is reprinted from Colin MacCabe (ed.), *Godard: Images, Sounds, Politics* (Macmillan, 1980).

'Visual Pleasure and Narrative Cinema' is reprinted from *Screen*, Autumn 1975 with the kind permission of the Society for Education in Film and Television.

'Melodrama Inside and Outside the Home' is reprinted from Colin MacCabe (ed.), *High Theory/Low Culture* with the kind permission of Manchester University Press.

'Film, Feminism and the Avant-Garde' is reprinted from Mary Jacobus (ed.), *Women Writing and Writing about Women* with the kind permission of Croom Helm Ltd Publishers.

'Frida Kahlo and Tina Modotti' is reprinted by the kind permission of the Trustees of the Whitechapel Gallery from the 1983 exhibition catalogue.

'Changes' is reprinted with the kind permission of the editors from *History Workshop Journal*, Spring 1987.

The author and publishers would like to thank Victor Burgin, Barbara Kruger, Karen Knorr, Mark Lewis, Geoff Miles, Olivier Richon and Mitra Tabrizian for permission to reproduce their work.

The author would like to thank Peter Wollen for help of very many practical kinds but especially for his conversation which has contributed to working through many of the ideas in this book and for his collaboration across film theory and film-making; and thanks also to Chad Wollen, particularly for finding the manuscript!   L. M.

Part I

Iconoclasm

1

The Spectacle is Vulnerable: Miss World, 1970

Margarita Jimenez and I wrote this account of the Miss World demonstration in Shrew *(the London Women's Liberation Workshop journal that each group edited in turn). We decided to use our very different styles of writing to give the piece two levels; she wrote a first person account of events, and I wrote an impersonal comment on our action. The piece was, of course, discussed with the whole group, collectively edited and published anonymously.*

* * *

The Miss World competition is not an erotic exhibition; it is a public celebration of the traditional female road to success. The Albert Hall on the evening of 20 November was miles away from the underground world of pornography. The atmosphere was emphatically respectable, enlivened by a contrived attempt at 'glamour'. The conventionality of the girls' lives and the ordinariness of their aspirations – Miss Grenada (Miss World): 'Now I'm looking for the ideal man to marry' – was the keynote of all the pre- and post-competition publicity. Their condition is the condition of all women, born to be defined by their physical attributes, born to give birth, or if born pretty, born lucky; a condition which makes it possible and acceptable, within the bourgeois ethic, for girls to parade, silent and smiling, to be judged on the merits of their figures and faces. (Bob Hope: 'Pretty girls don't have those problems' – that is, the problems that plain girls have in finding a husband or making a successful career. Women's Liberation girls must be plain, because only plain girls would have an interest in attacking the system.)

Demonstrating against Miss World, Women's Liberation struck a blow against this narrow destiny, against the physical confines of the way women are seen and the way they fit into society. Most of all it was a blow against passivity, not only the enforced passivity of the girls on the stage but the passivity that we all felt in ourselves. We were dominated while preparing for the demonstration by terror at what we were about to do. To take violent action, interrupting a carefully ordered spectacle, drawing attention to ourselves, inviting the hostility of thousands of people, was something that we had all previously thought to be personally impossible for us, inhibited both by our conditioning as women, and our acceptance of bourgeois norms of correct behaviour. It was also a revolt against the new safeness of our lives inside WL, the comfort of continual contact with like-minded people. The fact of joining WL shows a level of awareness of women's condition. But it's also possible within the movement to become sheltered by the support and understanding of a group, and/or friends. In the Albert Hall we were back in the previous isolation of the outside world, surrounded by people, men and women, who were there to participate in women's oppression, and who were outraged and bewildered by our challenge to it. The outside world is mystified, and consequently often hostile, but WL cannot, for that reason, fear communication with it. Women must be confident enough to challenge the distortion or indifference of the press, and transcend their own feelings of vulnerability.

The seating arrangements in the Albert Hall were completely different from what we had anticipated. For example, Sally and I found ourselves unexpectedly isolated the other side of the hall from most of the others; we had only managed to fill the two extra seats at the last moment; Laura found herself downstairs instead of upstairs. We had reduced our grandiose plans to the simplest strategy of aiming for the jury and the stage with the comic array of weapons with which we were armed. We got into the hall amazingly easily; we had thought, what with the Young Liberals' propaganda, the bomb scare and strict security, that a group of unescorted girls would never be allowed in. Once seated, Sally and I realised that the hall itself wasn't nearly as vast as our heightened imaginations had led us to believe. Above all we saw how ludicrously accessible the stage was, and that with the lights on throughout the show, the bouncers right behind us, our only possible plan could be to make for the stage. Our feelings ranged from complicity with the audience – a mixture of people backing their own national candidates, to over-dressed couples on a night out and the odd family outing – mixed with an intense feeling that we stood out and that everyone was staring at us. Conspiratorially, we had not acknowledged each other in the Ladies and the bar during the intermission – a silent solidarity. Mostly it was the feeling of being caged in, trapped in an absurd pantomime, surrounded by superficially 'nice' but basically hostile thousands.

In the hall Sally's and my conversation fluctuated wildly between frantically whispered consultations and mutual encouragement, and over-loud comments about the show, the judges, the girls, anything 'ordinary' and unsuspicious. We tried our best to laugh at Bob Hope's jokes, in a pathetic attempt to feel one with the audience at last. But as his jokes fell flat and left the audience cold, we were even isolated in our efforts at normality. Suddenly the signal which we had been waiting for so anxiously came at the perfect moment. It was our robot-like response which surprised us most of all. When the moment came it was easier to act than to consider; in the scuffle with the police, it was anger and determination that prevailed. As I was lifted bodily out of the hall, three Miss Worlds came running up to me, a trio of sequined, perfumed visions, saying 'Are you all right?', 'Let her go.'

When the policeman explained we were from WL and demonstrating against them, I managed to say that we weren't against them, we were for them, but against Mecca and their exploitation. 'Come on "Miss Venezuela"', we're on' and the trio disappeared down the corridor. Then I was dragged off, and taken to a room where, to my relief, I saw that Sally and the two girls who gave the signal had already been detained.

How was it, with so many odds against us, that the demonstration was successful? The spectacle is vulnerable. However intricately planned it is, a handful of people can disrupt it and cause chaos in a seemingly impenetrable organisation. The spectacle isn't prepared for anything other than passive spectators.

Bob Hope made more connections than we had ever expected to put across: his continual emphasis on Vietnam revealed the arrogance of imperialism behind the supposedly reassuring family-of-nations façade. The press, searching for sensation, turned a small demonstration into headline news. Let's leave the last words to Bob Hope: 'They said we were "using" women. I always thought we were using them right. I don't want to change position with them. Why do they want to change position with me? I don't want to have babies. I'm too busy.'

2

Fears, Fantasies and the Male Unconscious *or* 'You Don't Know What is Happening, Do You, Mr Jones?'*

* Written in 1972 and published in 1973 in *Spare Rib*.

To decapitate equals to castrate. The terror of the Medusa is thus a terror of castration that is linked to the sight of something. The hair upon the Medusa's head is frequently represented in works of art in the form of snakes, and these once again are derived from the castration complex. It is a remarkable fact that, however frightening they may be in themselves, they nevertheless serve actually as a mitigation of the horror, for they replace the penis, the absence of which is the cause of the horror. This is a confirmation of the technical rule according to which a multiplication of penis symbols signifies castration.   (Freud, 'The Medusa's Head')

In 1970 Tooth's Gallery in London held a one-man show of sculptures by Allen Jones which gained him the notoriety he now enjoys throughout the Women's Movement. The sculptures formed a series, called 'Women as Furniture', in which life-size effigies of women, slave-like and sexually provocative, double as hat-stands, tables and chairs. The original of *Chair* is now in the Düsseldorf home of a West German tycoon, whose complacent form was recently photographed for a *Sunday Times* article, sitting comfortably on the upturned and upholstered female figure. Not surprisingly, members of Women's Liberation noticed the exhibition and denounced it as supremely exploitative of women's already exploited image. Women used, women subjugated, women on display: Allen Jones did not miss a trick.

Since 1970 Allen Jones's work has developed and proliferated in the same vein. It has won increasing international acclaim, with exhibitions in Italy, Germany, Belgium and the United States, as well as Britain. He is one of the shining properties in the stable of Marlborough Fine Art, the heaviest and most prestige-conscious of the international art traders. He has expanded his interests beyond painting and sculpture proper into stage design, coffee-table books, luxury editions, film and television. The Allen Jones artistic octopus extends its tentacles into every nook and cranny where the image of woman can be inserted and spotlighted.

At first glance Allen Jones seems simply to reproduce the familiar formulas which have been so successfully systematised by the mass media. His women exist in a state of suspended animation, without depth or context, withdrawn from any meaning other than the message imprinted by their clothes, stance and gesture. The interaction between his images and those of the mass media is made quite explicit by the collection of source material which he has published. *Figures*[1] is a scrapbook of cuttings out of magazines, both respectable (*Nova*, *Harper's Bazaar*, *Life*, *Vogue*, *Sunday Times* supplement and so on) and non-respectable (*Exotique*, *Female Mimics*, *Bound*, *Bizarre* and so on). There are also postcards, publicity material, packaging designs and film stills (*Gentlemen Prefer Blondes*, *Barbarella*, *What's New, Pussycat?*). *Projects*,[2] his second book, records, sketches and concepts (some unfinished) for stage, film and TV shows, among them *Oh Calcutta!* and Kubrick's *A Clockwork Orange* and includes more source material as an indication of the way his ideas developed.

By publishing these clippings Allen Jones gives vital clues, not only to the way he sees women, but to the place they occupy in the male unconscious in general. He has chosen images which clearly form a definite pattern, which have their own visual vocabulary and grammar. The popular visuals he produces go beyond an obvious play on the exhibitionism of women and the voyeurism of men. Their imagery is that of a fetishism. Although every single image is a female form, not one shows the actual female genitals. Not one is naked. The female genitals are always concealed, disguised or supplemented in ways which alter the significance of female sexuality. The achievement of Allen Jones is to throw an unusually vivid spotlight on the contradiction between woman's fantasy presence and real absence from the male unconscious world. The language which he speaks is the language of fetishism, which speaks to all of us every day, but whose exact grammar and syntax we are usually only dimly aware of. Fetishistic obsession reveals the meaning behind popular images of women.

It is Allen Jones's mastery of the language of 'basic fetishism' that makes his work so rich and compelling. His use of popular media is important not because he echoes them stylistically (pop art) but because he gets to the heart of the way in which the female image has been requisitioned, to be recreated in the image of man. The fetishist image of women has three aspects, all of which come across clearly in his books and art objects. First: woman plus phallic substitute. Second: woman minus phallus, punished and humiliated, often by woman plus phallus. Third: woman as phallus. Women are displayed for men as figures in an amazing masquerade, which expresses a strange male underworld of fear and desire.

THE LANGUAGE OF CASTRATION ANXIETY

The nearer the female figure is to genital nakedness, the more flamboyant the phallic distraction. The only example of frontal nudity in his work, a sketch for *Oh Calcutta!*, is a history of knickers, well-worn fetishist items, in which the moment of nakedness is further retrieved by the fact that the girls are carrying billiard cues and an enormous phallus is incorporated into the scenery. In the source material, a girl from *Playboy* caresses a dog's head on her lap; another, on the cover of a movie magazine, clutches an enormous boa constrictor as it completely and discreetly entwines her. Otherwise there is an array of well-known phallic extensions to divert the eye: guns, cigarettes, erect nipples, a tail, whips, strategically placed brooches (Marilyn Monroe and Jane Russell in *Gentlemen Prefer Blondes*), a parasol, and so on, and some, more subtle, which depend on the visual effect of shadows or silhouettes.

Women without a phallus have to undergo punishment by torture and fetish objects ranging from tight shoes and corsetry, through rubber goods to leather. Here we can see the *sadistic* aspect of male fetishism, but it still remains fixated on objects with phallic significance. An ambiguous tension is introduced within the symbolism. For instance, a whip can be simultaneously a substitute phallus and an instrument of punishment. Similarly, the high heel on high-heeled shoes, a classic fetishist image, is both a phallic extension and a means of discomfort and constriction. Belts and necklaces, with buckles and pendants, are both phallic symbols and suggest bondage and punishment. The theme of *woman bound* is one of the most consistent in Allen Jones's source material: at its most vestigial, the limbs of pin-up girls are bound with shiny tape, a fashion model is loaded with chains, underwear advertisements, especially for corsets, proliferate, as do rubber garments from fetishistic magazines. Waists are constricted by tight belts, necks by tight bands, feet by the ubiquitous high-heeled shoes. For the television show illustrated in *Projects* Allen Jones exploits a kind of evolved garter of black shiny material round the girls' thighs, which doubles, openly in one case, as a fetter. The most effective fetish both constricts and uplifts, binds and raises, particularly high-heeled shoes, corsets or bras and, as a trimming, high neck bands holding the head erect.

In *Projects* the theme of punishment can be seen in the abandoned plan for the milkbar in the film of *A Clockwork Orange* (infinitely more subtle in its detailed understanding of fetishism than the kitsch design

Kubrick finally used for the movie). The waitress is dressed from neck to fingertip to toe in a rubber garment with an apron, leaving only her buttocks bare, ready for discipline, while she balances a tray to imply service. The same theme can be traced in his women-as-furniture sculptures. In *Figures*, the background and evolution of the sculptures is made clear. Gesture, bodily position and clothing are all of equal importance. *Hat-Stand* is based on the crucial publicity still from *Barbarella*, which unites boots, binding, leather and phallic *cache-sexe* in the image of a girl captive who hangs ready for torture, her hands turned up in a gesture which finally becomes the hat-peg. A similar design for an hors-d'oeuvre stand derives from a Vargas drawing of a waitress who sums up the spirit of service and depersonalisation.

Another aspect of the theme of punishment is that the castrated woman should suffer spanking and humiliation at the hands of the man–woman, the great male hope. Characterised in Eneg's drawings for *Bound* (reproduced in *Figures*) by tight belt, tight trousers, mask and constricted neck (while a female woman carries a soon-abandoned handbag), the man–woman emerges with full force of vengeance in *Projects* as Miss Beezley in *Homage to St Dominic's* ('to be played by a 7-foot woman – *or a man would do*. With 6-inch platform heels "she" would be 18 inches taller than the school "girls"'). And again in *The Playroom* (another abandoned stage project) the transvestite owner, 'an elderly "woman"' chases the children. A series of paintings shows sexually ambiguous figures in which a man walks into female clothing to become a woman or male and female legs are locked as one.

Finally, in *Männer Wir Kommen*, a show for West German television, which is illustrated in *Projects* by stills, notes and sketches, Allen Jones adds yet another dimension to his use of fetishistic vocabulary. The close-ups and superimpositions possible on television give him the chance to exploit ambiguities of changed scale and proportion. The spectator is stripped of normal perceptual defences (perspective, normal size relationships) and exposed to illusion and fantasy on the screen. As sections of the female body are isolated from the whole and shown in close-up, or as the whole body shrinks in size and is superimposed on a blown-up section, Allen Jones develops even further the symbolic references of woman to man and subjects her form to further masculinisation.

His previous work preserved the normal scale of the female body physically, although it distorted it symbolically. *Männer Wir Kommen* contains some imagery of this kind: *Homage to Harley* uses the motorcycle and the nozzle in their classic role as phallic extensions, with the women in natural proportion to them (women with boots and bound necks and black bands around their thighs). But by far the most striking image is that of the entire figure of one girl, shrunk in scale though symbolically erect, superimposed as a phallic substitute on the tight black shiny shorts of another. A series of freeze-frames from the show, female manikins strategically poised, makes Allen Jones's point blindingly clear.

More close-ups in the television sketch carry the female body further into phallic suggestion. Girls like human pillars supporting a boxing ring have bared breasts divided by shiny pink material fastened to their necks. A single frame, from breast to neck only, makes the breasts look like testicles with the pink material functioning as a penis. Female bodies and fragments of bodies are redeployed to produce fantasy male anatomies. A similar emphasis on breasts divided by a vertical motif can be seen in the source material: the torture harness in the *Barbarella* still, Verushka's single-strap bikini in a fashion photograph. There is a strong overlap between the imagery of bondage and the imagery of woman as phallus built into fetishism. The body is unified to a maximum extent into a single, rigid whole, with an emphasis on texture, stiffness caused by tight clothing and binding, and a general restriction of free movement.

In *Figures* there is a consistent theme of women as automata, with jerking, involuntary, semaphore-like movements, suggestive of erection. These automata often have rhythmic movements (Ursula Andress dancing in a series of stills like an animated doll, the Rockettes, Aquamaid water-skiers in Florida), uniforms in which the conception of duty and service is combined with strictness and rigidity (for instance, a cutting from the *Daily Express* in which 'Six Model Girls Step Smartly Forward for Escort Duty') and, most important of all, the stiffness induced by wearing tight clothes which constitute a second slithery skin (rubber garments transforming the body into a solid mass from fingertip to toe, one-piece corsets, synthetic garments ranging from perspex to nylon). An identification develops between the phallus and woman herself. She must be seen in her full phallic glory.

THE FETISHIST'S COLLECTION OF SIGNS

To understand the paradoxes of fetishism, it is essential to go back to Freud. Fetishism, Freud first pointed out, involves displacing the sight of woman's imaginary castration onto a variety of reassuring but often surprising objects – shoes, corsets, rubber gloves, belts, knickers and so on – which serve as *signs* for the lost penis but have no direct connection with it. For the fetishist, the sign itself becomes the source of fantasy (whether actual fetish objects or else pictures or descriptions of them) and in every case the sign is the sign of the phallus. It is man's narcissistic fear of losing his own phallus, his most precious possession, which causes shock at the sight of the female genitals and the subsequent fetishistic attempt to disguise or divert attention from them.

A world which revolves on a phallic axis constructs its fears and fantasies in its own phallic image. In the drama of the male castration complex, as Freud discovered, women are no more than puppets; their significance lies first and foremost in their lack of a penis and their star turn is to symbolise the castration which men fear. Women may seem to be the subjects of an endless parade of pornographic fantasies, jokes, day-dreams and so on, but fundamentally most male fantasy is a closed-loop dialogue with itself, as Freud conveys so well in the quotation about the Medusa's head. Far from being a woman, even a monstrous woman, the Medusa is the sign of a male castration anxiety. Freud's analysis of the male unconscious is crucial for any understanding of the myriad ways in which the female form has been used as a mould into which meanings have been poured by a male-dominated culture.

Man and his phallus are the real subject of Allen Jones's paintings and sculptures, even though they deal exclusively with images of women on display. From his scrapbooks we see how the mass media provide material for a 'harem cult' (as Wilhelm Stekel describes the fetishist's penchant for collections and scrapbooks in his classic psychoanalytic study) in which the spectre of the castrated female, using a phallic substitute to conceal or distract attention from her wound, haunts the male unconscious. The presence of the female form by no means ensures that the message of pictures or photographs or posters is about women. We could say that the image of woman comes to be used as a sign, which does not necessarily signify the meaning 'woman' any more than does the Medusa's head. The harem cult which dominates our culture springs from the male unconscious and woman becomes its narcissistic projection.

Freud saw the fetish object itself as phallic replacement so that a shoe, for instance, could become the object on which the scandalised denial of female castration was fixated. But, on a more obvious level, we could say with Freud in 'The Medusa's Head' that a *proliferation* of phallic symbols must symbolise castration. This is the meaning of the parade of phallic insignia borne by Allen Jones's harem, ranging from precisely poised thighs, suggestive of flesh and erection, through to enormous robots and turrets. Castration itself is only rarely alluded to in even indirect terms. In one clipping an oriental girl brandishes a large pair of scissors, about to cut the hair of a man holding a large cigar. In another, a chocolate biscuit is described in three consecutive pictures: *c'est comme un doigt* (erect female finger), *avec du chocolat autour* (ditto plus chocolate), *ça disparaît très vite* (empty frame), then larger frame and triumphal return, *c'est un biscuit: Finger de Cadbury* (erect biscuit held by fingers).

There is one exception to this: the increasingly insistent theme of women balancing. Female figures hang suspended, on the point of coming down (the phallic reference is obvious). Anything balanced upright – a woman walking a tightrope or balancing a tray or poised on the balls of her feet – implies a possible catastrophe that may befall. The sculptures of women as furniture, especially the hat-stand, freeze the body in time as the erect pose seems to capture a moment, and also they are suspended, cut off from any context, to hang in space. In addition, the formal structure of some of Jones's earlier paintings – three-dimensional flights of steps leading steeply up to two-dimensional paintings of women's legs poised on high heels – describe an ascension: erect posture and suspension and balance are fused into one illusionistic image.

In his most recent paintings, exhibited this summer at the Marlborough Galleries, Allen Jones develops the theme of balance much further. A number of the paintings are of women circus performers, objects of display and of balance. Here the equation 'woman = phallus' is taken a step further, almost as if to illustrate Freud's dictum that 'the remarkable phenomenon of erection which constantly occupies the human phantasy, cannot fail to be impressive as an apparent suspension of the laws of gravity (of the winged phalli of the ancients)'. In *Bare Me*, for example, the phallic woman, rigid and pointing upwards, holding her breasts erect with her hands, is standing in high heels on a tray-like board balanced on two spheres. She is on the way up, not down. Loss of balance is possible, but is not immediate.

But in other paintings this confidence is undercut. The defiance of gravity is more flamboyant than convincing. The same devices – high heels, walking on spheres – which compel an upright, erect posture can also point to its precariousness. The painting *Whip* is derived from a brilliant Eneg drawing of two women, castrator and castrated: a woman lassoed by a whipcord is slipping off a three-legged stool. In the painting, we can see only the toppling stool, but there can be no doubt from comparison with the Eneg source that the real absence – symbolic castration – is intended. In another painting, *Slip*, both figures from the same Eneg drawing are combined into one and loss of balance becomes the explicit theme. Dancers on points, waitresses carrying trays, women acrobats teetering on high heels or walking the tightrope – all are forced to be erect and to thrust vertically upwards. But this phallic deportment carries the threat of its own undoing: the further you strive up, the further you may fall.

In *Männer Wir Kommen* the reverse side of the phallic woman, the true horror of the fetishist, can be seen in one startling sequence. The female body, although still bound in a tight corset and with a snake necklace wound around her neck, has a flamboyant, scarlet scar over her genitals. The surrounding *mise en scène* consists of enormous eggs, containing bound women rising from a foetus-like position while, in another sequence, maggot-like women's limbs emerge from equally enormous apples. The scar breeds the putrescence of pregnancy and nothing but decay can come out of the apple. The apple and the egg are the only non-fetishistic images of women to appear in Allen Jones's work. Infested by manikin maggots, they are the eternal companions of the scar.

Most people think of fetishism as the private taste of an odd minority, nurtured in secret. By revealing the way in which fetishistic images pervade not just specialised publications but the *whole of the mass media*, Allen Jones throws a new light on woman as spectacle. The message of fetishism concerns not woman, but the narcissistic wound she represents for man. Women are constantly confronted with their own image in one form or another, but what they see bears little relation or relevance to their own unconscious fantasies, their own hidden fears and desires. They are being turned all the time into objects of display, to be looked at and gazed at and stared at by men. Yet, in a real sense, women are not there at all. The parade has nothing to do with woman, everything to do with man. The true exhibit is always the phallus. Women are simply the scenery onto which men project their narcissistic fantasies. The time has come for us to take over the show and exhibit our own fears and desires.

Notes

1. Allen Jones, *Figures* (Berlin: Galerie Mikro, and Milan: Edizioni O, 1969).
2. Allen Jones, *Projects* (London: Matheus Miller Dunbar, and Milan: Edizioni O, 1971).

3

Visual Pleasure and Narrative Cinema*

* Written in 1973 and published in 1975 in *Screen*.

I INTRODUCTION

(a) A Political Use of Psychoanalysis

This paper intends to use psychoanalysis to discover where and how the fascination of film is reinforced by pre-existing patterns of fascination already at work within the individual subject and the social formations that have moulded him. It takes as its starting-point the way film reflects, reveals and even plays on the straight, socially established interpretation of sexual difference which controls images, erotic ways of looking and spectacle. It is helpful to understand what the cinema has been, how its magic has worked in the past, while attempting a theory and a practice which will challenge this cinema of the past. Psychoanalytic theory is thus appropriated here as a political weapon, demonstrating the way the unconscious of patriarchal society has structured film form.

The paradox of phallocentrism in all its manifestations is that it depends on the image of the castrated women to give order and meaning to its world. An idea of woman stands as linchpin to the system: it is her lack that produces the phallus as a symbolic presence, it is her desire to make good the lack that the phallus signifies. Recent writing in *Screen* about psychoanalysis and the cinema has not sufficiently brought out the importance of the representation of the female form in a symbolic order in which, in the last resort, it speaks castration and nothing else. To summarise briefly: the function of woman in forming the patriarchal unconscious is twofold: she firstly symbolises the castration threat by her real lack of a penis and secondly thereby raises her child into the symbolic. Once this has been achieved, her meaning in the process is at an end. It does not last into the world of law and language except as a memory, which oscillates between memory of maternal plenitude and memory of lack. Both are posited on nature (or on anatomy in Freud's famous phrase). Woman's desire is subjugated to her image as bearer of the bleeding wound; she can exist only in relation to castration and cannot transcend it. She turns her child into the signifier of her own desire to possess a penis (the condition, she imagines, of entry into the

14

symbolic). Either she must gracefully give way to the word, the name of the father and the law, or else struggle to keep her child down with her in the half-light of the imaginary. Woman then stands in patriarchal culture as a signifier for the male other, bound by a symbolic order in which man can live out his fantasies and obsessions through linguistic command by imposing them on the silent image of woman still tied to her place as bearer, not maker, of meaning.

There is an obvious interest in this analysis for feminists, a beauty in its exact rendering of the frustration experienced under the phallocentric order. It gets us nearer to the roots of our oppression, it brings closer an articulation of the problem, it faces us with the ultimate challenge: how to fight the unconscious structured like a language (formed critically at the moment of arrival of language) while still caught within the language of the patriarchy? There is no way in which we can produce an alternative out of the blue, but we can begin to make a break by examining patriarchy with the tools it provides, of which psychoanalysis is not the only but an important one. We are still separated by a great gap from important issues for the female unconscious which are scarcely relevant to phallocentric theory: the sexing of the female infant and her relationship to the symbolic, the sexually mature woman as non-mother, maternity outside the signification of the phallus, the vagina. But, at this point, psychoanalytic theory as it now stands can at least advance our understanding of the *status quo*, of the patriarchal order in which we are caught.

(b) Destruction of Pleasure as a Radical Weapon

As an advanced representation system, the cinema poses questions about the ways the unconscious (formed by the dominant order) structures ways of seeing and pleasure in looking. Cinema has changed over the last few decades. It is no longer the monolithic system based on large capital investment exemplified at its best by Hollywood in the 1930s, 1940s and 1950s. Technological advances (16mm and so on) have changed the economic conditions of cinematic production, which can now be artisanal as well as capitalist. Thus it has been possible for an alternative cinema to develop. However self-conscious and ironic Hollywood managed to be, it always restricted itself to a formal *mise en scène* reflecting the dominant ideological concept of the cinema. The alternative cinema provides a space for the birth of a cinema which is radical in both a political and an aesthetic sense and challenges the basic assumptions of the mainstream film. This is not to reject the latter moralistically, but to highlight the ways in which its formal preoccupations reflect the psychical obsessions of the society which produced it and, further, to stress that the alternative cinema must start specifically by reacting against these obsessions and assumptions. A politically and aesthetically avant-garde cinema is now possible, but it can still only exist as a counterpoint.

The magic of the Hollywood style at its best (and of all the cinema which fell within its sphere of influence) arose, not exclusively, but in one important aspect, from its skilled and satisfying manipulation of visual pleasure. Unchallenged, mainstream film coded the erotic into the language of the dominant patriarchal order. In the highly developed Hollywood cinema it was only through these codes that the alienated subject, torn in his imaginary memory by a sense of loss, by the terror of potential lack in fantasy, came near to finding a glimpse of satisfaction: through its formal beauty and its play on his own formative obsessions. This article will discuss the interweaving of that erotic pleasure in film, its meaning and, in particular, the central place of the image of woman. It is said that analysing pleasure, or beauty, destroys it. That is the intention of this article. The satisfaction and reinforcement of the ego that represent the high point of film history hitherto must be attacked. Not in favour of a reconstructed new pleasure, which cannot exist in the abstract, nor of intellectualised unpleasure, but to make way for a total negation of the ease and plenitude of the narrative fiction film. The alternative is the thrill that comes from leaving the past behind without simply rejecting it, transcending outworn or oppressive forms, and daring to break with normal pleasurable expectations in order to conceive a new language of desire.

II PLEASURE IN LOOKING/FASCINATION WITH THE HUMAN FORM

A The cinema offers a number of possible pleasures. One is scopophilia (pleasure in looking). There are circumstances in which looking itself is a source of pleasure, just as, in the reverse formation, there is pleasure in being looked at. Originally, in his *Three Essays on Sexuality*, Freud isolated scopophilia as one of the component instincts of sexuality which exist as drives quite independently of the erotogenic zones. At this point he associated scopophilia with taking other people as objects, subjecting them to a controlling and curious gaze. His particular examples centre on the voyeuristic activities of children, their desire to see and make sure of the private and forbidden (curiosity about other people's genital and bodily functions, about the presence or absence of the penis and, retrospectively, about the primal scene). In this analysis scopophilia is essentially active. (Later, in 'Instincts and Their Vicissitudes', Freud developed his theory of scopophilia further, attaching it initially to pre-genital auto-eroticism, after which, by analogy, the pleasure of the look is transferred to others. There is a close working here of the relationship between the active instinct and its further development in a narcissistic form.) Although the instinct is modified by other factors, in particular the constitution of the ego, it continues to exist as the erotic basis for pleasure in looking at another person as object. At the extreme, it can become fixated into a perversion, producing obsessive voyeurs and Peeping Toms whose only sexual satisfaction can come from watching, in an active controlling sense, an objectified other.

At first glance, the cinema would seem to be remote from the undercover world of the surreptitious observation of an unknowing and unwilling victim. What is seen on the screen is so manifestly shown. But the mass of mainstream film, and the conventions within which it has consciously evolved, portray a hermetically sealed world which unwinds magically, indifferent to the presence of the audience, producing for them a sense of separation and playing on their voyeuristic fantasy. Moreover the extreme contrast between the darkness in the auditorium (which also isolates the spectators from one another) and the brilliance of the shifting patterns of light and shade on the screen helps to promote the illusion of voyeuristic separation. Although the film is really being shown, is there to be seen, conditions of screening and narrative conventions give the spectator an illusion of looking in on a private world. Among other things, the position of the spectators in the cinema is blatantly one of repression of their exhibitionism and projection of the repressed desire onto the performer.

B The cinema satisfies a primordial wish for pleasurable looking, but it also goes further, developing scopophilia in its narcissistic aspect. The conventions of mainstream film focus attention on the human form. Scale, space, stories are all anthropomorphic. Here, curiosity and the wish to look intermingle with a fascination with likeness and recognition: the human face, the human body, the relationship between the human form and its surroundings, the visible presence of the person in the world. Jacques Lacan has described how the moment when a child recognises its own image in the mirror is crucial for the constitution of the ego. Several aspects of this analysis are relevant here. The mirror phase occurs at a time when children's physical ambitions outstrip their motor capacity, with the result that their recognition of themselves is joyous in that they imagine their mirror image to be more complete, more perfect than they experience in their own body. Recognition is thus overlaid with misrecognition: the image recognised is conceived as the reflected body of the self, but its misrecognition as superior projects this body outside itself as an ideal ego, the alienated subject which, re-introjected as an ego ideal, prepares the way for identification with others in the future. This mirror moment predates language for the child.

Important for this article is the fact that it is an image that constitutes the matrix of the imaginary, of recognition/misrecognition and identification, and hence of the first articulation of the I, of subjectivity. This is a moment when an older fascination with looking (at the mother's face, for an obvious example) collides with the initial inklings of self-awareness. Hence it is the birth of the long love affair/despair between image and self-image which has found such intensity of expression in film and such joyous recognition in the cinema audience. Quite apart from the extraneous similarities between screen and mirror (the framing of the human form in its surroundings, for instance), the cinema has structures of fascination strong enough to allow temporary loss of ego while simultaneously reinforcing it. The sense of forgetting the world as the ego has come to perceive it (I forgot who I am and where I was) is nostalgically reminiscent of that pre-subjective moment of image recognition. While at the same time, the cinema has distinguished itself in the production of ego ideals, through the star system for instance. Stars provide a focus or centre both to screen space and screen story where they act out a complex process of likeness and difference (the glamorous impersonates the ordinary).

C Sections A and B have set out two contradictory aspects of the pleasurable structures of looking in the conventional cinematic situation. The first, scopophilic, arises from pleasure in using another person as an object of sexual stimulation through sight. The second, developed through narcissism and the constitution of the ego, comes from identification with the image seen. Thus, in film terms, one implies a separation of the erotic identity of the subject from the object on the screen (active scopophilia), the other demands identification of the ego with the object on the screen through the spectator's fascination with and recognition of his like. The first is a function of the sexual instincts, the second of ego libido. This dichotomy was crucial for Freud. Although he saw the two as interacting and overlaying each other, the tension between instinctual drives and self-preservation polarises in terms of pleasure. But both are formative structures, mechanisms without intrinsic meaning. In themselves they have no signification, unless attached to an idealisation. Both pursue aims in indifference to perceptual reality, and motivate eroticised phantasmagoria that affect the subject's perception of the world to make a mockery of empirical objectivity.

During its history, the cinema seems to have evolved a particular illusion of reality in which this contradiction between libido and ego has found a beautifully complementary fantasy world. In *reality* the fantasy world of the screen is subject to the law which produces it. Sexual instincts and identification processes have a meaning within the symbolic order which articulates desire. Desire, born with language, allows the possibility of transcending the instinctual and the imaginary, but its point of reference continually returns to the traumatic moment of its birth: the castration complex. Hence the look, pleasurable in form, can be threatening in content, and it is woman as representation/image that crystallises this paradox.

III WOMAN AS IMAGE, MAN AS BEARER OF THE LOOK

A In a world ordered by sexual imbalance, pleasure in looking has been split between active/male and passive/female. The determining male gaze projects its fantasy onto the female figure, which is styled accordingly. In their traditional exhibitionist role women are simultaneously looked at and displayed, with their appearance coded for strong visual and erotic impact so that they can be said to connote *to-be-looked-at-ness*. Woman displayed as sexual object is the *leitmotif* of erotic spectacle: from pin-ups to strip-tease, from Ziegfeld to Busby Berkeley, she holds the look, and plays to and signifies male desire. Mainstream film neatly combines spectacle and narrative. (Note, however, how in the musical song-and-dance numbers interrupt the flow of the diegesis.) The presence of woman is an indispensable element of spectacle in normal narrative film, yet her visual presence tends to work against the development of a story-line, to freeze the flow of action in moments of erotic contemplation. This alien presence then has to be integrated into cohesion with the narrative. As Budd Boetticher has put it:

> What counts is what the heroine provokes, or rather what she represents. She is the one, or rather the love or fear she inspires in the hero, or else the concern he feels for her, who makes him act the way he does. In herself the woman has not the slightest importance.

(A recent tendency in narrative film has been to dispense with this problem altogether; hence the development of what Molly Haskell has called the 'buddy movie', in which the active homosexual eroticism of the central male figures can carry the story without distraction.) Traditionally, the woman displayed has functioned on two levels: as erotic object for the characters within the screen story, and as erotic object for the spectator within the auditorium, with a shifting tension between the looks on either side of the screen. For instance, the device of the show-girl allows the two looks to be unified technically without any apparent break in the diegesis. A woman performs within the narrative; the gaze of the spectator and that of the male characters in the film are neatly combined without breaking narrative verisimilitude. For a moment the sexual impact of the performing woman takes the film into a no man's land outside its own time and space. Thus Marilyn Monroe's first appearance in *The River of No Return* and Lauren Bacall's songs in *To Have and Have Not*. Similarly, conventional close-ups of legs (Dietrich, for instance) or a face (Garbo) integrate into the narrative a different mode of eroticism. One part of a fragmented body destroys the Renaissance space, the illusion of depth demanded by the narrative; it gives flatness, the quality of a cut-out or icon, rather than verisimilitude, to the screen.

B   An active/passive heterosexual division of labour has similarly controlled narrative structure. According to the principles of the ruling ideology and the psychical structures that back it up, the male figure cannot bear the burden of sexual objectification. Man is reluctant to gaze at his exhibitionist like. Hence the split between spectacle and narrative supports the man's role as the active one of advancing the story, making things happen. The man controls the film fantasy and also emerges as the representative of power in a further sense: as the bearer of the look of the spectator, transferring it behind the screen to neutralise the extra-diegetic tendencies represented by woman as spectacle. This is made possible through the processes set in motion by structuring the film around a main controlling figure with whom the spectator can identify. As the spectator identifies with the main male protagonist, he projects his look onto that of his like, his screen surrogate, so that the power of the male protagonist as he controls events coincides with the active power of the erotic look, both giving a satisfying sense of omnipotence. A male movie star's glamorous characteristics are thus not those of the erotic object of the gaze, but those of the more perfect, more complete, more powerful ideal ego conceived in the original moment of recognition in front of the mirror. The character in the story can make things happen and control events better than the subject/spectator, just as the image in the mirror was more in control of motor co-ordination.

   In contrast to woman as icon, the active male figure (the ego ideal of the identification process) demands a three-dimensional space corresponding to that of the mirror recognition, in which the alienated subject internalised his own representation of his imaginary existence. He is a figure in a landscape. Here the function of film is to reproduce as accurately as possible the so-called natural conditions of human perception. Camera technology (as exemplified by deep focus in particular) and camera movements (determined by the action of the protagonist), combined with invisible editing (demanded by realism), all tend to blur the limits of screen space. The male protagonist is free to command the stage, a stage of spatial illusion in which he articulates the look and creates the action. (There are films with a woman as main protagonist, of course. To analyse this phenomenon seriously here would take me too far afield. Pam Cook and Claire Johnston's study of *The Revolt of Mamie Stover* in Phil Hardy (ed.), *Raoul Walsh* (Edinburgh, 1974), shows in a striking case how the strength of this female protagonist is more apparent than real.)

C1 Sections III A and B have set out a tension between a mode of representation of woman in film and conventions surrounding the diegesis. Each is associated with a look: that of the spectator in direct scopophilic contact with the female form displayed for his enjoyment (connoting male fantasy) and that of the spectator fascinated with the image of his like set in an illusion of natural space, and through him gaining control and possession of the woman within the diegesis. (This tension and the shift from one pole to the other can structure a single text. Thus both in *Only Angels Have Wings* and in *To Have and Have Not*, the film opens with the woman as object of the combined gaze of spectator and all the male protagonists in the film. She is isolated, glamorous, on display, sexualised. But as the narrative progresses she falls in love with the main male protagonist and becomes his property, losing her outward glamorous characteristics, her generalised sexuality, her show-girl connotations; her eroticism is subjected to the male star alone. By means of identification with him, through participation in his power, the spectator can indirectly possess her too.)

But in psychoanalytic terms, the female figure poses a deeper problem. She also connotes something that the look continually circles around but disavows: her lack of a penis, implying a threat of castration and hence unpleasure. Ultimately, the meaning of woman is sexual difference, the visually ascertainable absence of the penis, the material evidence on which is based the castration complex essential for the organisation of entrance to the symbolic order and the law of the father. Thus the woman as icon, displayed for the gaze and enjoyment of men, the active controllers of the look, always threatens to evoke the anxiety it originally signified. The male unconscious has two avenues of escape from this castration anxiety: preoccupation with the re-enactment of the original trauma (investigating the woman, demystifying her mystery), counterbalanced by the devaluation, punishment or saving of the guilty object (an avenue typified by the concerns of the *film noir*); or else complete disavowal of castration by the substitution of a fetish object or turning the represented figure itself into a fetish so that it becomes reassuring rather than dangerous (hence overvaluation, the cult of the female star).

This second avenue, fetishistic scopophilia, builds up the physical beauty of the object, transforming it into something satisfying in itself. The first avenue, voyeurism, on the contrary, has associations with sadism: pleasure lies in ascertaining guilt (immediately associated with castration), asserting control and subjugating the guilty person through punishment or forgiveness. This sadistic side fits in well with narrative. Sadism demands a story, depends on making something happen, forcing a change in another person, a battle of will and strength, victory/defeat, all occurring in a linear time with a beginning and an end. Fetishistic scopophilia, on the other hand, can exist outside linear time as the erotic instinct is focused on the look alone. These contradictions and ambiguities can be illustrated more simply by using works by Hitchcock and Sternberg, both of whom take the look almost as the content or subject matter of many of their films. Hitchcock is the more complex, as he uses both mechanisms. Sternberg's work, on the other hand, provides many pure examples of fetishistic scopophilia.

C2   Sternberg once said he would welcome his films being projected upside-down so that story and character involvement would not interfere with the spectator's undiluted appreciation of the screen image. This statement is revealing but ingenuous: ingenuous in that his films do demand that the figure of the woman (Dietrich, in the cycle of films with her, as the ultimate example) should be identifiable; but revealing in that it emphasises the fact that for him the pictorial space enclosed by the frame is paramount, rather than narrative or identification processes. While Hitchcock goes into the investigative side of voyeurism, Sternberg produces the ultimate fetish, taking it to the point where the powerful look of the male protagonist (characteristic of traditional narrative film) is broken in favour of the image in direct erotic rapport with the spectator. The beauty of the woman as object and the screen space coalesce; she is no longer the bearer of guilt but a perfect product, whose body, stylised and fragmented by close-ups, is the content of the film and the direct recipient of the spectator's look.

Sternberg plays down the illusion of screen depth; his screen tends to be one-dimensional, as light and shade, lace, steam, foliage, net, streamers and so on reduce the visual field. There is little or no mediation of the look through the eyes of the main male protagonist. On the contrary, shadowy presences like La Bessière in *Morocco* act as surrogates for the director, detached as they are from audience identification. Despite Sternberg's insistence that his stories are irrelevant, it is significant that they are concerned with situation, not suspense, and cyclical rather than linear time, while plot complications revolve around misunderstanding rather than conflict. The most important absence is that of the controlling male gaze within the screen scene. The high point of emotional drama in the most typical Dietrich films, her supreme moments of erotic meaning, take place in the absence of the man she loves in the fiction. There are other witnesses, other spectators watching her on the screen, their gaze is one with, not standing in for, that of the audience. At the end of *Morocco*, Tom Brown has already disappeared into the desert when Amy Jolly kicks off her gold sandals and walks after him. At the end of *Dishonoured*, Kranau is indifferent to the fate of Magda. In both cases, the erotic impact, sanctified by death, is displayed as a spectacle for the audience. The male hero misunderstands and, above all, does not see.

In Hitchcock, by contrast, the male hero does see precisely what the audience sees. However, although fascination with an image through scopophilic eroticism can be the subject of the film, it is the role of the hero to portray the contradictions and tensions experienced by the spectator. In *Vertigo* in particular, but also in *Marnie* and *Rear Window*, the look is central to the plot, oscillating between voyeurism and fetishistic fascination. Hitchcock has never concealed his interest in voyeurism, cinematic and non-cinematic. His heroes are exemplary of the symbolic order and the law – a policeman (*Vertigo*), a dominant male possessing money and power (*Marnie*) – but their erotic drives lead them into compromised situations. The power to subject another person to the will sadistically or to the gaze voyeuristically is turned onto the woman as the object of both. Power is backed by a certainty of legal right and the established guilt of the woman (evoking castration, psychoanalytically speaking). True perversion is barely concealed under a shallow mask of ideological correctness – the man is on the right side of the law, the woman on the wrong. Hitchcock's skilful use of identification processes and liberal use of subjective camera from the point of view of the male protagonist draw the spectators deeply into his position, making them share his uneasy gaze. The spectator is absorbed into a voyeuristic situation within the screen scene and diegesis, which parodies his own in the cinema.

In an analysis of *Rear Window*, Douchet takes the film as a metaphor for the cinema. Jeffries is the audience, the events in the apartment block opposite correspond to the screen. As he watches, an erotic dimension is added to his look, a central image to the drama. His girlfriend Lisa had been of little sexual interest to him, more or less a drag, so long as she remained on the spectator side. When she crosses the barrier between his room and the block opposite, their relationship is reborn erotically. He does not merely watch her through his lens, as a distant meaningful image, he also sees her as a guilty intruder exposed by a dangerous man threatening her with punishment, and thus finally giving him the opportunity to save her. Lisa's exhibitionism has already been established by her obsessive interest in dress and style, in being a passive image of visual perfection; Jeffries's voyeurism and activity have also been established through his work as a photo-journalist, a maker of stories and captor of images. However, his enforced inactivity, binding him to his seat as a spectator, puts him squarely in the fantasy position of the cinema audience.

In *Vertigo*, subjective camera predominates. Apart from one flashback from Judy's point of view, the narrative is woven around what Scottie sees or fails to see. The audience follows the growth of his erotic obsession and subsequent despair precisely from his point of view. Scottie's voyeurism is blatant: he falls in love with a woman he follows and spies on without speaking to. Its sadistic side is equally blatant: he has chosen (and freely chosen, for he had been a successful lawyer) to be a policeman, with all the attendant possibilities of pursuit and investigation. As a result, he follows, watches and falls in love with a perfect image of female beauty and mystery. Once he actually confronts her, his erotic drive is to break her down and force her *to tell* by persistent cross-questioning.

In the second part of the film, he re-enacts his obsessive involvement with the image he loved to watch secretly. He reconstructs Judy as Madeleine, forces her to conform in every detail to the actual physical appearance of his fetish. Her exhibitionism, her masochism, make her an ideal passive counterpart to Scottie's active sadistic voyeurism. She knows her part is to perform, and only by playing it through and then replaying it can she keep Scottie's erotic interest. But in the repetition he does break her down and succeeds in exposing her guilt. His curiosity wins through; she is punished.

Thus, in *Vertigo*, erotic involvement with the look boomerangs: the spectator's own fascination is revealed as illicit voyeurism as the narrative content enacts the processes and pleasures that he is himself exercising and enjoying. The Hitchcock hero here is firmly placed within the symbolic order, in narrative terms. He has all the attributes of the patriarchal superego. Hence the spectator, lulled into a false sense of security by the apparent legality of his surrogate, sees through his look and finds himself exposed as complicit, caught in the moral ambiguity of looking. Far from being simply an aside on the perversion of the police, *Vertigo* focuses on the implications of the active/looking, passive/looked-at split in terms of sexual difference and the power of the male symbolic encapsulated in the hero. Marnie, too, performs for Mark Rutland's gaze and masquerades as the perfect to-be-looked-at image. He, too, is on the side of the law until, drawn in by obsession with her guilt, her secret, he longs to see her in the act of committing a crime, make her confess and thus save her. So he, too, becomes complicit as he acts out the implications of his power. He controls money and words; he can have his cake and eat it.

IV SUMMARY

The psychoanalytic background that has been discussed in this article is relevant to the pleasure and unpleasure offered by traditional narrative film. The scopophilic instinct (pleasure in looking at another person as an erotic object) and, in contradistinction, ego libido (forming identification processes) act as formations, mechanisms, which mould this cinema's formal attributes. The actual image of woman as (passive) raw material for the (active) gaze of man takes the argument a step further into the content and structure of representation, adding a further layer of ideological significance demanded by the patriarchal order in its favourite cinematic form – illusionistic narrative film. The argument must return again to the psychoanalytic background: women in representation can signify castration, and activate voyeuristic or fetishistic mechanisms to circumvent this threat. Although none of these interacting layers is intrinsic to film, it is only in the film form that they can reach a perfect and beautiful contradiction, thanks to the possibility in the cinema of shifting the emphasis of the look. The place of the look defines cinema, the possibility of varying it and exposing it. This is what makes cinema quite different in its voyeuristic potential from, say, striptease, theatre, shows and so on. Going far beyond highlighting a woman's to-be-looked-at-ness, cinema builds the way she is to be looked at into the spectacle itself. Playing on the tension between film as controlling the dimension of time (editing, narrative) and film as controlling the dimension of space (changes in distance, editing), cinematic codes create a gaze, a world and an object, thereby producing an illusion cut to the measure of desire. It is these cinematic codes and their relationship to formative external structures that must be broken down before mainstream film and the pleasure it provides can be challenged.

To begin with (as an ending), the voyeuristic–scopophilic look that is a crucial part of traditional filmic pleasure can itself be broken down. There are three different looks associated with cinema: that of the camera as it records the pro-filmic event, that of the audience as it watches the final product, and that of the characters at each other within the screen illusion. The conventions of narrative film deny the first two and subordinate them to the third, the conscious aim being always to eliminate intrusive camera presence and prevent a distancing awareness in the audience. Without these two absences (the material existence of the recording process, the critical reading of the spectator), fictional drama cannot achieve reality, obviousness and truth. Nevertheless, as this article has argued, the structure of looking in narrative fiction film contains a contradiction in its own premises: the female image as a castration threat constantly endangers the unity of the diegesis and bursts through the world of illusion as an intrusive, static, one-dimentional fetish. Thus the two looks materially present in time and space are obsessively subordinated to the neurotic needs of the male ego. The camera becomes the mechanism for producing an illusion of Renaissance space, flowing movements compatible with the human eye, an ideology of representation that revolves around the perception of the subject; the camera's look is disavowed in order to create a convincing world in which the spectator's surrogate can perform with verisimilitude. Simultaneously, the look of the audience is denied an intrinsic force: as soon as fetishistic representation of the female image threatens to break the spell of illusion, and the erotic image on the screen appears directly (without mediation) to the spectator, the fact of fetishisation, concealing as it does castration fear, freezes the look, fixates the spectator and prevents him from achieving any distance from the image in front of him.

This complex interaction of looks is specific to film. The first blow against the monolithic accumulation of traditional film conventions (already undertaken by radical film-makers) is to free the look of the camera into its materiality in time and space and the look of the audience into dialectics and passionate detachment. There is no doubt that this destroys the satisfaction, pleasure and privilege of the 'invisible guest', and highlights the way film has depended on voyeuristic active/passive mechanisms. Women, whose image has continually been stolen and used for this end, cannot view the decline of the traditional film form with anything much more than sentimental regret.

Part II

Melodrama

4

Afterthoughts on 'Visual Pleasure and Narrative Cinema' inspired by King Vidor's *Duel in the Sun* (1946)*

* Presented as a paper at the conference *Cinema and Psychoanalysis* held at the Center for Media Studies, SUNY, Buffalo, and published in *Framework* in 1981.

So many times over the years since my 'Visual Pleasure and Narrative Cinema' article was published in *Screen*, I have been asked why I only used the *male* third person singular to stand in for the spectator. At the time, I was interested in the relationship between the image of woman on the screen and the 'masculinisation' of the spectator position, regardless of the actual sex (or possible deviance) of any real live movie-goer. In-built patterns of pleasure and identification impose masculinity as 'point of view'; a point of view which is also manifest in the general use of the masculine third person. However, the persistent question 'what about the women in the audience?' and my own love of Hollywood melodrama (equally shelved as an issue in 'Visual Pleasure') combined to convince me that, however ironically it had been intended originally, the male third person closed off avenues of inquiry that should be followed up. Finally, *Duel in the Sun* and its heroine's crisis of sexual identity brought both areas together.

I still stand by my 'Visual Pleasure' argument, but would now like to pursue the other two lines of thought. First (the 'women in the audience' issue), whether the female spectator is carried along, as it were by the scruff of the text, or whether her pleasure can be more deep-rooted and complex. Second (the 'melodrama' issue), how the text and its attendant identifications are affected by a *female* character occupying the centre of the narrative arena. So far as the first issue is concerned, it is always possible that the female spectator may find herself so out of key with the pleasure on offer, with its 'masculinisation', that the spell of fascination is broken. On the other hand, she may not. She may find herself secretly, unconsciously almost, enjoying the freedom of action and control over the diegetic world that identification with a hero provides. It is *this* female spectator that I want to consider here. So far as the second issue is concerned, I want to limit the area under consideration in a similar manner. Rather than discussing melodrama in general, I am concentrating on films in which a woman central protagonist is shown to be unable to achieve a stable sexual identity, torn between the deep blue sea of passive femininity and the devil of regressive masculinity.

There is an overlap between the two areas, between the unacknowledged dilemma faced in the auditorium and the dramatic double bind up there on the screen. Generally it is dangerous to elide these two separate worlds. In this case, the emotions of those women accepting 'masculinisation' while watching action movies with a male hero are illuminated by the emotions of a heroine of a melodrama whose resistance to a 'correct' feminine position is the critical issue at stake. Her oscillation, her inability to achieve stable sexual identity, is echoed by the woman spectator's masculine 'point of view'. Both create a sense of the difficulty of sexual difference in cinema that is missing in the undifferentiated spectator of 'Visual Pleasure'. The unstable, oscillating difference is thrown into relief by Freud's theory of femininity.

Freud and Femininity

For Freud, femininity is complicated by the fact that it emerges out of a crucial period of parallel development between the sexes; a period he sees as masculine, or phallic, for both boys and girls. The terms he uses to conceive of femininity are the same as those he has mapped out for the male, causing certain problems of language and boundaries to expression. These problems reflect, very accurately, the actual position of women in patriarchal society (suppressed, for instance, under the generalised male third person singular). One term gives rise to a second as its complementary opposite, the male to the female, in that order. Some quotations:

> In females, too, the striving to be masculine is ego-syntonic at a certain period – namely in the phallic phase, before the development of femininity sets in. But it then succumbs to the momentous process of repression, as so often has been shown, that determines the fortunes of a woman's femininity.[1]

> I will only emphasise here that the development of femininity remains exposed to disturbances by the residual phenomena of the early masculine period. Regressions to the pre-Oedipus phase very frequently occur; in the course of some women's lives there is a repeated alternation between periods in which femininity and masculinity gain the upper hand.[2]

We have called the motive force of sexual life 'the libido'. Sexual life is dominated by the polarity of masculine–feminine; thus the notion suggests itself of considering the relation of the libido to this antithesis. It would not be surprising if it were to turn out that each sexuality had its own special libido appropriated to it, so that one sort of libido would pursue the aims of a masculine sexual life and another sort those of a feminine one. But nothing of the kind is true. There is only one libido, which serves both the masculine and the feminine functions. To it itself we cannot assign any sex; if, following the conventional equation of activity and masculinity, we are inclined to describe it as masculine, we must not forget that it also covers trends with a passive aim. Nevertheless, the juxtaposition 'feminine libido' is without any justification. Furthermore, it is our impression that more constraint has been applied to the libido when it is pressed into the service of the feminine function, and that – to speak teleologically – Nature takes less careful account of its [that function's] demands than in the case of masculinity. And the reason for this may lie – thinking once again teleologically – in the fact that the accomplishment of the aim of biology has been entrusted to the aggressiveness of men and has been made to some extent independent of women's consent.[3]

One particular point of interest in the third passage is Freud's shift from the use of active/masculine as *metaphor* for the function of the libido to an invocation of Nature and biology that appears to leave the metaphoric usage behind. There are two problems here: Freud introduces the use of the word *masculine* as 'conventional', apparently simply following an established social–linguistic practice (but which, once again, confirms the masculine 'point of view'); however, secondly, and constituting a greater intellectual stumbling-block, the feminine cannot be conceptualised as different, but rather only as *opposition* (passivity) in an antinomic sense, or as *similarity* (the phallic phase). This is not to suggest that a hidden, as yet undiscovered femininity exists (as is perhaps implied by Freud's use of the word 'Nature') but that its structural relationship to masculinity under patriarchy cannot be defined or determined within the terms offered. This shifting process, this definition in terms of opposition or similarity, leaves women also shifting between the metaphoric opposition 'active' and 'passive'. The correct road, *femininity*, leads to increasing repression of 'the active' (the 'phallic phase' in Freud's terms). In this sense Hollywood genre films structured around masculine pleasure, offering an identification with the *active* point of view, allow a woman spectator to rediscover that lost aspect of her sexual identity, the never fully repressed bed-rock of feminine neurosis.

Narrative Grammar and Trans-sex Identification

The 'convention' cited by Freud (active/masculine) structures most popular narratives, whether film, folk-tale or myth (as I argued in 'Visual Pleasure'), where his metaphoric usage is acted out literally in the story. Andromeda stays tied to the rock, a victim, in danger, until Perseus slays the monster and saves her. It is not my aim, here, to debate the rights and wrongs of this narrative division of labour or to demand positive heroines, but rather to point out that the 'grammar' of the story places the reader, listener or spectator *with* the hero. The woman spectator in the cinema can make use of an age-old cultural tradition adapting her to this convention, which eases a transition out of her own sex into another. In 'Visual Pleasure' my argument took as its axis a desire to identify a pleasure that was specific to cinema, that is the eroticism and cultural conventions surrounding the look. Now, on the contrary, I would rather emphasise the way that popular cinema inherited traditions of story-telling that are common to other forms of folk and mass culture, with attendant fascinations other than those of the look.

Freud points out that 'masculinity' is, at one stage, ego-syntonic for a woman. Leaving aside, for the moment, problems posed by his use of words, his general remarks on stories and day-dreams provide another angle of approach, this time giving a cultural rather than psychoanalytic insight into the dilemma. He emphasises the relationship between the ego and the narrative concept of the hero:

> It is the true heroic feeling, which one of our best writers has expressed in the inimitable phrase, 'Nothing can happen to me!' It seems, however, that through this revealing characteristic of invulnerability we can immediately recognise His Majesty the Ego, the hero of every day-dream and every story.[4]

Although a boy might know quite well that it is most *unlikely* that he will go out into the world, make his fortune through prowess or the assistance of helpers, and marry a princess, the stories describe the male fantasy of ambition, reflecting something of an experience and expectation of dominance (the active). For a girl, on the other hand, the cultural and social overlap is more confusing. Freud's argument that a young girl's day-dreams concentrate on the erotic ignores his own position on her early masculinity and the active day-dreams necessarily associated with this phase. In fact, all too often, the erotic function of the woman is represented by the passive, the waiting (Andromeda again), acting above all as a formal closure to the narrative structure.

Three elements can thus be drawn together: Freud's concept of 'masculinity' in women, the identification triggered by the logic of a narrative grammar, and the ego's desire to fantasise itself in a certain, active, manner. All three suggest that, as desire is given cultural materiality in a text, for women (from childhood onwards) trans-sex identification is a *habit* that very easily becomes *second nature*. However, this Nature does not sit easily and shifts restlessly in its borrowed transvestite clothes.

The Western and Oedipal Personifications

Using a concept of character function based on V. Propp's *Morphology of the Folk-tale*, I want to argue for a chain of links and shifts in narrative pattern, showing up the changing function of 'woman'. The Western (allowing, of course, for as many deviations as one cares to enumerate) bears a residual imprint of the primitive narrative structure analysed by Vladimir Propp in folk-tales. Also, in the hero's traditional invulnerability, the Western ties in closely with Freud's remarks on daydreaming. (As I am interested primarily in character function and narrative pattern, not in genre definition, many issues about the Western as such are being summarily side-stepped.) For present purposes, the Western genre provides a crucial node in a series of transformations that *comment* on the function of 'woman' (as opposed to 'man') as a narrative signifier and sexual difference as personification of 'active' or 'passive' elements in a story.

In the Proppian tale, an important aspect of narrative closure is 'marriage', a function characterised by 'princess' or equivalent. This is the only function that is sex-specific, and thus essentially relates to the sex of the hero and his marriageability. This function is very commonly reproduced in the Western, where, once again, 'marriage' makes a crucial contribution to narrative closure. However, in the Western the function's presence has also come to allow a complication in the form of its opposite, 'not marriage'. Thus, while the social integration represented by marriage is an essential aspect of the folk-tale, in the Western it can be accepted . . . or not. A hero can gain in stature by refusing the princess and remaining alone (Randolph Scott in the Ranown series of movies). As the resolution of the Proppian tale can be seen to represent the resolution of the Oedipus complex (integration into the symbolic), the rejection of marriage personifies a nostalgic celebration of phallic, narcissistic omnipotence. Just as Freud's comments on the 'phallic' phase in girls seemed to belong in limbo, without a place in the chronology of sexual development, so, too, does this male phenomenon seem to belong to a phase of play and fantasy difficult to integrate exactly into the Oedipal trajectory.

The tension between two points of attraction, the symbolic (social integration and marriage) and nostalgic narcissism, generates a common splitting of the Western hero into two, something unknown in the Proppian tale. Here two functions emerge, one celebrating integration into society through marriage, the other celebrating resistance to social demands and responsibilities, above all those of marriage and the family, the sphere represented by woman. A story such as *The Man Who Shot Liberty Valance* juxtaposes these two points of attraction, and spectator fantasy can have its cake and eat it too. This particular tension between the double hero also brings out the underlying significance of the drama, its relation to the symbolic, with unusual clarity. A folk-tale story revolves around conflict between hero and villain. The flashback narration in *Liberty Valance* seems to follow these lines at first. The narrative is generated by an act of villainy (Liberty rampages, dragon-like, around the countryside). However the development of the story acquires a complication. The issue at stake is no longer how the villain will be defeated, but how the villain's defeat will be inscribed into history, whether the *upholder* of law as a symbolic system (Ranse) will be seen to be victorious or the *personification* of law in a more primitive manifestation (Tom), closer to the good or the right. *Liberty Valance*, as it uses a flashback structure, also brings out the poignancy of this tension. The 'present-tense' story is precipitated by a funeral, so that the story is shot through with nostalgia and sense of loss. Ranse Stoddart mourns Tom Doniphon.

This narrative structure is based on an opposition between two irreconcilables. The two paths cannot cross. On one side there is an encapsulation of power, and phallic attributes, in an individual who has to bow himself out of the way of history; on the other, an individual impotence rewarded by political and financial power, which, *in the long run*, in fact becomes history. Here the function 'marriage' is as crucial as it is in the folk-tale. It plays the same part in creating narrative resolution, but is even more important in that 'marriage' is an integral attribute of the upholder of the law. In this sense Hallie's choice between the two men is predetermined. Hallie equals princess equals Oedipal resolution rewarded, equals repression of narcissistic sexuality in marriage.

Woman as Signifier of Sexuality

In a Western working within these conventions, the function 'marriage' sublimates the erotic into a final, closing, social ritual. This ritual is, of course, sex-specific, and the main rationale for any female presence in this strand of the genre. This neat *narrative* function restates the propensity for 'woman' to signify 'the erotic' already familiar from *visual* representation (as, for instance, argued in 'Visual Pleasure'). Now I want to discuss the way in which introducing a woman as central to a story shifts its meanings, producing another kind of narrative discourse. *Duel in the Sun* provides the opportunity for this.

While the film remains visibly a 'Western', the generic space seems to shift. The landscape of action, although present, is not the dramatic core of the film's story, rather it is the interior drama of a girl caught between two conflicting desires. The conflicting desires, first of all, correspond closely with Freud's argument about female sexuality quoted above, that is: an oscillation between 'passive' femininity and regressive 'masculinity'. Thus, the symbolic equation, woman = sexuality, still persists, but now rather than being an image or a narrative function, the equation opens out a narrative area previously suppressed or repressed. Woman is no longer the signifier of sexuality (function 'marriage') in the 'Western' type of story. Now the female presence as centre allows the story to be actually, *overtly*, about sexuality: it becomes a melodrama. It is as though the narrational lens had zoomed in and opened up the neat function 'marriage' ('and they lived happily . . .') to ask 'what next?' and to focus on the figure of the princess, waiting in the wings for her one moment of importance, to ask 'what does *she* want?' Here we find the generic terrain for melodrama, in its woman-orientated strand. The second question ('what does *she* want?') takes on greater significance when the hero function is split, as described above in the case of *Liberty Valance*, where the heroine's choice puts the seal of married grace on the upholder of the law. *Duel in the Sun* opens up this question.

In *Duel in the Sun* the iconographical attributes of the two male (oppositional) characters, Lewt and Jesse, conform very closely to those of Tom and Ranse in *Liberty Valance*. But now the opposition between Ranse and Tom (which represents an abstract and allegorical conflict over Law and history) is given a completely different twist of meaning. As Pearl is at the centre of the story, caught between the two men, their alternative attributes acquire meaning *from* her, and represent different sides of her desire and aspiration. They personify the split in *Pearl*, not a split in the concept of *hero*, as argued previously for *Liberty Valance*.

However, from a psychoanalytic point of view, a strikingly similar pattern emerges, Jesse (attributes: books, dark suit, legal skills, love of learning and culture, destined to be Governor of the State, money, and so on) signposts the 'correct' path for Pearl, towards learning a passive sexuality, learning to 'be a lady', above all sublimation into a concept of the feminine that is socially viable. Lewt (attributes: guns, horses, skill with horses, Western get-up, contempt for culture, destined to die an outlaw, personal strength and personal power) offers sexual passion, not based on maturity but on a regressive, boy/girl mixture of rivalry and play. With Lewt, Pearl can be a tomboy (riding, swimming, shooting). Thus the Oedipal dimension persists, but now illuminates the sexual ambivalence it represents for femininity.

In the last resort, there is no more room for Pearl in Lewt's world of misogynist machismo than there is room for her desires as Jesse's potential fiancée. The film consists of a series of oscillations in her sexual identity, between alternative paths of development, between different desperations. Whereas the regressive phallic male hero (Tom in *Liberty Vallance*) had a place (albeit a doomed one) that was stable and meaningful, Pearl is unable to settle or find a 'femininity' in which she and the male world can meet. In this sense, although the male characters personify Pearl's dilemma, it is their terms that make and finally break her. Once again, however, the narrative drama dooms the phallic, regressive resistance to the symbolic. Lewt, Pearl's masculine side, drops out of the social order. Pearl's masculinity gives her the 'wherewithal' to achieve heroism and kill the villain. The lovers shoot each other and die in each other's arms. Perhaps, in *Duel*, the erotic relationship between Pearl and Lewt also exposes a dyadic interdependence between hero and villain in the primitive tale, now threatened by the splitting of the hero with the coming of the Law.

In *Duel in the Sun*, Pearl's inability to become a 'lady' is highlighted by the fact that the perfect lady appears, like a phantasmagoria of Pearl's failed aspiration, as Jesse's perfect future wife. Pearl recognises her and her rights over Jesse, and sees that she represents the 'correct' road. In an earlier film by King Vidor, *Stella Dallas* (1937), narrative and iconographic structures similar to those outlined above make the dramatic meaning of the film although it is not a Western. Stella, as central character, is flanked on each side by a male personification of her instability, her inability to accept correct, married 'femininity' on the one hand, or find a place in a macho world on the other. Her husband, Stephen, demonstrates all the attributes associated with Jesse, with no problems of generic shift. Ed Munn, representing Stella's regressive 'masculine' side, is considerably emasculated by the loss of the Western's accoutrements and its terrain of violence. (The fact that Stella is a mother, and that her relationship to her child constitutes the central drama, undermines a possible sexual relationship with Ed.) He does retain residual traces of Western iconography. His attributes are mapped through associations with horses and betting, the racing scene. However, more importantly, his relationship with Stella is regressive, based on 'having fun', most explicitly in the episode in which they spread itching powder among the respectable occupants of a train carriage. In *Stella Dallas*, too, a perfect wife appears for Stephen, representing the 'correct' femininity that Stella rejects (very similar to Helen, Jesse's fiancée in *Duel in the Sun*).

I have been trying to suggest a series of transformations in narrative pattern that illuminate, but also show shifts in, Oedipal nostalgia. The 'personifications' and their iconographical attributes do not relate to parental figures or reactivate an actual Oedipal moment. On the contrary, they represent an internal oscillation of desire, which lies dormant, waiting to be 'pleasured' in stories of this kind. Perhaps the fascination of the classic Western, in particular, lies in its rather raw touching on this nerve. However, for the female spectator the situation is more complicated and goes beyond simple mourning for a lost fantasy of omnipotence. The masculine identification, in its phallic aspect, reactivates for her a fantasy of 'action' that correct femininity demands should be repressed. The fantasy 'action' finds expression through a metaphor of masculinity. Both in the language used by Freud and in the male personifications of desire flanking the female protagonist in the melodrama, this metaphor acts as a strait-jacket, becoming itself an indicator, a litmus paper, of the problems inevitably activated by any attempt to represent the feminine in patriarchal society. The memory of the 'masculine' phase has its own romantic attraction, a last-ditch resistance, in which the power of masculinity can be used as postponement against the power of patriarchy. Thus Freud's comments illuminate both the position of the female spectator and the image of oscillation represented by Pearl and Stella:

> . . . in the course of some women's lives there is a repeated alternation between periods in which femininity and masculinity gain the upper hand.

> . . . (the phallic phase) . . . then succumbs to the momentous process of repression as has so often been shown, that determines the fortunes of women's femininity.

I have argued that Pearl's position in *Duel in the Sun* is similar to that of the female spectator as she temporarily accepts 'masculinisation' in memory of her 'active' phase. Rather than dramatising the success of masculine identification, Pearl brings out its sadness. Her 'tomboy' pleasures, her sexuality, are not fully accepted by Lewt, except in death. So, too, is the female spectator's fantasy of masculinisation at cross-purposes with itself, restless in its transvestite clothes.

Notes

1. S. Freud, 'Analysis Terminable and Interminable', *Standard Edition*, vol. xxiii (London: The Hogarth Press, 1964).
2. S. Freud, 'Femininity', *Standard Edition*, vol. xxii (London: The Hogarth Press, 1964).
3. Ibid.
4. S. Freud, 'Creative Writers and Day Dreaming', *Standard Edition*, vol. ix (London: The Hogarth Press, 1964).

5

Notes on Sirk and Melodrama*

* Presented as a paper for the SEFT weekend school *Melodrama* and published in *Movie* in 1977.

It has been suggested that the interest of Hollywood 1950s melodrama lies primarily in the way that, by means of textual analysis, fissures and contradictions can be shown to be undermining the films' ideological coherence.[1] These contradictions, whether on the level of form or of narrative incident, seem to save the films from belonging blindly to the bourgeois ideology which produced them. This argument depends on the premise that the project of this ideology is indeed to conjure up a coherent picture of a world and conceal contradictions which in turn conceal exploitation and oppression. A text which defies unity and closure would then quite clearly be progressive. Although this line of argument has been productive and revealing, there is a way in which it has been trapped in a kind of Chinese box quite characteristic of melodrama itself. Ideological contradiction is actually the overt mainspring and specific content of melodrama, not a hidden, unconscious thread to be picked up only by special critical processes. No ideology can ever pretend to totality: it searches for safety-valves for its own inconsistencies. And the 1950s melodrama works by touching on sensitive areas of sexual repression and frustration; its excitement comes from conflict, not between enemies, but between people tied by blood or love.

Melodrama as a safety-valve for ideological contradictions centred on sex and the family may lose its progressive attributes, but it acquires a wider aesthetic and political significance. The workings of patriarchy, and the mould of feminine unconscious it produces, have left women largely without a voice, gagged and deprived of outlets (of a kind supplied, for instance, either by male art or popular culture) in spite of the crucial social and ideological functions women are called on to perform. In the absence of any coherent culture of oppression, a simple fact of recognition has aesthetic and political importance. There is a dizzy satisfaction in witnessing the way that sexual difference under patriarchy is fraught, explosive, and erupts dramatically into violence within its own private stamping-ground, the family. While the Western and the gangster film celebrate the ups and downs endured by men of action, the melodramas of Douglas Sirk, like the tragedies of Euripides, probing the pent-up emotion, bitterness and disillusion well known to women, act as a corrective.

Roughly, there are two dramatic points of departure for melodrama. One is coloured by a female protagonist's point of view which provides a focus for identification. The other examines tensions in the family, and between the sexes and generations; here, although women play an important part, their point of view is not analysed and does not initiate the drama. Helen Foley's article 'Sex and State in Ancient Greece' analyses Greek drama in terms that illuminate the 'safety-valve' function of Hollywood's family melodramas. She argues that Aeschylus shows how overvaluation of virility under patriarchy causes social and ideological problems which the drama comments on and attempts to correct: 'male characters . . . overly concerned with military and political glory at the expense of domestic harmony and their own children', and 'the emotional domestic sphere cannot be allowed direct political power and the wife must subordinate herself to her husband in marriage; but the maternal or domestic claims are nevertheless central and inviolable, a crucial check on bellicose male-dominated democracy'.[2]

For family life to survive, a compromise has to be reached, sexual difference softened, and the male brought to see the value of domestic life. As art and drama deal generously with male fantasy, a dramatic rendering of women's frustrations, publicly acting out an adjustment of balance in the male ego, is socially and ideologically beneficial. A positive male figure who rejects rampant virility and opposes the unmitigated power of the father achieves (at least by means of a 'happy end') the reintegration of both sexes in family life. The phallocentric, misogynist fantasies of patriarchal culture are shown here to be in contradiction with the ideology of the family. These tensions are certainly present in both the Hollywood Western and melodrama; both tend towards a beneficial sacrifice of unrestrained masculine individualism in the interests of civilisation, law and culture. Rafe in *Home from the Hill* re-establishes the family and 'feminine' values on the grave of his over-bearing father. But, as Sirk has pointed out, the strength of the melodramatic form lies in the amount of dust the story raises along the road, the cloud of overdetermined irreconcilables which put up a resistance to being neatly settled, in the last five minutes, into a happy end.

Sirk, in the two films on which he had virtual independence (both produced by Albert Zugsmith), was able to turn his attention to the 'masculine' or family melodrama without conforming to a standard happy end. He turns the conventions of melodrama sharply. Roger Shumann in *Tarnished Angels* and Kyle Hadley in *Written on the Wind* (both played by Robert Stack) are tortured and torn by the mystique of masculinity, haunted by phallic obsessions and fear of impotence. Both are suicidal, finally taking refuge in death. In these two films Sirk provides an extremely rare epitaph, an insight into *men* as victims of patriarchal society. He shows castration anxiety, not (as is common) personified by a vengeful woman but presented *dread*fully and without mediation. In dealing with the male unconscious Sirk approaches complexity near to the tragic. His Universal movies deal more specifically with women, and work more clearly within melodramatic conventions.

Significantly, discussions of the difference between melodrama and tragedy specify that while the tragic hero is conscious of his fate and torn between conflicting forces, characters caught in the world of melodrama are not allowed transcendent awareness or knowledge.

> In tragedy, the conflict is within man; in melodrama, it is between men, or between men and things. Tragedy is concerned with the nature of man, melodrama with the habits of men (and things). A habit normally reflects part of nature, and that part functions as if it were the whole. In melodrama we accept the part for the whole; this is a convention of the form.[3]

Melodramatic characters act out contradiction to varying degrees and gradually face impossible resolutions and probable defeats. However, the implications and poignancy of a particular narrative cannot be evoked wholly by limited characters with restricted dramatic functions – they do not fully grasp the forces they are up against or their own instinctive behaviour. It is here that the formal devices of Hollywood melodrama, as analysed by Thomas Elsaesser,[4] provide a transcendent, wordless commentary, giving abstract emotion spectacular form, contributing a narrative level that provides the action with a specific coherence. *Mise en scène*, rather than the undercutting of the actions and words of the story level, provides a central point of orientation for the spectator.

Sirk allows a certain interaction between the spectator's reading of *mise en scène*, and its presence within the diegesis, as though the protagonists, from time to time, can *read* their dramatic situation with a code similar to that used by the audience. Although this device uses aesthetics as well as narrative to establish signs for characters on the screen as for the spectator in the cinema, elements such as lighting or camera movement still act as a privileged discourse for the spectator.

In the opening scene of *All That Heaven Allows*, Cary (Jane Wyman) looks at Ron (Rock Hudson) with the first inklings of desire. The emotion is carried through into the second scene through the presence of the autumn leaves he has given her, so that we, the spectators, share with Cary his secret importance. The touch of nature he has left behind marks the opening seconds of her preparation for what is to prove a barren evening at the Country Club. The children comment on Cary's red dress, interpreting it, as we do, as a sign of newly awakened interest in life and love but mistaking its object as the impotent and decrepit

Harvey, her date and their preferred future stepfather. The camera does not allow the spectator to make the same mistake, establishing in no uncertain terms the formal detachment with which Cary sees Harvey, in contrast to the way in which in the previous scene Ron had been subtly extracted from the background and placed in close face-to-face with Cary.

Lighting style clearly cannot be recognised within the diegesis, and in *All That Heaven Allows* it illustrates the basic emotional division which the film is actually about: Cary's world is divided between the cold, hard light (blues and yellows) of loneliness, repression and oppression and the warmer, softer light (red/orange) of hope, emotional freedom and sexual satisfaction. In keeping with the pace and emotion generated by a particular scene, Sirk occasionally changes lighting from one shot to the next, for instance, in order to use the dramatic potential of an intricate screen which dominates Cary's confrontation with her son Ned.

Although it is impossible to better Rainer Werner Fassbinder's plot synopsis of *All That Heaven Allows*,[5] it might be useful to bring out some different emphases. The story-line is extremely simple, if not minimal (concocted specifically to repeat the success of *Magnificent Obsession*)[6] and is told strictly from a woman's point of view, both in the sense of world view (the film is structured around female desires and frustrations) and point of identification (Cary, a widow with two college-age children and a standard of life in keeping with her late husband's elevated social and economic position). The narrative quickly establishes lack (her world is sexually repressed and obsessed simultaneously, offering only impotent elderly companionship – Harvey – or exploitative lechery – Howard). She then discovers love and a potentially physically and emotionally satisfying *country* way of life in Ron Kirby, her gardener (whose resonance shifts from that of the socially unacceptable in the Country Club world to that of the independent man in harmony with nature out by the old mill where he grows trees). Cary's transgression of the class barrier mirrors her more deeply shocking transgression of sexual taboos in the eyes of her friends and children. Her discovery of happiness is then reversed as she submits to pressure and gives Ron up, resulting in a 'flight into illness'. The doctor puts her on the road to success through self-knowledge and a happy end, but, by an ironic *deus ex machina* in reverse, their gratification is postponed by Ron's accident (caused by his joy at seeing Cary in the distance). A hidden shadow is cast implicitly over their perfect, joyful acceptance of love, although as the shutters are opened in the morning, the cold, hard light of repression is driven off the screen by the warm light of hope and satisfaction.

Jon Halliday points out the importance of the dichotomy between contemporary New England society – the setting for the movie – and 'the home of Thoreau and Emerson' as lived by Ron. 'Hudson and his trees are both America's past and America's ideals. They are ideals which are now unattainable. . . .'[7] The film is thus posited on a recognised contradiction within the American tradition. The contemporary reality and the ideal can be reconciled only by Cary moving, as it were, into the dream which, as though to underline its actual ephemeral nature, is then broken at the end by Ron's accident. How can natural man and woman re-establish the values of primitive economy and the division of labour when the man is bedridden and incapable? How can a mother of grown children overcome the taboo against her continued sexual activity in 'civilised society', when the object of her desire is reduced to child-like dependence on her ministrations?

In other films, particularly *All I Desire*, *Imitation of Life* and *The Tarnished Angels*, Sirk ironises and complicates the theme of the continued sexuality of mothers. The women perform professionally (from the depths of Laverne's parachute jump in *Tarnished Angels* to the heights of Lora's stardom in *Imitation of Life*) and attract the gaze of men and the curious crowd. Their problems are approached with characteristically Sirkian ambiguity as they try to brazen out their challenge to conformity as best they can. Cary, on the other hand, has no heroic or exhibitionist qualities, and the gaze and gossip of the town cause her agonies of embarrassment. It is only very occasionally that the setting and the narrative move away from Cary and, when they do, it is significant. The gaze of Cary's friends at Sara's party is established in a scene before Cary and Ron arrive. The camera takes in the prurient voyeurism which turns the sexual association of a middle-aged woman with a younger man into an act of public indecency (this view is then expressed and caricatured by Howard's drunken assault on Cary).

Melodrama can be seen as having an ideological *function* in working certain contradictions through to the surface and re-presenting them in an aesthetic form. A simple difference, however, can be made between the way that irreconcilable social and sexual dilemmas are finally resolved in, for instance, *Home from the Hill*, and are not in, for example, *All That Heaven Allows*. It is as though the fact of having a female point of view dominating the narrative produces an excess which precludes satisfaction. If the melodrama offers a fantasy escape for the identifying women in the audience, the illusion is so strongly marked by recognisable, real and familiar traps that escape is closer to a day-dream than to fairy story. Hollywood films made with a female audience in mind tell a story of contradiction, not of reconciliation. Even if a heroine resists society's overt pressures, its unconscious laws catch up with her in the end.

Notes

1. Paul Willemen, 'Distanciation and Douglas Sirk', *Screen*, vol. 12, no. 2. Paul Willemen, 'Towards an Analysis of the Sirkian System', *Screen*, vol. 13, no. 4. Stephen Neale, 'Douglas Sirk', *Framework*, no. 5.
2. Helen Foley, 'Sex and State in Ancient Greece', *Diacritics*.
3. R. B. Heilman, *Tragedy and Melodrama* (Seattle: University of Washington Press, 1968).
4. Thomas Elsaesser, 'Tales of Sound and Fury', *Monogram*, no. 4.
5. R. W. Fassbinder, 'Six Films by Douglas Sirk', Halliday and Mulvey (eds) *Douglas Sirk*, Edinburgh Film Festival Publication (Edinburgh, 1972).
6. Jon Halliday, *Sirk on Sirk* (London: Secker & Warburg, 1971).
7. Ibid.

6

Fassbinder and Sirk*

* Written as a review of *Fear Eats the Soul* for *Spare Rib* in 1974.

Rainer Werner Fassbinder is proving to be one of the most important directors of the 1970s, and his film *Fear Eats the Soul*, which launches London's new art cinema, the Gate, is a good example of his recent work. Fassbinder's films are not specifically feminist but they are of interest to women because they deal consistently with themes in which women have an independent importance, and have been emphasised by the women's movement: the family, hysteria, and the contradictions between the oppressed and the oppressor within a class. His particular interest, the individual's desire that finds itself in direct conflict with class and family ideology, links him to the Hollywood melodrama of the 1950s. Fassbinder acknowledges his debt to Hollywood. His understanding of the Hollywood melodrama, the way its greatest directors built up a picture of ideological forces and the insoluble problems of sex and desire within them, contributes to the complexity he achieves in his own work.

Fassbinder came to the American cinema through the influence of the French New Wave and its acknowledged debt to Hollywood. (His first feature was dedicated to Chabrol, Rohmer and Straub, showing in itself a sense of history and of heritage.) But much more than they, he has looked back to Hollywood melodrama in its own right. He takes it further along its own path, transposing and bringing out its essential themes with a clarity that comes from both the passing of time and freedom from studio supervision, and a bitterness that comes from his perception of contemporary German society. There are two important ways in which Fassbinder develops the American melodrama. First, he focuses on hysteria or the symptoms of repression in the oppressed. Although hysteria has traditionally been considered a female phenomenon, Fassbinder has brought out its meaning in men, by dealing with men who are an ambiguous and oppressed situation (most particularly in *Merchant of Four Seasons*) in relation to their class and family, men who are trapped, as women are, in a way they can neither grasp nor articulate.

Fassbinder uses role reversals and sex confusions in his own manner, but particularly to expand the American melodrama in a second direction, to take it outside the confines of the bourgeoisie. While Hollywood in the 1950s dealt above all with the oppression and frustrations of the bourgeois woman, Fassbinder goes into the repressions of bourgeois ideology within the working class, the lumpen proletariat and its tyranny within the *petite bourgeoisie*. Women still have an unusual importance in his films, maintaining the subtly subversive tradition of the Hollywood genre at its best (made about women and for women), where women are a sign of desire that makes them a potential weak link in the ideological structure.

Fassbinder has particularly acknowledged his debt to Douglas Sirk, pioneer director of some of the greatest melodramas, first in Germany in the 1930s and then reaching the peak of his career with his so-called 'women's weepies' in Hollywood in the 1950s. Both come from the theatre, both brought to the cinema a sense of theatrical distanciation (drama as spectacle) that works against the tendency of film to absorb the spectator into itself. (They are both also conscious that the cinema is in the camera. Fassbinder quotes Sirk as saying: 'A director's philosophy is his lighting and camera angles'.) *Fear Eats the Soul* is loosely based on Sirk's *All That Heaven Allows*, not as a re-make but as a transposition. The plot changes bring out, to begin with, the way in which working-class people are infinitely more trapped than the bourgeoisie when in an intolerable personal situation. Having no means of escape, no economic alternatives, their problem is not one of emotional choice but of facing the situation, going under, struggling against it, in a succession of desperate attempts at mastery over the world. At the same time, Fassbinder himself has pointed out that the escape of Sirk's hero and heroine contains the irony of the happy end: you cannot escape from yourself and your past as easily as all that.

In the Sirk film, a rich country club widow falls in love with the free-lance gardener (who comes to prune her trees), young, handsome, poor and from the wrong social class. The revulsion of her teenage children, her friends and her small town, country club community put her in a state of agonised conflict. Her love for the gardener is not only based on deep sexual re-awakening but on an identification with the Utopian dream of complete social and economic self-sufficiency he is attempting to create for himself (and for her, if she can break with her past) in the countryside. In the Fassbinder, an elderly working-class office-cleaner falls in love with a Moroccan immigrant worker. They marry and she tries to incorporate him into her world, thus bringing down racist ostracism from her grown-up children, her fellow workers and her whole neighbourhood. But the greatest crisis comes after the couple have finally become accepted; it is difficult for her, in her gratitude at being allowed to *belong* again, to stay uncontaminated by the racism that pervades her surroundings. Both films bring the couple together at the end, as they realise how much they mean to each other, but the man falls victim to the stress of the relationship and ends an invalid, with the woman at his bedside.

The two films have more in common than a romantic love story of an older woman ostracised for her love for a younger man of different social status. They both depict the contradictions of a woman's economic position within her own class, and the way she is torn apart by trying to move outside a predestined path. In these two relationships, the women are culturally dominant, belonging by birth and marriage to a dominant class, in *All That Heaven Allows*, the higher bourgeoisie, in *Fear Eats the Soul*, the white, indigenous working class. But both have a lower economic status than the men of their own class; one is a housewife living off her dead husband's legacy and the other is an office-cleaner (Emmi is reluctant at first to admit what she does). There is an implicit identity in both films between the economic position of the woman and that of the man she falls in love with. In *Fear Eats the Soul* the two protagonists belong to the main sectors of casual, unorganised labour that capitalist society depends on but refuses to recognise as an integral part of the work-force. Nor are they treated as serious workers by the unions, who see only the casual intermittent nature of the work, ignoring both the degree of exploitation involved and its meaning for the capitalist economy as a whole.

The lower antinomy in the polarisations – man/woman, indigenous worker/immigrant worker – creates an unexpected parallel between the two terms, underlining the closeness of indigenous woman/immigrant man. Although the Sirk film takes place within a bourgeois milieu, there is also a parallel economic interest between the protagonists. The isolated unproductive labour of the housewife is comparable to the isolated unproductive labour of the gardener. But together they can achieve social independence through economic self-sufficiency, outside capitalism and its urban services: the gardener to control his own labour power and the widow to find her place as an equal and useful partner in the primaeval division of labour that has always played a part in the rural American dream. Fassbinder acknowledges the power of Sirk's film, and brings out its social implications as he transforms it.

The sexual implications of both films are complex. The woman's higher social status contributes to her sexual fulfilment and allows her to find equality and solidarity with a man for the first time. But an active/passive role reversal is no solution. The man loses dignity, risking stereotyping as sex-object, for example, when Emmi asserts her triumph over the other women and displays Ali to them as a man would a woman. And Sirk has often dealt with the humiliation heaped on a mother (not necessarily, even, an 'older woman') who still publicly asserts her active sexuality. Cary's romance becomes a source of scandal and gossip. The *mother* who refuses to be made a back number attracts the otherwise indifferent gaze of her neighbours. In *Fear Eats the Soul* the spectator has the sense of staring along with the whole neighbourhood; the heroine has literally made a spectacle of herself.

It is satisfying to see the hidden strengths of the American melodrama brought out so vigorously. Sirk's clear sense of the oppression of family life, the repressive nature of bourgeois society, his irony and unusual grasp of the dilemma of women, should be used and remembered. And Fassbinder does not work, as Sirk did, with one hand tied behind his back by the restrictions of Hollywood. Finally, in structure and composition Fassbinder has learnt from Sirk this crucial fact, as he quotes: 'Sirk has said: you can't make films about things, you can only make films with things; with people, with light, with flowers, with mirrors, with blood, in fact with all the fantastic things that make life worth living'.

7

Images of Women, Images of Sexuality: Some Films by J. L. Godard*

* Co-written with Colin MacCabe.

Do you know, madame, that despite your very light brown hair, you make me think of a beautiful redhead. *La Jolie Rousse* is a poem by Apollinaire. 'Soleil voici le temps de la raison ardente . . .' Well, that burning-bright reason which the poet is looking for . . . when it does appear, it takes on the form of a beautiful redhead. That is what can be seen on a woman's face, the presence of awareness, something which gives her a different, an extra beauty. Feminine beauty becomes something all-powerful, and it's for that reason, I believe, that all the great ideas in French are in the feminine gender.

(From *Une femme mariée*)

Are there objects which are inevitably a source of suggestiveness as Baudelaire suggested about women?

(Roland Barthes)

Following this line of thought, one might reach the conclusion that women have escaped the sphere of production only to be absorbed the more entirely by the sphere of consumption, to be captivated by the immediacy of the commodity world no less than men are transfixed by the immediacy of profit. . . . Women mirror the injustice masculine society has inflicted on them – they become increasingly like commodities.

(Theodor Adorno on Veblen)

In the twenty years that Godard has been making movies one of the remarkable features of his work has been its closeness to the contemporary moment. Perhaps the most striking example of this is *La Chinoise*, apparently aberrant when it appeared, yet confirmed in its actuality less than a year later by the events of May 1968. But all his films are inextricably locked in with the moment of their making, existing on the sharp edge between observing the world taking and changing shape and, in giving it concrete form in representation, being part of the changing shapes.

During these twenty years, and particularly in the last ten, feminism has emerged as a crucial new cultural and political force. Feminists have considered images and representations to be a political issue. Godard has always been in the forefront of debates on politics and representation. And women have always been central to his films. Yet, on this point, Godard's practice seems to be out of sync with feminist arguments on the representation of women. Perhaps the necessary exclusiveness of the Women's Movement, the need for women to develop their own positions, diminishes the influence of feminism on an established film-maker such as Godard, open, otherwise, to the political developments and conflicts of his moment. It is not that Godard's movies have remained untouched by the growth of feminism – quite the contrary – but his use of images of women continues, from his early through to his late films, to raise problems for those who have followed the logic of feminist arguments. Two examples, from very different periods, can serve to indicate both the interest and the problems of Godard's representations of women.

The first example goes straight to the heart of the matter. In *A bout de souffle* Patricia goes to a press conference given by the novelist M. Parvulesco, who has just published an erotic novel. He is surrounded by journalists bombarding him with questions about love and the relations between the sexes and his responses can be taken as enigmatic or simply banal. When Patricia asks, 'Do you believe that women have a role to play in modern society?' we recognise that the question is as clichéd as the others but, at the same time, through our knowledge of the narrative, that it represents a real dilemma for Patricia herself. Should she try to pursue her career as a journalist or let herself be absorbed into Michel's world? His world is a gangster movie made up of violence and his love for her. He is on the run from the police but promises dreams of freedom and fortune in Italy. Parvulesco's answer is short and to the point. He takes off his glasses, leans forward, giving Patricia a privileged look, and says: 'Yes, if she is charming, and is wearing a striped dress and dark glasses'. Patricia answers his look with a complicit smile. The deliberate misunderstanding becomes the deliberate suggestion: women's contribution to the modern world can be measured according to their sex appeal. This is a point that Godard returns to repeatedly in his films. He understands the forces that mould women into a stereotype and reduce them to impotence.

More than any other single film-maker Godard has shown up the exploitation of woman as an image in consumer society. For Godard this image is the very basis of consumer society, a relation he captures in his description of the contemporary world as *la civilisation du cul*. But his own relation to that image raises further problems. The scene from *A bout de souffle* demonstrates but is also complicit with an equation of woman and sexuality. In his later work Godard breaks down the equation to reveal its construction – that is, how the female form and its connotations are used in the circulation of images. But this investigation always risks producing another equation in which women represent *the problem of sexuality in capitalist society*. And this position can be traced back to Godard's romantic heritage in which woman is divided into an appearance that can be enjoyed and an essence that is only knowable at risk, deceptive and dangerous.

Ten years later Godard made *British Sounds*. Nothing could be further from *A bout de souffle*, a gangster genre movie (commented on, distanced, but still strongly within the magnetic radius of Hollywood), than this relentless political investigation of Britain in 1969. As Godard used and transformed the gangster movie in *A bout de souffle*, so he uses and transforms the documentary in *British Sounds*, and as *A bout de souffle* shows Godard influenced by Hollywood and bringing Hollywood to Europe, so *British Sounds* is a product of the period of revolutionary commitment around 1968 and Godard's rigorous application of current ideas to the cinema. Both in their different ways show his involvement with his moment and the necessary unity, for him, of theory and practice. The film critic becomes director, the political militant makes movies.

This combination of theoretical rigour and commitment to applying theory in his films makes Godard continually fascinating, as one watches dilemmas and contradictions being courageously tackled in the course of his films. But it is not only a commitment to the interrelation of theory with practice that links *A bout de souffle* and *British Sounds*; a concern with the contemporary situation of women is common to both. After a long opening travelling shot along a production line of cars over which a voice pronounces a classic Marxist analysis of capitalism, the sound-track prefaces the next section by announcing that 'the relation between man and man is dependent on the relation between man and woman'. The sounds of this second sequence are already more complex. While a middle-class woman's voice talks of the subjective benefits and problems of women's liberation, a working-class man's voice juxtaposes the discourses of politics and sexuality, the distance between the two grotesquely exemplified in his demand for a 'Marxist–Leninist analysis of the natural position to fuck'. The images which accompany these voices contrast with the populous and noisy factory floor that we have just seen. The opening shot is of a silent interior of a suburban house in which a naked woman moves from room to room and goes up and down stairs. This static shot is followed by another, this time a close-up of the body framed from waist to thigh, and the sequence ends with a head-and-shoulders shot of the woman talking on the telephone, her conversation repeating with minor differences what the woman's voice-over is saying.

The struggle between images and sounds which composes the film starts here. If the image of the factory has a sound to go with it – the classic Marxist analysis of capitalism – there is no sound for these images of silence, of women. For Godard, the voice of women's liberation and the voice of Marxism cannot be simply added one to the other, not least because, he considers, the silence of the house and the body of woman have not yet found a place in political discourse. Godard's presentation still simply identifies woman and sexuality. He ignores the evident fact that a contrast with male labour in factory production would, in the home, be domestic labour, that of wife and mother as producer and reproducer of labour power, with the all-too-strident noises that accompany it. It is not that Godard's investigation lacks interest but it is finally a masculine investigation, ignoring the complex social determination of women's position in favour of an image of woman outside any social or economic context.

The limitations of Godard's position are evident in the images themselves. For many, the use of a naked female body immediately casts doubt on Godard's project. The very image for the most visible exploitation that women endure in a sexist society cannot be used with impunity, cannot be used without a certain complicity. Once again, the position is not straightforward. It is possible to argue that Godard's use of the image of the body is resolutely unexploitative. The length of the shots and the fact that the image of the body is not presented as spectacle makes us uneasy in our position of the voyeur. If we look at this woman's body then we are aware of our own look, which is not hidden in the folds of the narrative and the movement of the camera. Similarly there is none of that titillation of vision on which exploitation depends. What we see is not the product of an unveiling; we gaze at a female body for several minutes. But although these arguments are valid they do not resolve the problem. The shot of the naked woman is a good example. On the one hand its length and form are an attempt to demystify the very source of our images of women and yet, at the same time, the potency of that image is such that it is doubtful that any simple demystification is possible. To use that image is immediately to run the risk of introducing the discourse in which the enigma of woman will offer the truth of the male situation; to reveal the truth of the image is to risk the inevitable demand for a true voice to complete it.

Godard slides continually between an investigation of the images of woman and an investigation which uses those images. It could be argued that since his collaboration with Anne-Marie Miéville this sliding has to a certain extent diminished as the problems of male sexuality have been introduced directly into the content of the films. *Numéro deux* is the most important example of their collaboration, from this perspective, but before looking at *Numéro deux* Godard's earlier films should be considered.

It is illuminating to examine the effect that sexing of point of view has on the narrative of particular films. There is an important difference between films organised around a male central protagonist and those around a female one, and a difference between the worlds they depict. Although this rule holds greater sway in Hollywood genre movies, its effect, infinitely more nuanced and sometimes consciously defied,[1] can also be seen in Godard's films. For instance, in *Pierrot le fou*, in which Ferdinand acts as central consciousness, the narrative referent is fiction and fantasy. The action does not develop in terms of logical relations of time, space and verisimilitude but in great sweeps ('We crossed France'), picaresque adventure ('Look, Pierrot, a Ford Galaxy. . . . Go on, show me you're a man'), generic violence ('detective stories') and Utopian escape ('the island of Mystery'). On the other hand the narrative of *Une femme mariée*, in which Charlotte acts as central consciousness, is acted out on a considerably smaller scale. Charlotte's story is literally a slice of life, with a beginning, middle and end, that is highly organised on the level of narrative form and symmetry, but not on the level of narrative action. The end provides no solution, no rounding off of the drama. And, unusually for Godard, there is no violence. The dramatic space of *Une femme mariée* is social and analytic, emerging out of Rouch and Rossellini rather than Sam Fuller and *film noir*. Sometimes, as in *Masculin/féminin*, for instance, the intimacy of the human relations observed is abruptly broken by bizarre outbreaks of violence. But this interweaving never merges two different worlds. Godard's use of interior space functions both figuratively and fictionally to limit the world of women's day-dreams. It is only when she is projected in a man's fantasy that her body takes on an image of power. The spatial limitations introduced by the woman's point of view have no necessary link with 'realism', but Godard uses this reduced space to analyse woman in relation to her social formation, the home.

Godard makes an important attempt to depict woman 'inside', but this position implies an 'outside', an alternative, masculine sphere and point of view where woman's threatening qualities predominate. This image does not refer to 'women' but is a phantasm of the male unconscious (familiar from the romanticism of 'La Belle Dame sans Merci' to the heroines of the *film noir*). In *Pierrot le fou*, Marianne is the origin of violence. Godard depicts woman outside in the world of action, in a fantasy based on the fear and desire of a male protagonist. She is mysterious, ultimately elusive, fascinating and destructive; this 'otherness' follows from a narrative centred on the hero's point of view. Marianne is as mysterious to the spectator as to Ferdinand. The hero leaves his home and family to follow her into a world of violence and *amour fou*, referring to the *film noir* tradition: Marianne's frantic search for money seems to throw back to *Double Indemnity* (Wilder), her treachery to *The Lady from Shanghai* (Welles), her powers of destruction and self-destruction to *Out of the Past* (Tourneur).[2]

Une femme mariée presents a marked contrast to *Pierrot le fou*. The spectator watches the development of the film alongside Charlotte; we *know* with her, not with her husband or lover. But, at the same time, the image of Charlotte is distanced, re-presented as the problem of woman's image in consumer society. On the one hand Godard takes a situation recognisable through our own direct experience of life, dilemmas *within* society, similar to and familiar from, the real world. On the other, he examines the cinematic image in order to demonstrate how far that direct experience is already an experience of images. The film's foregrounding of its own process of production and its break with the conventions of verisimilitude are not at the service of a formalist aesthetic. They allow Godard to confront the way that consumer society moulds woman's image so that it conforms to a given concept of female sexual appeal.

The female body has become industrialised; a woman must buy the means to paint on (make-up) and sculpt (underwear/clothes) a look of femininity, a look which is the guarantee of *visibility* in sexist society for each individual woman. Advertisements sell the means of production of the look, sealing it in with the mark of feminine desirability, attainable by means of lipsticks, bras, scents and so on – magic formulae depending on novelty for appeal just as the market depends on turnover for profit. Magazines provide the know-how, techniques and expertise; sealing the association of *woman* and *sexuality* in the minds of women themselves. It is almost as though woman herself were a factory, feeding in the means of production, painting on the mask and emerging transformed with value added in the process, a commodity ready for consumption. *Une femme mariée* contains a great many references in dialogue to male concepts of female beauty and their mediation through the image:

> *Robert*　　You ought to do like they do in Italian films. . . . Have you
> seen any? The women don't shave under their arms.
>
> *Charlotte*　I prefer American films. Hollywood ones . . . they're
> prettier.
>
> *Robert*　　Yes, but less arousing.

There is also a recurrent emphasis throughout the films on images of the female breasts, from advertisements of brassières to 'the ideal breasts of Venus de Milo', and both Charlotte and Mme Céline try to measure themselves to see how they compare with this ideal figure.

Charlotte is nothing more than a perfect image. But this perfect image, this mask of visibility (which, composed of make-up, clothes and so on, has an indexical relationship to the woman's body) is furthermore a symbolic sign. It represents the concept of woman in a given social formation – that is, the equation woman = sexuality. This feminine mask is the passport to visibility in a male-dominated world. Her mask of visibility conceals behind it the diverse and complex nature of woman's place in the social and economic order, where sexual difference is a matter of division of labour, differences and divisions which have no image, no form. The invisible women in factories, homes, schools, hospitals, are formless and unrepresentable.

As observer of woman as image, and analyser of the moulding, masking process evolved by consumer capitalism, Godard is acute and rigorous. His consciousness of image as cultural product, consciousness of himself as part of and torn by cultural traditions, gives him access to levels of meaning that the image of woman has acquired in history like the grime on an ancient monument. He takes things a step further. In *Une femme mariée*, Godard is interested in the relationship between advertising and the body, the commodities produced for women and the image which sells the commodities. He then indicates how that image functions in relation to the home and to the place of the woman in the home as *the* consumer in advanced capitalist society. Charlotte and Pierre present their apartment to their dinner guest in the language of the advertising brochure. The image on the screen, showing Pierre sitting down on the sofa next to Charlotte, establishes Godard's perception of the married couple as the basic unit of consumer capitalism, and the home they construct about them as its essential market outlet. The married woman's function is to provide a rationale for this economic process, and simultaneously to be, herself, *prima inter pares* of her husband's possessions. Her body's mass-produced perfection expresses his position in the world outside, the world of production and achievement.

Within the bourgeoisie a woman's physical appearance, elegance and fashionableness have complemented her husband's economic position. Illustrating the shifts inherent in the changing nature of 'subsistence' under capitalism, *Deux ou trois choses que je sais d'elle* concentrates not on the bourgeoisie as in *Une femme mariée*, but on the effects of consumer capitalism on the Parisian working class. The family lives in a new housing estate, a concrete jungle on the outskirts of the city, a new world similar to that of *Une femme mariée*; but the different social context is indicated by the fact that the husband is a car mechanic rather than a pilot. In *Deux ou trois choses que je sais d'elle* the landscape functions as *mise en scène*, echoing the changing world around Juliette. In *Une femme mariée* the language and landscape of advertising seemed to shape people and their lives like a sculpting force. In *Deux ou trois choses que je sais d'elle* the landscape has become gigantic, disproportionate to the people who scuttle like ants among motorways and housing complexes. The screen of *Deux ou trois choses que je sais d'elle* is filled with earth-movers and bulldozers which are changing the city's spatial relations. The anthropomorphic proportions of Paris are disappearing. As Godard's voice announces on the sound-track:

> One thing is obvious: that the structuring of the Paris region will enable the government to carry out its class policy with even greater ease and that the monopolies will be able to direct and organise the economy without really taking into account the aspirations to a better life of those eight million inhabitants.

The film is set at the moment when luxury goods came within the economic sphere of the working class, during the boom in consumer durables (before rampant inflation, before depression). Once again Godard sees advertising as playing a crucial role in forming people's desires, creating a new market for expanding production. Once again, the family and the home are the point of consumption and it is the wife's job to 'manage' the process. In *Deux ou trois choses que je sais d'elle*, loosely based on a news item that attracted Godard's attention, the wife, Juliette, takes to casual prostitution to earn the extra money needed to keep up with this new 'image' of a correct standard of living. *Deux ou trois choses que je sais d'elle* marks a move away from the exotic perception of a woman's selling of her sexuality present in *Vivre sa vie* or *Une femme est une femme*, where the heroine is a stripper. However, the centrality of sexuality to any image of woman is, if anything, more marked in *Deux ou trois choses que je sais d'elle*.

Godard's perception of women in the economy is simultaneously illuminating and obscurantist. His analysis of the place of the image in relation to consumption, to our patterns of living, is acute and succeeds in linking the oppression of capitalism and the alienation of sexuality. There is, however, a crucial flaw in the analysis because, although it shows up the close relations between sexuality and an economic system, it finally reproduces the equation between woman and sexuality which, at another level, it displaces. If one series of Godard's films assumes a woman's point of view, it is a point of view that is determined by her sexuality. In the tradition of the apocryphal Jesuit dictionary containing the entry '*Woman*: see *Sin*', Godard's films conflate woman and sexuality. With the very important exception of *Tout va bien* Godard never shows women placed in an economic or social role that is not an aspect of their sexual function or its social rationalisation, marriage. It is as though woman can only be of interest through her sexuality.

At the point where the most rigorous challenge is necessary, Godard's own cultural traditions, the legacy of romanticism, his place in a system of desire, overdetermine his analysis of woman. Going back to *Pierrot le fou*, escape from the confines of the home, the advertising language of his elegant wife and friends, lies for Ferdinand in the world of fantasy: nineteenth-century romanticism or twentieth-century popular culture. And in this tradition woman, once again, becomes the sign for the sexual desires and fears of men. The phantasm recurs, an image of mystery, essential otherness and, very often, violence and deceit. From *Pierrot le fou* until 1968 this crisis became more and more acute. Godard's attempt to articulate the cultural traditions of classical art and the popular cinema was disintegrating under the more immediate pressures of the war in Vietnam. It was no longer possible to separate the romantic violence of Hollywood from the violence of imperialism, and the high cultural traditions from Velasquez to Picasso lead to a beautiful but arid dead-end on a Mediterranean island, cut off from history. In the more political films that followed, the privileging of sound over image went together with, one could almost say determined, a decreased interest in images of woman.

Indeed, Godard did not return specifically to the question of women until 1975, when he made *Numéro deux* in collaboration with Anne-Marie Miéville. It is his most thorough and self-conscious attempt to depict the problem of sexuality under capitalism, but at the same time it leaves the spectator with a sense of hesitancy and pessimism. The changes brought about in the working-class family by the post-war development of capitalism seem to have stabilised. Goods such as a television or a washing-machine which, in *Deux ou trois choses que je sais d'elle*, might have stood for the *embourgeoisement* of the consumer boom are now part of the basic subsistence of working-class life. Pierre's earphones for listening to music appear to be his status symbol. The concrete blocks of flats mushrooming everywhere in the earlier films have grown roots and lost any promise of a new way of life. In fact, the new way of life is one of claustrophobic imprisonment. Godard's old sensitivity to the limits of women's mobility in the world now focuses on the rigid division between inside and outside. The housewife is tied more tightly to the home and the camera echoes her imprisonment, never moving outside the confines of the flat, except to show her once, returning from a doomed search for work, refusing to give her attention to the demands of the outside world, unable to listen to a woman campaigning against the coup in Chile. The camera registers this scene from the balcony above, maintaining its own sense of imprisonment. This same camera position is used for the other exterior scene in the film. Emphasising the interior/exterior division as one of sexual difference, the screen juxtaposes Pierre, in successive shots, leaving for and returning from work with an image of Sandrine lying asleep in bed. The bed evokes a space more intimate yet more confined, the cosiness of the home inside the prison block, but at the same time takes us back to essential associations between women and sexuality.

Numéro deux opens with a long introductory sequence. First Godard himself presents the film, its apparatus (film and video combined) and tells how it was financed by his old friend and producer Georges Beauregard. Then the themes of the film are presented in a pre-diegetic sequence. Using two video monitors with voice-over commentary and written titles, Godard brings together an assortment of ideas and images that are suggestive rather than coherently argued. Cinema, sex, politics are the recurring images that start to work together almost subliminally for the spectator but actually define quite explicitly the film's area of interest. One monitor shows documentary footage of a May Day parade, the other shows scenes from kung fu movies, porno movies and trailers, finally posing the issue (voice off): 'No, it's not about politics, it's about sex.' 'No, it's not about sex, it's about politics.'

The diegetic section of the film keeps the video format, sometimes juxtaposing two monitor screens within the single cinematic space. The film uses rolling superimposition, direct superimposition and vision-mixing in which one image appears as an insert in another. This allows the action of the film to exist on different spatial levels simultaneously, developing a kind of montage within the single image itself, providing the spectator with the kind of pleasure in juxtaposition that can be obtained from the best use of deep-focus cinema.

Numéro deux is about the family unit, with the couple in the centre, children (a boy and a girl) coming after them and a grandmother and grandfather before them. Here we see the basic unit for production and reproduction of labour power, with the woman in the home, the 'factory' that carries out the domestic process. However, the film is not primarily concerned with the question of domestic labour under capitalism, but rather with the effects of capitalism on sexual relations and the oppression of the working class on this personal, emotional level. Work is one factor that disrupts Pierre and Sandrine's enjoyment of sex. Pierre comes home reduced to virtual impotence by the hierarchical chain of command at the factory, and is unable to satisfy Sandrine (she says 'If I was rich I'd pay for it') or do more than feel a mixture of sympathy and resentment at her complaints. But there is also a theme which has been important in Godard's earlier works involving relations between the sexes: that of female deception and the violence provoked as a result. Pierre rapes Sandrine anally in revenge for her sleeping with another man. The scene is probably the most important in the film, repeated often with

varied presentations, unequivocally shown as a scene of male violence
and assault on a woman, and a scene witnessed by their little daughter
Vanessa.

> *Pierre*   One day something terrible happened. Sandrine had fucked
> another guy. She wouldn't tell me who. I wanted to rape
> her. She let me and finally I buggered her. Then she started
> screaming. Afterwards we realised that Vanessa had seen it
> all. I suppose that's what family life is all about.

The little girl's witnessing of this act of sexual violence reproduces a
cliché, shocking in its visual realisation, of Freud's concept of the primal
scene. But the presence of the little girl acts almost as a distraction from
the underlying force and importance of the rape. It is here that Godard
shows the hatred and disgust, the virulent rejection of sexual difference,
that brings the romantic concept of woman to life. It is only a moment
of violence that gives Pierre sexual potency. Later on he says, 'Sometimes
she is the man and I am the woman. But seeing that I'm a guy,
sometimes with her it's . . . it's as though I was fucking another guy. It
must be because I like her putting her finger up my arse. I often ask
her to do it'.

It is these moments that mark a crucial shift in the terms of Godard's
presentation of sexuality. For the first time the chickens come home to
roost. The problem of sexuality is not *wholly* signified by a woman; the
problems of male sexuality, and the attendant undercurrents of misogyny
and violence, come out into the open. Godard and Miéville now explicitly
investigate the nature of the male sexuality that turns woman into an
image of its desire and, crucially, the repression of homosexuality as
one of the founding moments of that sexuality. The violence against
women, the emphasis on anal sex, turns around this ambiguous relation
to other men. It is another man's penis in Sandrine's body that makes
her body desirable but also makes it an object that must be punished
for arousing that desire. It could be objected that Godard's treatment of
this problem presents this repression and the subsequent violence as
inevitable. In one of the key scenes of the film the mother and daughter
dance while the son is eating. When the mother attempts to persuade
the boy to join them, she is angrily repulsed in a gesture of sexual
shame and disgust. This image of male self-exclusion from a female
world in which the body is more easily accepted is one that recurs in
the script of *The Story* and in *Sauve qui peut*.

There is a sense in which *Numéro deux*, at its most pessimistic, shows
people trapped within a given sexual identity which they neither
understand nor have any hope of transcending, and breeding a new
generation into the same pattern. And the given sexual identity is

sealed, not by personal desire, but by the needs of the social formation that defines their lives. It is not a question of conditioning: both Pierre and Sandrine are bitterly aware of their own shortcomings and seem to intuit the sources as coming from outside themselves. But as an isolated unit imprisoned in a concrete block they can do no more than act out their anger against one another. Pierre attacks Sandrine. Sandrine rejects Pierre. The film shows the interconnected frustrations of sex and violence as permeating every aspect of 'ordinary' life. This is, perhaps, one of its more radical points: a relentless insistence on *showing*, on the cinema screen, the place of sex in the home: in front of the children, explained to the children, de-mystified to the children, part of everyday language, the nudity of the young, the nudity of the old and so on.

In *Une femme mariée* and *Deux ou trois choses que je sais d'elle*, Godard showed women within a social formation, her sexuality functioning as part of an economic chain. In the second part of *Numéro deux*, Sandrine takes on a rather more symbolic function. Whereas the first part of the film is dominated by the image of the anal rape, the second part is dominated by Sandrine's constipation: 'When you can't get on with a man you can always leave him. But what do you do when it's a state? When a whole social system rapes you?'

Her blocked body comes to stand for the blockage in the social system as a whole; she consumes but she cannot produce. She eats but she is unable to defecate. Sandrine is simultaneously at the bottom of the line, a woman defined by passivity, and elevated, as the image of woman has so often been elevated before, to an abstraction or an emblem. Godard and Miéville have centred on Sandrine, acknowledging that sexuality is not fantasy and escape from the 'inside' into day-dreams and fiction, but is rooted deeply into the home. Sandrine is allowed her own desires beyond what she may represent for men but there is a sense in which she still represents a tautology. The tendency to define woman in terms of sexuality, however much that definition is given social complexity, is still familiar from Godard's earlier films. The film sets up an opposition between male/female, home/work that distorts the reality of working-class life. Working-class women have generally worked before and after childrearing – and often during it – and play a vital part in the labour force. The fact that the labour movement is itself reluctant to recognise women at work in production and services is like yet another level of masking: women visible in relation to man, invisible in the factories, hospitals, offices and so on. Woman's vulnerable place in the labour force is linked to her place in the home, producing and reproducing labour power, but they are two sides of the same coin. In one of the first films ever shot the Lumière brothers recorded workers leaving their factory. Most of the people going out of the factory gates on that day in 1895 were women.

There is another juxtaposition in *Numéro deux* that Godard and Miéville suggest and yet seem to skirt around. The two old people, grandmother and grandfather, have their own moments to speak. Both are shown naked, the woman washing accompanied by her voice off, the man sitting at a table with a drink and speaking straight to camera. The woman's speech is about woman; it is divided into two parts, seeming to represent the two sides of the paradox. The first part is about oppression and woman as victim of male violence, the need for her, herself, to make things change. The second part is about violence done to the natural world in the name of female narcissism, a litany of death and destruction for the adornment of her body. The man's speech is about his experience in the world, journeys to distant lands, adventure, politics and class consciousness. Here again one sees the spatial difference between male and female expectations of life, one tied to the body and the other free to roam and take action. This paradox takes us back to the original point of departure, the difference between the spatial representation of social relations in *Une femme mariée* and fantasy in *Pierrot le fou*.

Questions emerge, questions that Godard has always offered, hard to face, difficult to answer: how can we effect a conscious and political interaction between the cultural forms of representation on the one hand and economic and social relations on the other? How does one affect the other? Should one show what is, what should be, or the dreams that escape from what is and what should be? All these questions pose the issue of the relations between appearance in the real (for instance, the mask of femininity produced by society) and fantasy within the psyche (for instance, the phantasm of femininity projected by men) and how those relations are caught in the image. This conjuncture has always fascinated Godard and has acted as a key point for his inquiries.

In *Numéro deux*, despite the radical presentation of sex and the family, Sandrine's body is shown without questioning traditional uses of female beauty and sexual allure in the dominant forms of image production. Yet the film rigorously undercuts its own imagery by its refusal of the use of an image which we can simply gaze at. Female nakedness carries associations of the exploitation of women that almost no degree of formal subversion can displace. How far can the fragmentation of the image in *Numéro deux*, reminiscent in some ways of the fragmentation of Charlotte's body in *Une femme mariée*, undercut the iconography of woman contained within the separate images?

The contradictions apparent within Godard's depiction of women, the contradiction between his use of the female form to signify sexuality and his rigorous questioning of the film form itself constitute a statement of the confusions and difficulties surrounding images of woman. This lack of coherence is a productive spring-board both as a starting-point for understanding how and why woman's image accumulates its particular meanings and also as a basis for further development, the construction of a cinema which challenges those meanings and assumptions.

Notes

1. Thus, for example, Anna Karina plays the Humphrey Bogart character in *Made in USA.*
2. Sylvia Harvey has noted the crucial absence of the family in the *film noir,* and the association of woman with sexual excess and destruction (Sylvia Harvey (ed.), *Women in Film Noir* (London: British Film Institute, 1973)).

8

Melodrama Inside and Outside the Home*

* Published in C. MacCabe (ed.), *High Theory/Low Culture*, 1986.

In the 1950s, the Hollywood studio system was faced with three massive crises: the impact of the HUAC (House of UnAmerican Activities Committee) investigation, indictment as a monopoly under the anti-trust laws, and the coming of television. The first two provided an ideological and economic background to the third, which broke the genealogical links connecting different forms of popular theatrical entertainment that stretched back to the early days of urban industrial-ised culture. Television revolutionised the conditions of spectatorship associated with mass entertainment. Urban cultures of spectacle had always previously depended on a communal audience, collected together in larger or smaller spaces, from the vast theatres of the London melodrama, the Keith Vaudeville Bijou in Boston or the small shop-front nickelodeons of early cinema. The cinema's birth as a mass art can be fixed at the moment when the Kinetoscope gave way to communal theatrical viewing.[1] Television broke up this audience, to create a home-based mode of consumption that was prefigured by radio but without precedent as mass visual entertainment. Whereas the appeal of films was posited on 'going out', television appeals to 'staying in'. The draw of the city lights at night, the neon, the names of the stars, the glamour of the Palaces are at an end.

The success of television as a means of mass entertainment was historically secondary to its success as a consumer durable. The 1950s saw a swing to domesticity that complemented the US economy's expansion in production. And then, as *Rosie the Riveter* has evoked so vividly, American women were being tempted and dragooned back into the home to readjust the unsettling effects of the Second World War on the division of labour between the sexes. Conservative retrenchment, epitomised by McCarthy, was reinforced by the war in Korea and confidence in the dollar, the post-war international currency. In Douglas Sirk's words, 'America was feeling safe and sure of herself, a society primarily sheltering its comfortable achievements and institutions'.[2] Hollywood acknowledged the nature of the crisis by resorting desper-ately to technical innovations and gimmicks to lure audiences away from the television and out of the home. It is perhaps no accident that the 1950s are marked by the particular resurgence of the family melodrama, the Hollywood genre associated with the dramas of domesticity, woman, love and sexuality. While Hollywood put a brave and colourful face on its difficulties, filling the wide screen with Western landscapes and spectacular casts of thousands, the melodrama drew its source material from unease and contradiction within the very icon of American life, the home, and its sacred figure, the mother.

For me, the melodrama is represented first and foremost by Douglas Sirk and the movies he made during the 1950s. The final phase of Sirk's Hollywood career coincides with this pivotal phase in the film industry. He signed a contract with Universal studios in 1950 and left the US for ever in 1959. In 1955 he directed *All That Heaven Allows*. In the movie's central scene, Jane Wyman, playing a widow in her forties, is given a television set by her grown-up children. This Christmas gift celebrates her decision to stay and live in their old family home, renouncing her sexuality and reaffirming the property-based values of her bourgeois milieu. The television set becomes charged with metaphor and connotation linking middle-class interior, motherhood, prosperity and repression. But the formal staging of the scene, its dramatic construction, evokes something more: the fact that television sprang, Minerva-like, fully grown into the American home, into the midst of the American family, the source material of the Hollywood melodrama itself. It is as though, at the moment of defeat, Hollywood could afford to point out the seeds of decay in its victorious rival's own chosen breeding ground.

How things end can throw previous experience into unexpected perspective. The home, as a social place and mythologised space, has a special significance for the new medium, and can thus draw attention to the way that oppositions of inside/outside have given order and pattern to the centrifugal/centripetal tensions in urban, industrialised, capitalist life. Imagery of place and space can, perhaps, link the complex strands interconnecting the class and sexual politics of popular entertainment. The worker, the raw material of the labour force, is culturally marginalised, often immigrant and literally displaced. Spheres of male space (outside the home) or female space (inside the home) reflect economic and social aspects of sexual difference. Popular entertainment has been increasingly absorbed by and drawn into an ordered national consensus (in which the 'home' plays an important iconographic role). But its origins lay on the margins of society among the first urban, industrialised proletariat, and the early nineteenth-century melodrama provided the first means of collective cultural expression for this new class, in a new social and economic order.

ECONOMICS

A jump from the Hollywood melodrama of the 1950s to the early nineteenth-century melodrama brackets a particular strand of popular culture, from its birth in the crowded city streets to its death in the television-dominated home. But the chaotic crowds in the streets and the contained privacy of the home both have their origins in an urban industrialised environment, and are bound together as each other's other side of the coin. The family audience, under the aegis of the mother, provided a rhetorical excuse to broaden, step by step, the appeal of popular theatrical entertainment out of the margins into the sphere of respectability, while simultaneously placing it on a firm capitalist and entrepreneurial basis.

In a remarkable chapter on Coney Island, in his book *Delirious New York*, Rem Koolhaas analyses three stages in the cultural and economic development of the amusement park that provides a suggestive paradigm for the more complex and extended transitions in popular theatrical entertainment:

> The triad of personalities and professions that Tilyou, Thompson and Reynolds represent – amusement expert/professional architect/ developer politician – is reflected in the character of the three parks:
> *Steeplechase*, where the park format is invented almost by accident under the hysterical demand for entertainment;
> *Luna*, where the format is invested with thematic and architectural coherence; and finally
> *Dreamland*, where the preceding breakthroughs are elevated to an ideological plane by a professional politician.
>
> Reynolds realises that to succeed, Dreamland must transcend its compromised origins and become a post-proletarian park 'the first time in the history of Coney Island Amusement that an effort has been made to provide a place of amusement that appeals to all classes'.[3]

Clearly, there are no exact parallels (Boucicault probably outshines Thompson, while Reynolds's perverse, deviant, carnivalesque Dreamland could not have survived in the Hays-dominated world of the film moguls) but the phasing suggests similar patterns of development in other entertainment media.

The first, spontaneous phase can be compared with the early phases of the British working-class melodrama, the immigrant vaudeville in the US and the nickelodeon days of the cinema. Here, profits are limited by small-scale investment and the audience restricted to a sizeable but ideologically marginalised sector of the population. The early British

melodrama celebrated transitional, liminal themes that included memories of feudal oppression with reflection on the lot of the working man.
The melodrama turned the world of everyday normality upside-down;
the innocent and oppressed suffered at the hands of the dominant,
while arbitrary turns of plot and fate reflected the arbitrary, relentless
nature of class justice. There was a direct appeal to the concerns and
preoccupations of a recently urbanised working class. By mid-century
the social themes of the melodrama went into abeyance as the repeal of
the Licensing Act in 1843 brought an end to the legal formal class
distinction in British culture (as will be discussed below). This transition
was marked by the great rebuilding of the London melodrama theatres
in the 1850s, directing the poorer and less respectable towards the
developing music-halls until they, in turn, acquired Palace status in the
1880s.

In the early vaudeville, unlike the melodrama, words and language
played a central role. Comic monologues, jokes and sketches reflected
the immigrant audience's own fascination and difficulty with the English
language. Ethnicity and difference could be kept alive while a collective
obeisance to the new country alleviated the trauma of immigration and
urbanisation: 'the slang of the cities, the rough coinage of the labouring
classes, the pidgin English of the European immigrants, back-country
archaisms and provincial dialects. It is also the language of unarticulated
emotion and uncommunicable ideas'.[4]

This entertainment belonged to a no man's land, in between the old
world and the new, neither one nor the other and both at once. The
experience of marginality and transition is suspended between memory
and loss on the one hand and aspiration to something new on the other.
Once the demands of industrial production and the experience of urban
living are internalised, the spectacle offered by popular entertainment
changes its significance. It keeps alive the values of the new life, so that
they will seem to be within reach, and celebrates wealth, social mobility,
success and the machine age. The new world, now reached but still so
far away, exists as the 'other world' of glitter, stars and glamour. Similar
in some ways to the early British melodrama, the first phase should not
be seen as a lost 'Golden Age' of working-class culture but a moment of
elongated transition in which heightened awareness and political self-
consciousness characterise a position on the margins of society, looking
in. Albert McLean describes the changed mood of the later vaudeville:

The fantasy ran on according to the laws of its own being, inviting
the spectator to identify but not to participate, leaving him at the close
with the sense of some inchoate dream, the order and meaning of
which lay buried beneath the threshold of consciousness. The dream
might be repeated but it was not to be dissected or understood.[5]

From the 1850s, the British melodrama rose above its specifically working-class audience and acquired an equivalently higher level of capitalisation. In 1852 *The Corsican Brothers* was presented in London, pioneering a new emphasis on spectacle and special effects. Lavish productions demanded investment that went hand in hand with investment in the spectacular buildings themselves. The amazing illusions of the mid-century gave way later to equally grandiose and expensive enactments of natural reality. This emphasis on surface appearance is reminiscent of Koolhaas's description of the architect Thompson's Luna Park development at Coney Island:

Thompson had designed the appearance, the exterior of a magic city. But . . . he is finally unable or unwilling to use his private realm, with all its metaphorical potential, for the design of culture. He is still an architectural Frankenstein whose talent for creating the new far exceeds his ability to control its contents.

Luna's astronauts may be stranded on another planet, in a magic city, but they discover in the sky-scraper forest the over-familiar instruments of pleasure – the Bunny Hug, the Burros, the Circus, the German Village, the Fall of Port Arthur, the Gates of Hell, the Great Train Robbery, the Whirl-the-Whirl.

Luna Park suffers from the self-defeating laws that govern entertainment: it can only skirt the surface of myth, only hint at the anxieties accumulated in the collective unconscious.[6]

When the cinema grew out of the nickelodeons into the age of feature films and picture palaces, with consequent increases in finance, nearly a century's development in popular theatrical spectacle existed as a tradition and a point of reference. The move towards a more monied audience had already produced the great spectacular melodramas of the late nineteenth century and the respectable vaudeville of, for instance, B. F. Keith. Naturally the presence of this popular cultural tradition contributed to the complexity and variety of the cinema but it also acted as a break, a pressure towards conservatism. When D. W. Griffith emerged as the major 'stage manager' of the cinema's shift into the formal, thematic and aesthetic conventions of the big picture, he looked back beyond the comedy and fantasy of the primitive one-reelers to the great theatrical productions of the late melodrama. In doing so he brought a conscious political stance, that was already conservative and nostalgic, to bear on a dramatic form that had already, itself, been refined into spectacle and sentiment. There seems, in Griffith's work, to be a desperate refusal to acknowledge the modernity of the cinema, the contemporary world and its aesthetics and, particularly, a new and changing concept of womanhood. It is as though the consolidation and coming of age this new form of popular entertainment could only take place under the aegis of an exaggerated emphasis on tradition. In this light it seems appropriate that the cinema's first great director should have grown up in a South that was already steeped in the process of creating a nostalgic myth for the *ante-bellum* period, generating an image of the lost 'feudal' South that became standard fare from the Broadway musicals of the 1890s to Griffith's own contribution, *Birth of a Nation*. Although Eisenstein pays tribute to the energy and modernity of Griffith's montage, he traces even this innovation back to a nineteenth-century influence, to Dickens.

The theatrical tradition of popular culture constructed its 'post-proletarian phase' around a process which dovetails money and morals. In the vaudeville this had involved banning liquor 'to encourage ladies to attend', and raising the level of decency in the acts and of respectability in the surroundings. 'Christy's Minstrels, Barnum and Pastor all represented attempts to capture the mass audience, and all acknowledged that the secret lay in providing a family entertainment acceptable to the middle class that would also appeal to a general audience.'[7]

B. F. Keith, the greatest of all the vaudeville entrepreneurs, precursor of the film moguls, censored his acts not only from the point of view of decency but also ethnicity, so the moment of transition from immigrant to family audience is marked not only by the presence of ladies, but also of the nation. The audience as now taken to be sufficiently integrated to react to an ethnic joke with laughter at, rather than laughter with. Once again this tradition provided a model for the cinema:

> Most important, when [film] exhibitors imagined the new audience, they usually thought of the vaudeville audience – a cross-section of urban and sub-urban American life. They preferred this audience to the new, unfashionable audience that had discovered them . . . the problem was, how to lure that affluent family audience, so near and yet so far. The answer was through the New American Woman and her children. . . . In a trade hungry for respectability, the middle-class woman was respectability incarnate. Her very presence in the theatre refuted vituperative accusations lodged against the common show's corrupting vulgarity.[8]

Architectural changes are one means of marking moments of transition in the economics of popular entertainment. The 'palace' signifies a new level of investment; it also invites a new audience able to pay for quality entertainment. All the great forms of popular theatrical entertainment seem to be affected by this 'drift up', to be then replaced at the lower social level by another type of spectacle. In each case, respectability attracts the general audience, and the presence of wife and mother seals the change. It is as though this self-conscious new grouping, constituted, pampered, even imagined, by entrepreneurs, is the sign that a form of entertainment that was previously on the margins of society has arrived on the 'inside', within the national consensus.

MYTHOLOGIES

A jump from the Hollywood melodrama of the 1950s to the early nineteenth-century melodrama brackets a particular strand of popular culture from its birth in the crowded city streets to its death in the television-dominated home. But the chaotic crowds in the street and the contained privacy of the home both have their origins in the same urban industrialised environment, and are bound together as each other's other side of the coin. The Manichaean aspect of nineteenth-century culture flourished on oppositions, in Peter Brooks's apt phrase 'the logic of the excluded middle'. Problems of class difference and sexual difference are translated into mythology through a series of spatial metaphors: interior/exterior, inside/outside, included/excluded. The oppositions exist on the level of fear and of reassurance, and give an order to the contradictions that haunted the cities of industrialised society.

> Under Louis-Philippe the private citizen was born . . . . For the private citizen, for the first time the living space became distinguished from the place of work. The former constituted itself as the interior. The office was its complement. The private citizen who in the office took reality into account, required of the interior that it support him in his illusions. The necessity was all the more pressing since he had no intention of adding social preoccupations to his business ones . . . . From this sprang the phantasmagorias of the interior.[9]

The separation of public and private spheres within the bourgeoisie gave order to the new experience of industrialised city life and the pressures of production, while also establishing the home as the area for commodity consumption. Advertising would soon make use of the 'phantasmagorias of the interior'. But the neat public/private antinomy concealed tensions and contradictions on both sides of its opposition. Benjamin does not mention the fact that the private sphere, the domestic, is an essential adjunct to bourgeois marriage and is thus associated with woman, not simply as female, but as wife and mother. It is the mother who guarantees the privacy of the home by maintaining its respectability, as essential a defence against outside incursion or curiosity as the encompassing walls of the home itself. But the social space of the interior contains a number of receding levels of privacy. Its front drawing-room becomes the public within the private, while the emotional terrains of motherhood and family relations are torn between façade and repression. Hidden away, invisible and unspeakable, at the point where the private becomes the secret, is the sphere of sexuality. The repression of the sexual within the private citizen's home is complemented by another hidden world, the underworld of prostitution, the marginal area outside the ordered opposition between public and private, between consumption and production, between male and female.

The workplace is no threat to the home. The two maintain each other in a safe, mutually dependent polarisation. The threat comes from elsewhere, from the seething mass of the urban environment, from its working-class tenements and, most of all, from its night-time pleasures. Over and over again, the mysterious, fascinating and frightening image of the city recurs throughout the nineteenth century. It represents an outside to the rule of order. To the individual swallowed up in the crowd, to the law in search of a criminal, to morality faced with a profusion of bars and prostitutes, the city at night epitomises chaos and uncertainty. The image of the city was that of the jungle, and the detective story provided an adventurer hero who could penetrate, tame and interpret it. The private citizen easily conflated the misery of the urban masses with criminality and degeneracy. Sites of entertainment were infested with the chaotic working or unemployed crowd, outside order and discipline to be shunned above all by the bourgeois woman and her family.

The early nineteenth-century melodrama presented a different moral and political perspective. The experience of the city presented dangers that needed to be represented, interpreted and understood by the poor undergoing the miseries and traumas of early industrial urbanisation.

> Innocence (a vanished moral heritage from the village) is tainted and lost in the world of London, a world of moral squalor and physical and mental suffering, as well as the spectacle of life. Hundreds of nineteenth-century plays deal with this theme and scores of them name that City of Dreadful Night in their titles. These plays teem with the life and people of the streets, of the homeless poor, of the cheap lodging houses, the taverns, the gambling dens, and the cold pavement beneath Waterloo Bridge.[10]

The melodrama's narratives caught the irrational reality of city life and class exploitation with the sharp turns of fortune in plot dependence on coincidence, and a sharp, vivid division between good and evil. But the industrialised city that produced both the Manichaean view of the masses and that of the private citizen began to negotiate a new terrain of the imagination, towards a popular culture of general melodramatic appeal.

> The crowd – no subject was more entitled to the interest of the nineteenth century writers. It was getting ready to take shape as a public in broad strata who had acquired the facility of reading: it wished to find itself portrayed in the contemporary novel. . . . Victor Hugo was the first to address the crowd in his titles *Les Misérables*, *Les Travailleurs de la Mer*. In France, Hugo was the only writer to compete with the serial novel. As is generally known, Eugene Sue was the master of the genre, which began to be a source of revelation to the man in the street. In 1850, an overwhelming majority of working men elected him to Parliament as the representative of the city of Paris.[11]

By the second half of the century, social changes in Britain were indicating a new pattern that would shift the mythology of class relations within the city and male/female relations within the proletariat. The division between home and workplace that had formerly characterised the bourgeois private citizen began to extend to other areas of society:

> Workers [had] generally lived in the immediate vicinity of their work. Political discussion, drinking and conviviality took place either at the work-place itself or at the local pub which served as a house of all and a centre for union organisation. . . . In the second half of the century, this work-centred culture began to yield to a culture orientated towards the family and the home. . . . By the mid-1870s, weekly hours of work had been substantially reduced in most skilled trades . . . the growth of sea-side excursions, sporting interests, working men's clubs and music-halls from about this time is not accidental. In London, however, this increase in leisure time should be seen in connection with another tendency – the growing separation between home and work-place . . . Increased earnings were not generally spent in late drinking customs but handed over to the wife who became the decision maker in all aspects of household expenditure.[12]

The opposition between the respectable privacy of the bourgeois home and the 'other' world of the urban poor gradually eroded. In mass entertainment, the new entrepreneurs ensured consensus and respectability: a safe passage out of the home within a national popular culture.

AESTHETICS

A jump from the Hollywood melodrama of the 1950s to the early nineteenth-century melodrama brackets a particular strand of popular culture, from its birth in the crowded city streets to its death in the television-dominated home. A comparison between the two, very different, melodramatic modes draws attention to limits of verbal articulation. These limits are central to the melodramatic aesthetic and to a popular culture where the struggle to speak from and about the margins is constantly displaced under the centrifugal forces of commercial expansion and censorship. Peter Brooks's chapters on the nineteenth-century melodrama in *The Melodramatic Imagination* make an illuminating juxtaposition with Thomas Elsaesser's invaluable article on Hollywood melodrama 'Tales of Sound and Fury'. Both argue that a melodramatic style of aesthetic value and significance exists in its own right. Both associate the formal characteristics of the style with a crisis of expression, in which language is either inappropriate or inadequate to the emotional burden of the subject matter at stake. Both point out the links between the melodramatic mode of expression and the language of the unconscious which must speak through symptom, on the knife-edge between meaning and silence, demanding interpretation rather than a direct, unmediated understanding of what is said.

When the melodrama developed in Paris in the aftermath of the Revolution, it was quickly imported and had an immediate impact on the London working class. The popular theatre of the early nineteenth century was a product of Britain's division into two nations, in which the ruling class extended its hegemony to a divided culture. Under the Licensing Act only three theatres in London were allowed to perform 'legitimate' drama, described later by the actor/manager William McCready as 'plays of poetic quality and supposed literary worth'. The popular 'illegitimate' theatre was defined in precise opposition to the qualities that characterised high cultural production. The law ensured that it should be non-literary entertainment in which words must be accompanied by music. Command over language, reading, writing and authoritative speech is a mark of political and economic dominance. But out of these circumstances the melodrama developed an important aesthetic of its own that bears witness to the energy of contemporary popular culture. The plays were watched by massive audiences of London's poor in theatres that could hold 2000 or more. (Dickens has described the magical transition from chaos and tumult to hushed attention as the play started.)

Peter Brooks shows how the melodrama's aesthetic strength lies precisely in its displacement of the power of the word. This 'low cultural' form could reflect on human struggle with language and expression, and thus influence the development of romantic theatre. The aesthetics of the popular melodrama depend on grand gesture, tableaux, broad moral themes, with narratives of coincidence, reverses and sudden happy endings organised around a rigid opposition between good and evil. Characters represent forces rather than people, and fail to control or understand their circumstances so that fate, rather than heroic transcendence, offers a resolution to the drama. A highly inflected narrative of passion and surprise must replace words with gestures and language with a visual representation of meaning. While the aesthetics of melodrama evolved for a non-literate audience, the style throws doubt on the adequacy of speech to express the complexities of passion and, instead, offers a wide range of semantic alternatives:

> Gesture in all forms is a necessary complement and supplement to the word, tableau is a repeated device in the summary of meaning acted out, and the mute role of the virtuoso is an emblem of the possibilities of meaning engendered in the absence of the word.[13]

A whole terrain of the 'unspeakable' can thus be depicted.

The melodramatic style had a strong influence on the cinema, partly through the genealogy of popular theatrical spectacle; but also, the movies were born mute, distanced from language by technology rather than the law. These constraints placed an emphasis on gesture, dramatic action, and expression through visual meaning that is reminiscent of the theatrical melodrama. Even the tableau's elongation of time is reflected in the cinematic convention of intercutting between looks and gestures within a scene, extending the possibilities for audience reading and interpretation. This cinematic style survived, along with musical accompaniment, expression through colour and lighting and *mise en scène* so that the popular cinema is suffused with the traditions of melodrama far beyond the particular genre that has inherited its name.

The Hollywood melodrama throws further light on melodramatic aesthetics. The subject matter that defines the genre is associated above all with woman, the family, the home, passion and so on. Peter Brooks argues that the early melodrama's language of signs relates it to the language of the unconscious. The drama gives visibility to material that evades conscious articulation: 'mute gesture is an expressionistic means – precisely the means of melodrama – to render meanings that are ineffable, but none the less operative in the sphere of human ethical relationships'.[14] In the 1950s family drama this relationship becomes more explicit and touches directly on the raw nerve of the psychoanalytic. The social sphere of the family provides a ready-made *dramatis personae* of characters whose relations are by very definition overdetermined and overlaid with tension and contradiction, destined to act out Oedipal drama, generational conflict, sibling rivalry, the containment and repression of sexuality. The family is the socially accepted road to respectable normality, an icon of conformity, and at one and the same time, the source of deviance, psychosis and despair. In addition to these elements of dramatic material, the family provides a physical setting, the home, that can hold a drama in claustrophobic intensity and represent, with its highly connotative architectural organisation, the passions and antagonisms that lie behind it. Here the text of muteness is produced not by the material constraints of the law or technology but by a proximity to the mechanisms of repression, that is aggravated in, for instance, the suburban expansion of Eisenhower's America with its desperate concern for appearances.

Thomas Elsaesser gives a further aesthetic dimension to the Hollywood melodramatic style. He distinguishes the cinema of cathartic action from the cinema of the domestic interior, which acts as a space that confines rather than providing a wide terrain for escape and realised conflict. The space of the home can then relate, metaphorically, to the inside space of human interiority, emotions and the unconscious.

> In one case, the drama moves forward to its resolution by having the central conflicts successively externalised and projected into direct action. A jail-break, a bank robbery, a Western chase or cavalry charge and even a criminal investigation all lend themselves to psychologised, thematised representations of the heroes' inner dilemmas. . . . Not so in the domestic melodrama: the social pressures are such, the frame of respectability so sharply defined that the range of 'strong' actions is limited. The tellingly impotent gesture, the social gaffe, the hysterical outburst replaces any more directly liberating or self-annihilating action and the cathartic violence of a shoot-out or chase becomes an inner violence, often one which the characters turn against themselves. The dramatic configuration, the pattern of the plot makes them, regardless of any attempt to break free, constantly look inwards, at each other and themselves.[15]

This sense of overdetermined gesture is there when Kyle Hadley throws his whisky at his mirror image, when Cary Scott breaks the Wedgwood pot that Ron has so painstakingly mended for her, when Sara-Jane Johnson kicks Susie's little white lamb across the floor. But in addition to the actions of individual characters, the constraints of plot, setting and expression spill over onto the cinematic image itself, so that meaning is infused into objects, colours, lighting, framing, camera movement and so on.

Hollywood has considerably naturalised the mode of performance associated with the theatrical melodrama. The family melodrama, however, produces a new variant of self-conscious, stylised acting. Through social and generic logic, the melodrama produces a preponderance of female protagonists. The presence of this woman, in contradiction with her sexuality, suffering from passion and repression, is in an uneasy tension with the conventions that order woman's image on the screen as erotic object of visual pleasure. Sexuality is presented as a problem and its Hollywood glamour falls away in pieces. The protagonist, with whom our sympathy and understanding lie, is subjected to the curious and prurient gaze of intrusive community, neighbours, friends and family so that the spectator's own look becomes self-conscious and awkward. A conventional expectation of voyeuristic pleasure is transformed into embarrassment. Fassbinder uses this distanciation device in *Fear Eats the Soul*, his remake of Douglas Sirk's *All That Heaven Allows*. (He also elongates the last moments of particular scenes into tableaux reminiscent of the nineteenth-century theatrical melodrama.) In the Hollywood melodrama there is a delicate balance between the protagonists' self-consciousness and the actresses' mastery over a self-conscious performance. This is achieved above all, perhaps, by Lana Turner acting Lora Meredith acting being an actress in *Imitation of Life*.

. . .

Feminist theory of popular culture has concentrated on the processes that produce the image of woman as 'signifier of sexuality' and has striven to create a sexual politics around representation that displaces and alters previous discourses. Significantly, feminism has also concentrated political attention on women's place in the home and family. Throughout, words, written and spoken, have been a political weapon for the Women's Movement, from the days of consciousness-raising to recent feminist preoccupation with linguistic and psychoanalytic theory. The question of how and where women are positioned in relation to language and dominant cultural production has highlighted women's marginality, near silence, and other, dispersed moves towards hesitant speech. This is not to say that women are, or at any point were, outside language (or the law) but that a given, limited vocabulary, characteristic of the oppressed, simply failed to provide the words needed to articulate the experience of oppression. . . . A shift towards a collective ability to articulate is a crucial political step, but what is said and how this speech relates to that of the 'centre' has continued or increased importance. There is a moment that might approximate to the threshold of speech, where conscious articulation is prefigured by the oblique forms of metaphor, symbolism and complex, semiotically charged systems of signification. But the desire for conscious articulation symptomatised by extra verbal systems of communications gives way to the centrifugal forces that cannot acknowledge the existence of margins. Paradoxically, this process has been negotiated primarily through the figure of the mother as 'signifier of censorship'. There are two strands of silence at stake here, doubling up and intertwined like a double helix: the mother who represents the silence imposed by censorship and the mother's own containment and constraint within the language of patriarchal domination. These complex processes and cultural patterns might now be breaking apart. The long-standing tension between inside and outside is resolved as television finally brings popular entertainment into the home itself.

Television arrived within the home, within censorship, for a family audience, tailored to front-parlour size. It also challenged the previous, well-established separation between public and private by turning political events into spectacular drama acted out within the confines of the home. Television was well and truly launched in the United States by two events symptomatic of the conservatism that swept the country in the early 1950s: the televised McCarthy hearings, and the televised proceedings of the United Nations investigation into the Korean War. It arrives with the backing and presence of national authority, without any awkward, difficult period on the limits that must have marked its predecessors. It represents the apotheosis of the home as point of commodity consumption within capitalism under the aegis of the housewife. But the mother has been challenged as the main source of commodity spending power by her teenage children. The youth market has established an autonomous cultural sphere, leading gradually to a new breakup of the old centrifugal forces of consensus centralisation. New 'margins' have emerged. In the music market, for instance, small companies can, for some time at least, resist the pull of the major producers and distributors; 16 mm film has made film-making available to women's groups and political activists; video gives people some control over what they see on their television screens. At the same time the national consensus is itself being threatened from above, literally from the sky, by satellite broadcasting that challenges legal and national boundaries. It seems appropriate that both threats to national broadcasting should be seen in terms of a sexual threat to the integrity of the home. Both video boom and satellite have been associated with an influx of pornography. Once again this rhetoric conceals the real contradictions, the dangers and possibilities that are hidden in these historical developments.

Notes

1. Judith Mayne, 'Immigrants and Spectators', *Wide Angle*, vol. 5, no. 2.

2. Jon Halliday, *Sirk on Sirk* (London: Secker & Warburg, 1971).
3. Rem Koolhaas, *Delirious New York* (London: Academy Editions, 1978).
4. Albert F. McLean, *American Vaudeville as Ritual* (Lexington: University of Kentucky Press, 1965).
5. McLean, *American Vaudeville as Ritual.*
6. Koolhaas, *Delirious New York.*
7. McLean, *American Vaudeville as Ritual.*
8. Russel Merritt, 'Nickelodeon Theatres 1905–1914. Building an Audience for the Movies', Tino Balio (ed.), *The American Film Industry* (Madison: The University of Wisconsin Press, 1976).
9. Walter Benjamin, *Charles Baudelaire* (London: New Left Books, 1973).
10. Michael Booth (ed.), *The Magistrate and Other Nineteenth-Century Plays* (London: Oxford University Press, 1974).
11. Benjamin, *Charles Baudelaire.*
12. Gareth Stedman Jones, *Languages of Class* (Cambridge: Cambridge University Press, 1983).
13. Peter Brooks, *The Melodramatic Imagination* (New York: Columbia University Press, 1983).
14. Brooks, *The Melodramatic Imagination.*
15. Thomas Elsaesser, 'Tales of Sound and Fury', *Monogram*, no. 4.

Part III

On the Margins

9

Frida Kahlo and Tina Modotti*

* Co-written with Peter Wollen. Written as the catalogue text for the exhibition *Frida Kahlo and Tina Modotti* held at the Whitechapel Gallery in 1983, which subsequently travelled to the Hausamwaldsee in Berlin, the Kunstverein in Hamburg, the Kustverein in Hannover, the Kulturhuset in Stockholm, the Grey Art Gallery in New York, and the Museo Nacional de Arte in Mexico City.

André Breton went to Mexico, as to a dreamland, to find there that magic 'point of intersection between the political and the artistic lines beyond which we hope that they may unite in a single revolutionary consciousness while still preserving intact the identities of the separate motivating forces that run through them'.[1] Fatal point, we may think as we survey its histories in this century: art corroded and destroyed by politics; politics smothered and sweetened by art. Yet the hope is necessary. Breton found it particularly in the paintings of Frida Kahlo, in Mexico, in 1938, work which blended reverie, cruelty and sexuality – the surrealist virtues, whose enchantment was heightened for Breton by the connection with Trotsky (then living in Frida Kahlo's 'Blue House', her self-portrait hanging on his study wall).[2]

Others found the point of intersection elsewhere. The critic of *30/30*,[3] reviewing an exhibition of Tina Modotti's photographs in Mexico City, in 1929, described how she had found 'a clear and concrete solution' to the problem of joining art with propaganda in her emblematic photographs of sickle, corn-cob and bandolier, and other combinations with guitar or the numbers 27 and 123, referring to the articles in the Mexican Constitution concerning the ownership of land and the rights of labour. She had shown how 'we can make a social art without giving up pure art', how the production of a 'pure aesthetic emotion' through plastic form can be combined with 'revolutionary anecdotism'. Modotti took the formal lessons she had learned from Edward Weston and found a point of intersection with the revolutionary politics she had learned in Mexico.

Breton's hope, the dialectical unity of art and revolution, is one that has haunted the modern period. The fact that it is still no more than a hope for us today demonstrates that none of the solutions sought, by Breton or by others of different tendencies, succeeded with any degree of permanence. The initial *élan* at the moment of intersection has not persisted or been generalised. We are left with a series of talismans, clustered most often at certain places and certain periods – Soviet art of the immediate post-revolutionary years, Berlin dadaism, French surrealism, the Mexico renaissance – to which we may turn back for encouragement and understanding. We need to know what has been achieved and how it was checked and deflected, to construct our own history in its own incompleteness. That is the purpose of this exhibition.

Why Mexico? An exhibition of work by Frida Kahlo and Tina Modotti automatically invites questions about 'marginality' – the status, in terms of mainstream art history as presented in books and museum displays, assigned to Mexican art and to women's art and (in Modotti's case) to photography. The centres of art history are in Europe and the United States; Paris and New York are the last links in a chain which reaches back through Rome and Florence to the classical civilisations of antiquity. Breaks and diversions are to be smoothed over or bracketed off, the 'heterogeneous' to be admitted only as an influence. In this way the originality, scope and richness of Mexican art have been overlooked or underestimated.

THE MEXICAN RENAISSANCE

It is important to remember that Diego Rivera during his second stay in Paris (1911–20)[4] was one of the best and most original of cubist painters. At the same time, in New York, the Mexican Marius de Zayas was central to the Stieglitz group, the first American avant-garde. He was a crucial contributor to *291* and was its main link with Paris.[5] In the 1920s after Rivera's return to Mexico, the decade of the Mexican renaissance, there was an extraordinary surge of energy in the arts, which attracted foreign visitors and admirers – among them Edward Weston and with him, Tina Modotti, who stayed after his return to California. This was the decade too in which, while Alfred Barr Jr went to Moscow, René d'Harnoncourt went to Mexico City.[6]

Then, in the 1930s, the muralists were able to launch themselves 'up there', north of the border, with works and workshops which had an enormous effect, as one would expect of a movement which provided the example of a distinctive and energetic American version of modern art. Surely 'the crisis of the easel picture',[7] which Clement Greenberg notes in 1948, had something to do with the impact of Mexican muralism? In particular, Siqueiros had a crucial and direct influence on Pollock, who studied with him. What is truly remarkable is the way in which Mexican art was shunted into the shadows after the New York art world had achieved its triumph.

It is worth comparing the art-historical fate of the Mexican renaissance

with that of Russian art of the 1920s. There are similarities between the
two experiences. In both countries the example of cubism enabled artists
independently to develop a specific culture of modern art. In both
countries the overthrow of an *ancien régime* (tsarism, the *porfiriato*[8]) and
the recasting of the society after political revolution and civil war gave
the avant-garde a particular vision of its role, to produce the new art
for the new society.

Through Rivera there were, in fact, close links between the Russian
and Mexican avant-gardes. Rivera lived in the Russian art colony of La
Ruche in Paris[9] – he was the model for Ehrenburg's novel *Jurio Jurenito* –
and was invited to the Soviet Union by Shterenberg after the October
revolution. Later in the 1920s, on a long visit to the Soviet Union, Rivera
took part in the debates on the relation between avant-garde art and
revolutionary politics. Rivera's visit to Russia was matched by those of
Mayakovsky and Eisenstein to Mexico.

Recent years have seen a great revival of interest in the Russian avant-
garde and particularly in the ways in which art and politics converged
and clashed. Many of the same issues and problems arose in Mexico at
the same time – the relationship of the avant-garde artist with the mass
audience, the role of collective work, the relationship between art and
craft, the absorption of cubism into a complex national culture, the
relationship between propagandist content and innovative formal concerns, and so on.

Yet while the Soviet artists' and theorists' search for answers to these
problems has been recognised as of renewed importance for artists and
theorists today, the Mexican experience has been only superficially
introduced into the debate. The work of Kahlo and Modotti focuses
particular questions about art and politics – feminist politics, in the
contemporary sense, as well as classical revolutionary politics – in ways
which are fruitful for those concerned by the same kind of questions
now, since the resurgence of a conscious feminist art.

WOMEN, ART AND POLITICS

The second issue of marginality posed by this exhibition is that of
women's art. At this point, the focus of attention shifts away from the
actual historical context in Mexico that influenced Tina Modotti and
Frida Kahlo and moves towards the debates which have developed
around feminist aesthetics. It is here that the importance of the juxtaposition between the two artists comes into relief. An exhibition of either
artist alone would have asserted her individual importance, her specific
contribution to an artistic practice (painting or photography) and to
women's cultural traditions. But the decision to bring the work of Frida

Kahlo and Tina Modotti together is based on something more than the fact that they have been unjustly neglected and that their art and their lives are of great intrinsic interest. The juxtaposition is designed to raise a series of ideas and arguments that are relevant to questions about women's art and feminist aesthetics.[10]

Thus the contrasts, as well as the parallels, suggested by the work of both artists provide a starting-point for the exhibition's line of interest to anyone concerned with art from a feminist perspective. Both were influenced by radical tendencies in contemporary Mexican politics and culture. They were both politically militant. Both found or developed their own aesthetic from under the shadow of a male artist of international repute. Both implicitly challenge 'high art', dominant traditions. It is here that their work has an immediate excitement and interest.

Feminism has always been deeply concerned with questions about representation, with the politics of images. This concern is with the way that 'woman' has been used in male representation, and (the necessary other side of the coin) with women's relegation to a marginal area of culture, specifically excluded from 'high art'. So work on women's art has proceeded on two fronts, both of which are relevant here. First comes a process of archaeological excavation, uncovering women artists overlooked and forgotten by male-dominated criticism. Secondly, there is the confrontation of the questions of value posed by the split between high art and applied arts and the examination of the rationale behind the unbridgeable gap that seems to divide them. In the present context this last point doubles with the discovery of popular traditions of Mexican art during this period (the background to Kahlo's work) and with an avant-garde desire to bring art into dialogue with the modern world and its technology (a contributing factor to Modotti's use of photography as political reportage).

Both Kahlo and Modotti worked in 'dialects' rather than the language of high art. Modotti learnt photography from Edward Weston, whose aesthetic was based on the desire to raise photography from a lesser art and give it the status of high art. Tina's own work shows a steady movement away from this principle. She returned rather to the documentary aspects of photography. The content changed as her work developed but she never lost or compromised her formal aesthetic position. Frida Kahlo's 'dialect' was drawn from folk art and naïve painting, both as part of a contemporary movement to the popular but also as a source of imagery and emotion that was very close to her own preoccupations. The contemporary political and cultural background is essential for an understanding of Frida Kahlo and Tina Modotti's work. But it is the present interest in radical aesthetics, in the breakdown of high art, in the breakup of art under the impact of other media such as photography, that gives the Mexican background an immediate relevance.

The relationship between the lives and work of both women raises the question of how women come to be artists. The Mexican revolution provided a special context, a stimulus. This is the contribution of history. But in each case, an arbitrary element entered into their lives, changing its normal course and directing them towards unusual choices. This arbitrary element introduces the question of the woman's body, its place in representation and the woman artist's relation to the woman's body in representation. Kahlo had an accident as a teenager that left her permanently in pain and unable to have children. Her paintings are a visual record of the effect this had on her. Modotti was a great beauty; Edward Weston fell in love with her and used her as a model. It was her journey to Mexico with him that changed her life. When he went back to the United States, she stayed on, joining the Communist Party and becoming a photographer in her own right. The perspective offered by feminism is in terms of this emphasis on the body, on woman's body as a particular *problem* both as the vehicle for childbearing and as an object of beauty.[11] This perspective takes the arbitrary or chance element back into the political context of history.

Their relationship to the Mexican cultural background was necessarily rather different. Kahlo was an important Mexican artist, given added prominence by the fact that she was married to Diego Rivera, the leading mural artist. Modotti was a foreigner, drawn to Mexico by the events taking place there (as so many foreigners were), arriving as Weston's companion, and then utterly changed by what she found. But this point only highlights the series of contrasts and differences that provide the basis for the second level of argument at stake here. It is here that the juxtaposition between the two became crucial. Through their differences they can spark off a new line of thought or argument (like montage in the cinema, where bringing two images together can produce a third idea in the mind of the spectator).

Looking at the work of Tina Modotti and Frida Kahlo side by side, with this hindsight, one is struck immediately by the contrasts between them. While both produced work that is recognisably that of a woman (Modotti sometimes less so than Kahlo), the stance taken up by each as an *artist* is very different. On the one hand Frida Kahlo's work concentrates primarily on the personal, the world of the interior, while Modotti's looks outward, to the exterior world. She photographed the street, women and children in the streets, men at public political meetings. In total contrast, Kahlo's subject is herself. She painted her private world of emotional relationships, she found images for her personal experience of pain and her tortured relationship with her body, her obsession with her own image. The types of work they produced, therefore, stand in apparent opposition to each other, suggesting two different roads for feminist art: a concern with social problems on the one hand, and private ones on the other. Two points can be introduced here to break down this apparent polarity. First of all, the feminist slogan 'the personal *is* political' recasts Kahlo's private world in a new light. Secondly, Modotti's work as a photographer can only be understood in the context of *her* private life and position as a woman. The intention here, then, is to switch over, or rather to blur the distinctions set up by the polarity between them and to bring out the ways in which Kahlo's work is political and Modotti's is personal.

Looking at Frida Kahlo and Tina Modotti's work in relation to their lives and experience as women it is clear that conscious decisions about artistic stance are only to a limited extent the result of conscious, controllable choice. Two other forces are of utmost importance: that of historical heritage and that of individual accident. The relation between these two can be described as that between the necessary and the contingent. The differences between a working-class Italian immigrant to California and a Mexican bourgeois intellectual are of great importance. These social-historical conditions contribute to the artist's stance, to Kahlo's desire to explore herself and her colonised cultural roots through her art, and to Modotti's desire to change the conditions of exploitation and oppression she saw around her, then to devote herself to the international working-class movement. These differences are clear and visible in the two women's places of birth and death.

REVOLUTION AND RENAISSANCE

The Mexican renaissance was the progeny of the Mexican revolution, an event – or rather a historic phase – which is not easy to characterise or describe in simple terms.[12] The overthrow of the *ancien régime* of Porfirio Díaz unleashed uncontrollable forces and counter-forces for nearly a decade of civil war, *putsch* and counter-*putsch*, peasant rising and landlord repression, convention, charter and constitution-writing. It was a period of mingled cruelty, surprise and hope in which great masses travelled through Mexico on military campaigns and many millions died, others surviving to march in triumph through the capital, wreak merciless vengeance on the defeated or thank their luck or their cunning.

There are five things, at least, worth emphasising about the Mexican revolution. First, it was a genuine revolution. It swept aside the attempts of political leaders to limit or control its effects. Peasants and workers played a leading role in breaking careers, changing *régimes* and, eventually, recasting the entire political order, inspired by schemes for their own betterment and the destruction of old enemies. In the end, after many checks and long delays, Mexico emerged with the power of the old ruling class broken. Its three pillars – landlords, army, church – were shattered and the institutions of debt peonage and the old *hacienda* system were destroyed. What took their place, however, was not workers' and peasants' power, not socialism, but a new type of state, answering many workers' and peasants' demands but nurturing an indigenous capitalism at the same time, under the harmonising protection of a civilian and lay bureaucracy.

Second, during the period of the revolution, organised labour fought on the opposite side to the most militant peasant forces. The House of the World Worker, the centre of the anarcho-syndicalist trade-union movement, enlisted with Carranza and Obregon, and battalions of workers fought against the armies of Villa and Zapata, who in different ways represented the aspirations of the peasantry. This meant that the labour unions were integrated rapidly into the new post-revolutionary structure of power after Obregon became president in 1920, long before land reforms of any scope were carried out. It was a division which made possible the deceleration of revolutionary impetus until both workers and then peasants could be integrated into the new state system.

Third, the Mexican revolution occurred before the Russian revolution. The armies which fought their way across the country had many a *corrido* to sing and demands formulated in many a *plan*, but they had no revolutionary theory of a Marxist, or even socialist type. Nor of course did they have the Russian revolution before them as a model; there was no Communist Party in Mexico till after the end of the revolution. The Constitution of 1917 was a compromise document, whose famous articles 27 and 123 offered in reality less than they seemed to promise. They produced radical liberalism rather than a step towards socialism, and democratic rights dependent on a state power which was destined to sediment into self-perpetuating one-party rule, though much less murderous and pervasive than that which came to prevail in the Soviet Union.

Fourth, the revolution made possible the release of a great surge of national feeling, the culture of *mexicanidad*. This aspect aligns it with the wave of third-world revolutions which have characterised the middle of the twentieth century: in Turkey, Argentina or Egypt, for instance. The wish to be rid of the *porfiriato* represented in part a wish to assert national independence, in the face principally, of course, of the United States which only sixty or seventy years before had seized and annexed the whole northern half of the country and had continually intervened in Mexican politics, both by military incursions and through diplomatic and economic pressure. In this sense, the Mexican revolution was a national revolution, disfigured and enfeebled by internal divisions and civil war. Certainly this is how the revolution is officially presented, with varying degrees of vigour.

Fifth, the revolution coincided with a cultural revival, not so much political as philosophical. In reaction against the positivism which had become an official part of Porfirian ideology, the succeeding generation, that of the *Ateneo* of 1909,[13] embraced a militant, not to say Promethean idealism. The tradition of classical humanism and idealist metaphysics was harnessed to a mystical vitalism and voluntarism, which grew to epic proportions with the revolution. Vasconcelos, the Minister of Education in the early 1920s who launched the programme of mural painting and cultural renewal from which the Mexican renaissance developed, was a leader of the *Ateneo* and the promulgator of a visionary teleology of the cosmic man, in which Mexican nationalism was blended with elements of Saint-Simon and Bergson, in an exalted amalgam of art, will and the destiny of *la raza*.

It was Vasconcelos who summoned Rivera and Siqueiros back from Europe to play their part in the cultural programme he had planned. (Rivera had been in Europe throughout the revolution; Siqueiros had fought on Obregon's side in the Red Battalions of workers.) Modelling himself on the example of Lunacharsky in the Soviet Union, Vasconcelos launched a mass literacy campaign, a reform of the education system and state patronage for the arts, which were to display the new national culture on a monumental scale. It was Vasconcelos's good fortune to find in Diego Rivera, especially, an artist who could match his own grandiose ambitions with the appropriate energy.

More than any of the other artists involved, many of them of great talent and ability, Rivera set his stamp on the Mexican renaissance (to the exasperation of his rival, Orozco). He set about creating an art which would be modern, monumental and American, worthy of the revolution and with the ideological and political aim of impelling it further forward. Unlike his fellows in Russia, Rivera determined to stay with figurative art and to reject abstraction. As far as content was concerned, Rivera revived the lost genre of history painting, on an unprecedentedly vast scale – the scale of the revolution and eventually the history of Mexico from its first beginnings, through every period up to the present, combined in one massive composition. Formally, he fused a mural style derived mainly from the early Italian renaissance (Giotto especially) with elements of cubism, of Gauguin and Cézanne, of the caricature tradition and of Mexican pre-Columbian and popular art.

While Rivera dominated Mexican painting of the 1920s, it is important to realise that there were many others who flourished at the same time, with widely varying styles and types of subject matter. None the less it was the concept of a monumental civic art, displaying in public places the history of Mexico, in a modern but distinctively national style, drawing on Indian and popular forms, which came to represent the core of the Mexican renaissance. Rivera's aim was to reverse the current of art history so that instead of the exotic or the primitive feeding into European art, the reverse would happen: the lessons of European art he had brought back with him would feed into the native Mexican tradition.

These strands formed the background of both Frida Kahlo's painting and Tina Modotti's photography (in Modotti's case in tension with the influence of her teacher, Edward Weston). The contrast between their work – its smallness of scale, both in subject matter and actual physical size – and the monumentalism of the muralists is immediately striking. Yet this 'smallness' is deceptive. It springs in part from the traditional constraints of women's art, which the Mexican revolution had done nothing to loosen. Yet within these constraints they were able to produce work quite as innovative and explosive in its implications as the mammoth productions of their *confrères*.

THE INTERIOR AND THE EXTERIOR

The slogan 'the personal is political' dates back to the days when the Women's Movement was organised around consciousness-raising. The phrase is emphatic and assertive. But in announcing what now *is*, it contains within it the residual ashes, the memory, of what previously *was not*. This argument has been forcefully restated in *Beyond the Fragments*:

> Before the women's movement, socialist politics like all other sorts of politics, seemed something separate from everyday life, something unconnected with looking after children, worrying about the meals and the housework, finding ways of enjoying yourself with your friends and so on. It was something professional for men among men, for the shop steward or the party activist. The activities of the women's movement have begun to change that as far as women are concerned. But it's meant a different way of organising which does not restrict political activity to the 'professional'.[14]

The phrase 'the personal is political' rejects the traditional exclusion and repression of the personal in male-dominated politics. And it also asserts the *political* nature of women's private individualised oppression. The main achievement of consciousness-raising lay in providing a structure for women to discover that their problems were no longer 'problems', no longer anybody's 'fault', but were political issues. Out of this immediate experience feminism revalued the private and the personal, challenging the division of the sexes into separate spheres.

These political arguments also influenced feminist aesthetics, and are relevant to any attempt to transform an experience of oppression into a theory of oppression. The principal question is this: what relationship should a new, feminist aesthetic have to the culture of oppression and marginality which has traditionally moulded women's artistic work? This marginality brings particular repercussions in its wake, when it is attached to an ideological concept of femininity and the 'feminine sphere'. Here a metonymic chain of meanings and resonances come into play, fettering women's cultural possibilities. The chain is a series of loose, associative links: woman, stability, the home, private emotion, family, domestic labour and decorative arts. But these links can only acquire meaning in opposition to another chain: man, mobility, work, transcendence, politics, productive labour and art. Thus an opposition develops between the interior and the exterior, the private female and public male as though the feminine sphere was there primarily to give meaning and significance to its opposite.[15]

Walter Benjamin comments on the institutionalisation of the public/private distinction around the home:

> Under Louis-Philippe the private citizen was born. . . . For the private citizen, for the first time the living-space became distinguished from the place of work. The former constituted itself as the interior. The office was its complement. The private citizen who in the office took reality into account, required of the interior that it should support him in his illusions. The necessity was all the more pressing since he had no intention of adding social preoccupations to his business ones. In the creation of his private environment he suppressed them both. From this sprang the phantasmagorias of the interior.[16]

Benjamin omits to mention that these phantasmagorias could only exist under the management of a wife. The home, on the scale envisaged here by the private citizen, only materialises as an effect of marriage.

It can be argued that, as women had been 'relegated', so had their creativity. Woman decorated her sphere with applied arts; the personal, private and domestic are the raw material of her self-expression. There is a danger here that a creativity produced by a social condition (the interior/exterior split) should then be theorised as *specific* to women and naturally expressive of 'femininity' as such. There is an important difference between 'femininity as such' and exploring a sphere which is not only assigned to women in a social division of labour, but is neglected and despised by men. In this sense the domestic, and the private lives it generates, are like uncolonised territory or virgin soil, untouched by the masculine. There are several positions that feminist aesthetics can adopt in response to this quandary. Women artists can embrace the domestic and personal, accepting their sphere and using it as a source of imagery and experience, simultaneously paying tribute to the historic relegation of women. But this position can, and should, lead very quickly to analysis of the female condition rather than a celebration of it.

Frida Kahlo's paintings emerge directly out of her life – her physical suffering and her emotional suffering. Living and working within the confines of her childhood home, she took herself as the main subject matter of art and painted her own image and her immediate relationships. Her art forms a material manifestation of her interior experiences, dreams and fantasies. It also seems to act as a 'decoration' of her life and relationships in a similar manner to the way she decorated herself and her house with the colours and objects of Mexican folk art. She painted her friends' portraits and gave her self-portraits (such as the one she painted for Trotsky) to friends.

This private, personalised world that gave rise to her art seems encapsulated by the fact that she often actually painted from her bed, the most private part of the private world of the home. Kahlo continually gives the impression of consciously highlighting the interface of women's art and domestic space, as though in her life (and in her dress) she was drawing attention to the impossibility of separating the two. However, her art also acts as an ironic, bitter comment on women's experience. The feminine sphere is stripped of reassurance. The haven of male fantasy is replaced by the experience of pain, including the pain associated with her physical inability to live out a feminine role in motherhood. This pain is shown not only in *Childbirth* (1932) and *Henry Ford Hospital* (1932) but also in the theme of a 'mask' inherent in her self-portraits. The masks fall away, revealing the wounds inflicted by physical illness and accident (her damaged spine, her fractured leg) merging with the wounds inflicted by Rivera, the pain caused by his infidelities, as, for instance, in *Unos Cuantos Piquetitos* (A Few Small Snips) (1935), where a man is shown inflicting the wounds on a woman's body.

In her *Self-Portrait with Cropped Hair* (1940), painted after Rivera left her in 1939, she makes yet another leap from the interior pain caused by her love for Diego to the wound left on the female body by castration. Here, surely, is a direct reference to Freud. Kahlo's painting seems to move through a process of stripping away layers, that of the actual skin over a wound, that of the mask of beauty over the reality of pain, then moving, like an infinite regress, out of the physical into the interior world of fantasy and the unconscious. Perhaps the most important aspect of this stripping away is its implicit rejection of any separation between the real and the psychoanalytic, an assertion of the reality of forces and fantasies that are of all the greater significance because they cannot be seen. Her use of metaphor and iconography is the means that enables her to give concrete form, in art, to interior experience. In this sense she takes the 'interior', offered as the feminine sphere, the male retreat from public life, and reveals the other 'interior' behind it, that of female suffering, vulnerability and self-doubt. Frida Kahlo provides an extremely rare voice for this sphere which, almost by definition, lacks an adequate means of expression or a language.

Tina Modotti gradually transformed herself from an object of beauty, used in the art of others, into a professional photographer. As Weston's model, assistant and, finally, artistic apprentice, her concept of photography was initially dominated by his aestheticism. Gradually her work shows her searching for her own direction, and gaining confidence as her political commitment changed her way of looking at the world. Her photographs do not lose their sense of form; but her priorities change.

During the period when she was deeply absorbed in Mexican political life, Tina's photographs reveal two rather different strands. These different approaches seem to reflect and comment on both the social and political division between the sexes and Tina's own position as a woman photographer. Politics was primarily the sphere of men. In her photographs of Mexican political life, Tina used her background of formal aestheticism to produce an ordered and abstract rhetoric of revolutionary imagery. Her 'slogan' photographs reflect this aspect of her work, but her photographs of workers and political meetings show the same approach. The use of formal patterns gives a sense of detachment from the people photographed and a commitment to the political ideas expressed. She must very often have been the only woman at the meetings she photographed. On the other hand, a different approach produces another strand of work in her photographs of women and children. The images of hunger, the oppression of being a child and childbearing speak for themselves. The images are posed and composed but the gaze of the subjects themselves strikes directly into the camera and out of the print.

Tina's photographs are predominantly of people in public, exterior space. In her own life, she was continually on the move: an immigrant in one country, adopting the politics and culture of another, then, as an exile, travelling through Europe as a Communist Party militant. She did not decorate the places she lived in. Manuel Alvarez Bravo recalled, 'The walls of her studio were white and clean. Later she started to write some of Lenin's and Marx's phrases on them.'[17]

The fact that Kahlo and Modotti's choices were not developed within a consciousness of women's art diffuses a polemic or antagonism between them. Furthermore the choices they made, consciously or unconsciously, were clearly linked to their own conditions of existence, class, sex, history, even chance, showing up the contingent aspects of artists' work that can so easily disappear under a cloud of genius. Particularly, what they wanted to do and what was possible for them to do, their desires and limitations, were defined by the fact that they were women, however different the kinds of work they produced may have been.

ROOTS AND MOVEMENTS I: FRIDA KAHLO

Frida Kahlo was born and died in the same house in Coyoacan, on the outskirts of Mexico City. The house is now the Frida Kahlo Museum. It is depicted in one of the paintings Frida Kahlo made of her family tree. The infant Frida stands naked in the courtyard, holding the blood-red ribbon which connects her to her grandparents. On her mother's side the ribbon leads up into the volcanic mountains of Mexico, on her father's across the sea to an invisible Europe. The motif of the ribbon is repeated in the twisting form of the umbilical cord which joins Frida's foetus to her mother, superimposed on her bridal gown. Below the foetus, another twisting form, that of a sperm, is penetrating an ovum, which at the same time is being pollinated by a blood-red cactus flower. The imagery is typical of her work; not only is she placed in her family house but rooted in a landscape and, more generally, in the process of nature, participating in a compound animal, vegetable and mineral life.

In another painting, *Roots* (1943), Frida Kahlo paints herself stretched out on the *pedregal*, the volcanic rock of Mexico, leaning on one elbow, her hair loose, her long dress cut away to reveal an intricate web of branches growing in a large green leaf and connected by root tendrils with the earth below. Artery, umbilical cord, root, tendril: in Frida Kahlo's paintings these symbolic connections merge into a single image as the life force is carried precariously between soil, stem and body along convoluted and precarious veins. In the *Self-Portrait as a Tehuana* (1943) the lace of her head-dress merges into the fronds of plants in the background through a tracery of tendrils.[18] In *The Two Fridas* (1939) the vein which connects to a locket of her loved one, held in one hand by the 'Indian' Frida, is being severed with scissors by the hand of her counterpart, the 'European' Frida, so that the blood drips down onto her white dress.

It would be wrong to think of Frida Kahlo as cloistered or secluded, despite the injuries which physically inhibited her movements, and her intense attachment to her native home and land. In some ways it would be easily possible to exaggerate the 'rootedness' of Frida Kahlo. She travelled extensively in the United States, firstly with Rivera, then on her own account when she was recognised as a painter in her own right, and also for medical reasons. She visited Europe after André Breton returned to Paris full of enthusiasm for her work. Nor did she live continuously in the Blue House even while she was in Mexico. It was there that Trotsky lived and the Dewey Commission prepared its report on Stalin's trials and purges of the late 1930s.

None the less, Frida Kahlo developed her own sense of 'rootedness' and 'Mexican-ness' to an extreme degree. She wore Mexican dress and Mexican jewellery, transforming herself, so to speak, into a Mexican artefact. She was noted especially for her use of Tehuana costume – the long dresses of the women of Tehuantepec in southern Mexico who enjoyed a mythic reputation for their personal and economic independence. For a while, when she visited New York and Paris for her exhibitions, Frida Kahlo's style was even taken up in high-fashion circles, featured in *Vogue* and adapted as a 'look' by Schiaparelli.[19] In a way, this suggests how much artifice there was in her 'rootedness', the extent to which her presentation of self *como Tehuana* was inextricably bound up with masquerade and a taste both for the archaic and the ornamental.

The same structure of feeling and sense of style comes out in her choice of art-historical models and pictorial schemes. At first sight, Frida Kahlo's paintings could be taken for those of a 'naïve'. There is an element of this appreciation in Breton's celebration of Frida Kahlo as a spontaneous surrealist. It is true, too, that she never had any formal tuition as a painter and was largely self-taught – she began painting as something to do while bed-ridden after the road accident which incapacitated her in 1925. Her first paintings could perhaps be properly called 'naïve'. But after her entry into the milieu of the muralist renaissance and her marriage to Diego Rivera, it is clear that she could hardly have remained naïve about the kind of artistic choices that she made, even if they were suited to a reliance on intensity and vigour of conception rather than technical skill or painterly touch.

The Mexican renaissance saw a revival of interest in certain specific forms of popular and traditional art: *pulqueria* painting, *retablos* and *ex-votos*, traditional portraiture and popular prints, as well as a more general interest in folk art.[20] This aesthetic 'going to the people' served the aims both of popular nationalism and political radicalism, on the one hand, and of the modernist attack on academicism and the institution of 'fine arts' on the other. Popular forms were celebrated and praised by most of the leading Mexican artists of the time – Rivera, Orozco, even Weston – but nobody took them to heart as much as Frida Kahlo, who not only reproduced their conventions but found ways of assimilating their typical subject matter in her own personal preoccupations and 'symptoms'.

Ex-voto paintings were particularly important to her. Dozens of them which she collected are still on display in the Kahlo house today. They were paintings made on sheets of tin to be nailed up in church as thanks-offering after a miraculous recovery from accident or disaster.[21] They are usually in three parts. At the top is the figure of the saint, the saviour or the virgin whose aid was invoked and who effected the miracle. In the middle is a graphic and often gory depiction of the disaster or affliction. At the base is a written inscription expressing gratitude and recounting the details of the incident. Frida Kahlo uses this form particularly directly in the painting titled *Marxism Can Cure the Sick* (n.d.), in which Marx is shown in the place of the holy figure and Frida Kahlo herself is being cured, throwing away her crutches. Other works, like *Henry Ford Hospital* (1932), show the catastrophe in savage detail, without offering any hope of recovery or amelioration.

It is worth stressing that *ex-voto* painting was already long in decline when rediscovered during the 1920s. The paintings emulated by Frida Kahlo had their heyday in the mid-nineteenth century. *Pulqueria* painting (murals on the walls of *pulque* shops, where the cheapest form of alcohol was sold) and popular print-making still existed during the 1920s, though they were to become extinct very soon afterwards, except for conscious revival by artists – Frida Kahlo herself painted a *pulqueria* with a team of students in the 1940s, when it was already a clearly archaising project. The discovery of popular forms was essentially a discovery of what was already in danger of being lost, their adoption by artists a conscious revival and prolongation beyond their normal historical span. Later *ex-votos* showed an influence of 'chromos' and comic strips which is absent from Frida Kahlo's 'historicist' use of the type.

In fact, the 'historicist' aspect of modernism comes out with great clarity in Mexico. In the first place, 'ancient' history was chronologically much closer and also in many ways culturally closer. The archaism of the Paris avant-garde took painters either back beyond antiquity – to Ancient Egypt or, as with Picasso, pre-Latin Spain – or else out to the colonies, to forms of art which were brought back to the metropolis as the cultural plunder of imperialism. In Mexico the situation was very different. Aztec culture was only centuries rather than millennia in the past. By the time that the Aztec capital of Tenochtitlan was taken and razed by the Spanish, Michelangelo had already completed the Sistine Chapel, and Raphael and Leonardo were both dead. Pre-Columbian is much more nearly co-extensive with pre-Raphaelite than with Egyptian or Mycenaean. The city of Tenochtitlan was founded in the thirteenth century and fell in the early *cinquecento* – the Aztec era was simultaneous with the Italian renaissance, and the sack of Tenochtitlan by Cortes took place in the same decade as the sack of Rome by his overlord, Charles V.

Thus the murals of Giotto, Piero and Mantegna which Rivera and Siqueiros studied and sketched were directly contemporary with the Aztec civilisation to which they turned back in the 1920s. Moreover, the actual language of the Aztecs (Nahuatl) was still being spoken and the Indian substructures of Mexican culture ('idols behind altars' in Anita Brenner's phrase)[22] was still clearly visible. Finally the Indian peoples had at last re-entered the mainstream of Mexican history during the Revolution. Zapata's demands for land reform were posed and understood as demands for a return to pre-Conquest forms of village organisation. A political history was being discovered and revived as well as an artistic one. Just as in the English Revolution appeals were made to the Saxon past before the Conquest and feudal rule identified with the Norman yoke, so in the Mexican revolution, appeals to the pre-Conquest Indian past still had a political value. It is for this reason, among others, that it was possible for political and artistic avant-gardes to overlap in Mexico in a way that they never could in Europe.

Hence the artistic avant-garde, once the crucial decision had been taken to retreat from any move into abstraction, was able to use popular forms not as a means of facilitating communication but as a means of constructing a mythic past whose effectiveness could be felt in the present. Thereby it brought itself into line with the revolutionary impetus towards reconstructing the mythic past of the nation. Though Frida Kahlo was not herself a 'history painter' like Rivera, she also worked from the point where 'avant-garde modernism', 'popular historicism' and 'mythic nationalism' met, in her own favourite genre – self-portraiture. Popular forms made it possible for her to develop a form of self-portraiture which transcended the limits of the purely iconic and allowed her to use narrative and allegory. In this way she created a mode of emblematic autobiography steeped in *mexicanidad*.

Frida Kahlo's roots in Mexico allowed her to participate in the avant-garde precisely because the Mexican revolution was not just the destruction of an old Porfirian, feudal, colonial past, but at the same time the creation of a new one, rooted in the suppressed pre-Columbian culture and the rejected popular traditions. In her painting *My Nurse and I* (1937) the Indian form of the nurse, reminiscent of an Aztec goddess, is fused with the colonial Catholic motif of the madonna and child. She uses the popular non-academic form in which the child is depicted out of proportion in relation to the mother with enlarged, and adult head – a self-portrait in fact. Thereby she both allegorises her own life and represents a mythic Mexican history in formal as well as figurative terms. In the background drops, like the drops of milk from the breasts, are falling like rain or manna: thus the world of nature is

1. Victor Burgin, **As in a fairy tale**, from **Hotel Latone**

2. Victor Burgin, **In the hotel**, from **Hotel Latone**

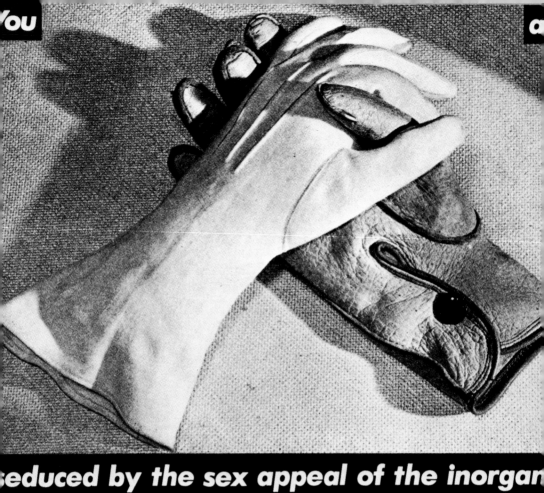

3. Barbara Kruger, **You are seduced by the sex appeal of the inorganic**

4. Barbara Kruger, **You transform prowess into pose**

5. Frida Kahlo, **Self-portrait with a monkey** *(Albright-Knox Art Gallery, Buffalo, New York. Bequest of A. Conger Goodyear)*

6. Frida Kahlo, **Self-portrait with cropped hair** (The Collection, Museum of Modern Art, New York. Gift of Edgar Kaufmann Jr/Centre Georges Pompidou, Paris)

7. Tina Modotti, **Bandolier, guitar and corn-cob** *(Comitato Tina Modotti, Trieste/Carlos Vidali Carbajal, Mexico)*

8. Tina Modotti, **Pregnant woman carrying a child** *(Comitato Tina Modotti, Trieste/Carlos Vidali Carbajal, Mexico)*

HIS HAND CARESSED THE PAGES OF THE ANCIENT MANUSCRIPTS

AS HIS EYE TRACED A PASSAGE THAT BEGGED HIS INTERPRETATIVE MOVES

9. Mark Lewis, from **Another love story 1985/6**

10. Karen Knorr, **Pleasure as a serious pursuit for the unemployed**, from the series **Country**

11. Oliver Richon, **In the West,** from the series **The Grand Tour**

He woke up feeling anxious.
Why was he put 'on the ground floor',
when it was his brother,
not *him*
who had lost
his money and position?
Suddenly he remembered a young man,
a great admirer of women
telling him of the beautiful wet-nurse
who had suckled him as a child:
'I'm sorry', he said,
'I didn't make better use of my opportunity'.

12. Mitra Tabrizian, from the series **Correct Distance**

The game was easy,
posing,
no real threat to the trapper.

The language I speak "within myself"
is not of my time;
it is prey, by nature,
to ideological suspicion.

13. Geoffrey Miles, from the series **The Trapper's Fear of the Text**

given its role as nourishing mother. Autobiography is encompassed by history and history by nature.

ROOTS AND MOVEMENTS II: TINA MODOTTI

Tina Modotti's relationship to Mexican culture was quite different from Frida Kahlo's though she took part in the same artistic movement. Tina Modotti's life was (almost) nomadic – born in Italy, emigrated with her family to the United States, moved from San Francisco to Los Angeles and then from California to Mexico, expelled from Mexico on a ship bound for Rotterdam, political asylum in Berlin, flight to Moscow where her work for the Comintern sent her first to Paris, then to Spain and finally flight again to France, after the defeat of the Republic by Franco and the Fascist forces in the Civil War, and a final exile, back in Mexico, where she died in 1942, only forty-five years old. The ten years or so which she spent in Mexico (first visit in 1922, a second more or less settled stay from 1923 to 1930, the final exile from April 1939 until her death) was the longest period spent in a single country during her adult life. It is also the period when almost all her work as a photographer was done.

While she was still in Los Angeles, Tina Modotti was part of a group interested in Mexico and Mexican art. Her first husband, the artist and poet Roubaix de l'Arbrie Richey, died in Mexico during a visit in 1922. Tina Modotti went to Mexico City to join him but he died of smallpox before she arrived. He had already made friends among Mexican artists and Tina Modotti too found herself increasingly drawn towards Mexico. In the autumn of the same year, after her return to the United States, an exhibition of Mexican folk art was sent to Los Angeles, and her determination to return grew. The next year she left again for Mexico, this time with Edward Weston, the photographer. Robo Richey had already urged Weston to come to Mexico, just before he died, and join him in what he called 'an artists' paradise'.

Weston's ideas about photography were essentially decided before he left for Mexico. In the first place, he was in reaction against 'pictorialist' photography, with its lack of focus, its atmospheric effects and its imitation of etching and painting. He wanted a photography which was clean and sharply outlined. Weston revered the modernist slogan 'Form follows function' and he wanted photographic forms which followed the function of the camera in its capacity to record with detail and accuracy. But besides distrusting pictorialism, Weston also rejected documentary realism and avant-garde photography – Man Ray or Moholy-Nagy. Documentary was not art and avant-gardism was another way of seeking effect and using camera trickery rather than straightforward photography. Weston's particular contribution was to find a different path: photographing ordinary objects or locations in the real world, clearly and straightforwardly, in order to bring out the formal values normally overlooked; to see with a trained and artistically sensitive eye the abstract formal compositions and textures of light and shade which could be elicited from ordinary reality and capture them precisely and without interference or mediation on his photographic plate. It was this aesthetic legacy which Tina Modotti, as his pupil, apprentice and eventually colleague, was to inherit.

In retrospect we can see close analogies between Weston's ideals for photography and those of Renger-Patsch and the 'New Objectivity' photographers in Germany or post-cubist purism and *l'esprit nouveau* in Paris. But Weston himself was very conscious of his own Americanism, of the need to break with European models of art. In fact, this was the driving force behind his modernism. The connection between Americanism, photography and avant-garde art had already been made in New York by Stieglitz, who took a similar line. At the same time he felt stifled by the philistinism he felt in Los Angeles, where both avant-gardism and the claims of photography to art were still worse than suspect. He was naturally impressed by what he found in Mexico City, where cubist artists, such as Rivera, had rejected the Parisian aspects of cubism without abandoning avant-gardism – and at the same time been given massive public commissions. Even better – Rivera and the other muralists accepted photography as an equal art form.

Weston, however, could not accept revolutionary politics. He retained his North American individualism and distrust of socialism. Tina Modotti, whose Italian immigrant family was already socialist, identified rapidly with the political aspects of the Mexican revolution as well as the artistic. She joined the Communist Party and was active in political campaigns – in support of Sandino, for instance, and in opposition to Mussolini. It was during this period in fact that she met Frida Kahlo, through the Communist Party (Frida Kahlo was then in the youth movement) and, according to Kahlo's biographer, Hayden Herrera,[23] introduced her to Diego Rivera, also of course a party member at that time. At any event, for Tina Modotti Mexico provoked both a rapid politicisation and a rapid development as a photographer in the manner of Weston. These two dimensions of her life and work, however, were in tension and part of the fascination of Modotti's photography lies in her efforts to overcome this tension.

During his time in Mexico Weston's preferred choices of subject for his photography were female nudes, Mexican folk toys and artefacts, clouds, plant and architectural forms, domestic objects (such as the toilet bowl he likened to the Victory of Samothrace). He also did many portrait heads, though he had a strong dislike for the idea of commercial portraiture (his main source of livelihood for much of the time). Weston also undertook some commissions – to photograph *pulqueria* paintings for the magazine *Mexican Folkways* and, jointly with Tina Modotti, to provide the illustrations for *Idols Behind Altars*. His human subjects, then, were limited mainly to socially neutral objects, though with a definite bias towards the 'classically' rather than ornamentally folkloric (where, as he saw it, 'form followed function').

Tina Modotti's style of photography is clearly indebted to Weston. Like him she used a large-view camera or a Graflex, slightly more portable but still necessitating a tripod. Her compositions were consciously geometrical, or 'elemental' as Weston might have put it. She did not crop photographs and she went for the same clean sharp-focus look as Weston. She used the same printing technique (like Weston, she frequently made palladium prints). Some of her photographs are on the verge of abstraction, as are many of Weston's – one of bamboo constructed simply around the parallel verticals of the stems or one of the rims of glasses (though this photograph is a double exposure, something Weston would never have allowed himself. Indeed, he half-remonstrated with Tina at one point in his *Daybooks* because she made a print negative).[24]

However, Tina Modotti soon showed a much greater range of subject matter in her photographs than is to be found in Weston's work. To begin with, she took her camera out into the street and photographed people there. There are series of photographs of women in Tehuantepec, of scenes of mothers with infant children, of the poor (especially children) in Mexico City, of peasants on demonstrations or reading the Communist Party paper *El Machete*. These photographs retain the same formal preoccupations as Weston's despite their very different subjects. The hats of peasants on a demonstration echo the same circular forms as the glasses on a table. The formal composition of a photograph of a pregnant woman holding a naked infant on her hip is arranged with great geometrical clarity and without showing the faces of either mother or child. The geometrical character of her compositions is shown at its clearest in four photographs originally published in *Forma* in 1927[25] and described there as illustrations for a book of *estridentista* poetry by German List Arzubide.[26] These are of telephone wires, a gas tank, a construction worker among girders and the corner of a staircase. All are composed with an emphasis on the geometrical outlines and tracings of their subjects. Except for the staircase, however, they are all scenes of modern industry. This is in accord with the tenets of *estridentismo* which of all Mexican art movements was closest to European constructivism and futurism in its emphasis on the urban, the modern and the industrial as well as the revolutionary. But it is quite unlike Weston's response to Mexico. Just before his journey south Weston had been photographing industrial scenes but in Mexico he returned to domestic subjects. Modotti also photographed workers loading bananas and carrying timber with the same formal concerns.

The most remarkable geometrical compositions which Modotti used were in her series of photographs which used as elements objects emblematic of the Mexican revolution; bandolier, corn-cob, sickle, guitar. In this series the subject matter is clearly not found *in situ* but the product of deliberate *mise en scène*. The choice is determined not for its denotation but for its connotation – there is a move towards conceptual as well as formal abstractions. The connotations involved are those not only of *mexicanidad* but also of revolution – the sickle (especially as a composed element) and the bandolier. Weston also, albeit with a slightly uneasy conscience, took to arranging his subject matter to bring out its formal qualities, but Modotti not only did this but also selected subject matter to reflect her political commitment.

After Tina Modotti was expelled from Mexico, on the grounds that she conspired to assassinate the President, she continued her photography in Germany (where it had already been published) but was discouraged by finding that photographers there used the Leica rather than the heavy camera she was used to. Her decision to abandon photography seems connected with her inability to change her whole style of work as a photographer, as the move from Graflex to Leica would have demanded, rather than simply assigning photography a lower priority in favour of direct political work. Workers' photography movements in Germany had developed around news magazines in an attempt to match the use of photography in the Establishment news media. The preconceptions of this style of photography were completely different from those implicit in Tina Modotti's work, which had been much closer in many respects to 'New Objectivity' photography.

In Mexico, Tina Modotti had worked with Workers International Relief, the world-wide organisation founded and directed by Willi Münzenberg. WIR not only ran mass-circulation photo-journals and magazines but produced films, both in Germany and the Soviet Union (the Dudow/Brecht *Kuhle Wampe*, for instance), and published books.[27] It was an enormously complex and far-reaching organisation which acted both as a propaganda machine and a patron of the arts. It was also financially independent, which gave Münzenberg the possibility of pursuing a more flexible policy than would have been possible if he had had to rely directly on either the German or the Soviet Communist Party for his operations.

Münzenberg's talents as an entrepreneur were suited to an age of mechanical reproduction. Within the mass media photography is just an element, juxtaposed with print, part of a layout, without the singularity which is the mark of the aesthetic object. Tina Modotti's background had trained her to see a photograph as an art object, to be looked at in its own right, with its own intrinsic value, rather than as one component of a wider mosaic. While in Germany her photographs were taken up and published in illustrated magazines; in Mexico they were shown in exhibitions, mounted and hanging on a wall, like paintings. This was not simply a question of art in opposition to journalism, but of quite different ways of contextualising and looking at photographs. In a famous essay Walter Benjamin supplied the theoretical arguments underpinning the priority which Münzenberg gave to the mass media, arguing in favour of the 'journalisation', but it is clear from his essay that he is really concerned with the latter and 'politicisation' is a supplement: 'In some cases today's films can also promote revolutionary criticism of social conditions, even of the distribution of property. However, our present study is no more specifically concerned with this than is the film production of Western Europe.'[28]

Faced with the pressure to 'journalise' her art Tina Modotti gave it up altogether. She belonged, in a sense, to a previous epoch, in which photography was an artisanal product, closer, despite the modernity of its technology, to folk art or popular urban art than to the mass media. The photographer had a small studio or workshop, received personal commissions, held public exhibitions, and so on. The photographs took a long time to conceive and even to make as a result of the detailed attention paid to the making of each print. Benjamin assumed that, in a secular society, this kind of activity would most naturally be justified in terms of 'art for art's sake' or 'pure' art. Certainly Weston's example does support this assumption. But Tina Modotti showed how this kind of photography could itself be politicised, without necessarily being 'journalised', Moreover, her work had a crucial influence on other artists: Manuel Alvarez Bravo, the leading Mexican photographer of the next generation, and Sergei Eisenstein, whose interest in Mexico was awakened by reading *Idols Behind Altars*. In fact, Modotti's 'emblematic' political photographs and her photographs of life in Mexico are analogous in a number of ways to Eisenstein's own practice – in terms of *typage*, the mode of composition and even the concept of 'intellectual montage'.

THE DISCOURSE OF THE BODY

The art of both Kahlo and Modotti had a basis in their bodies: through injury, pain and disability in Frida Kahlo's case, through an accident of beauty in Tina Modoti's. Frida Kahlo sought an iconic vocabulary which could both express and mask the reality of the body. Tina Modotti, whose career began as a film-actress and a model, redirected the look which had focused on her outwards when she herself became a photographer. Kahlo's art became predominantly one of self-portraiture; Modotti's one of depiction of others – predominantly women, but seen with an eye quite different from the one that had looked at her.

Frida Kahlo had about thirty operations in the years between her accident in 1925 and her death in 1954. In the accident her spine was fractured, her pelvis shattered and her foot broken. For long periods she was bed-ridden, in pain and incapacitated. She was unable to have the child she desired and suffered miscarriages and medical abortions. In some respects her painting was a form of therapy, a way of coping with pain, warding off despair and regaining control over the image of her crushed and broken body. Painting brought pleasure, hope and power over herself. It made possible both a triumphant reassertion of narcissism and a symbolisation of her pain and suffering. She painted originally for herself and it was not really till Breton recognised the value and fascination of her work for others that she conceived the possibility of holding exhibitions and marketing the paintings.

The vocabulary which Frida Kahlo found and used was primarily that of traditional Mexican Catholic art, especially depictions of martyrdom and of the Passion. There is an explicit use of the imagery of the Passion: the wounds of the scourging and the crucifixion, the knotted cord, the ring of thorns, the simultaneous shining of sun and moon during the tenebrae. The style and iconography are those of popular baroque, in which intensity of expression is given precedence over beauty or dignity, and like most popular forms there is an archaic, almost medieval aspect to the representation, a love of minute detail, a disparity between foreground figure and background setting, a disregard for proportion and perspective. The graphic is systematically favoured rather than the perceptually realistic.

In particular, Kahlo uses the device of the 'emblem'. In *Henry Ford Hospital* her body on the bed is surrounded by a set of emblematic objects, like those surrounding the crucified Christ in an allegory of redemption. Emblems and attributes are graphic signs which carry a conventional meaning, often in reference to a narrative subtext (attributes) or a common set of beliefs (emblems). At times, Frida Kahlo used complex allegorical schemes, as in *Moses* (1945) with an idiosyncratic personal iconography. Through the resources of emblems, she was able to transcribe her physical pain and suffering into a form of graphic language, which could be read by the spectator. The appeal is not to an imaginary identification with herself as subject of pain but as a symbolic reading of herself as vehicle for suffering as in *The Little Deer* (1946).[29] Hence the common reaction of horror rather than pity, itself associated more with 'low' than 'high' art.

Another mode of representing the body which she used was to draw detailed imagery from anatomical textbooks. Before her accident she had intended to study medicine and her injuries gave her a further reason for studying anatomy. Anatomical organs are often used as emblems – the bleeding heart of Catholic tradition, or the pelvis in *Henry Ford Hospital*. The accuracy of anatomical depiction contrasts with other stylistic aspects of her painting, drawn from an epoch and a milieu without precise anatomical knowledge. The effect produced is not only one of physical fragmentation and dislocation but also a kind of anachronism.

Beauty is another form of accident, one that is prized rather than feared. Yet it is one which can bring with it its own burdens. After her expulsion from Mexico, the ship on which Tina Modotti was deported docked in New Orleans and she was detained for eight days in the Immigration Station there. She wrote to Weston:

> the newspapers have followed me, and at time preceded me, with wolf-like greediness – here in the U.S. everything is seen from the 'beauty' angle – a daily here spoke of my trip and referred to me as 'a woman of striking beauty' – other reporters to whom I refused an interview tried to convince me by saying they would just speak of 'how pretty I was' – to which I answered that I could not possibly see what 'prettiness' had to do with the revolutionary movement nor with the expulsion of Communists – evidently women here are measured by a motion picture standard.[30]

It is ironic, in a way, that this letter should have gone to Weston who did more than anyone else to promote and perpetuate the legend of Tina Modotti's beauty, both through his daybooks and through the photographs for which she was model, culminating with the famous series of her lying nude on the *azotea* in 1924. Tina Modotti also acted as a model for Diego Rivera when he was painting murals in the Agricultural College at Chapingo in 1926. Earlier she had been an actress – playing the fiery Latin vamp in early Hollywood Westerns. When Tina Modotti herself became a photographer she photographed primarily women, but the contrast with Weston's approach could not be greater.

Weston became famous as a photographer of the female nude. He claimed that it was the formal quality of the shape of the female body which interested him and that any erotic motive (and there certainly was one, because he had affairs with the great majority of his models) was suspended in the photographic work. His particular form of voyeurism, of taking woman as an object of gaze, was justified in the terms of pure aesthetic form. About the comments of others on the erotic quality of his work he wrote: 'Others must get from them what they bring to them: evidently they do!'[31] implying also that an erotic interpretation might follow from the 'sexual suppression' he himself did not suffer from. The fact remains, however, that his nude photographs of Tina Modotti are often taken from above, looking down on her as she lies passively, sunbathing or asleep, on the ground, in a conventional pose.

Tina Modotti's photographs were not of 'beauties' but of peasant and proletarian women, marked by the conditions of their life. Often they are mothers with small children, their bodies framed to emphasise not their own form but that of their interaction with the children. That is to say, they are represented in the process of activity and work, rather than isolated in a pose for the camera. The camera position is often below head height (it is only men who are photographed from above, partly to bring out the circular shape of their hat-brims). In her photographs of women especially the careful organisation of the composition is not allowed to override the directness of the look.

For Frida Kahlo beauty was inextricably bound up with masquerade. In her self-portraits, whatever the degree of pain implied, by tears or even wounds, her face remains severe and expressionless with an unflinching gaze. At the same time the mask-like face is surrounded by luxuriant growths, accoutrements, ornaments and familiars – a monkey, a doll, a hairless dog. The ornament borders on fetishism, as does all masquerade, but the imaginary look is that of self-regard, therefore a feminine, non-male and narcissistic look. There is neither coyness nor cruelty, none of the nuance necessary to the male eroticisation of the female look. The masquerade serves the purpose of displacement from a traumatic childhood of the subject herself, ever-remembered, ever-repeated.

Throughout Kahlo's work there is a particular fetishisation of nature, an imagery of fecundity and luxuriant generation which is clearly a defence against her knowledge of her own barrenness, one of the products of her childhood accident. Veins, fronds and vines often merge in the body itself. There are three modes of self-portraiture: the body damaged, the body masked and ornamented, the body twined and enmeshed with plants. In some paintings even the rays of the sun are incorporated in the web. Fruit in still lifes become part of the body, flesh-like, or like skulls with vacant eyes. It is as though compensation for her barrenness, and a defence against trauma, are condensed in pullulating images of cosmic and natural vitality sometimes counterposed with images of barrenness itself, of lava rock and broken ligneous forms.

In a sense, nature is being turned into a complex of signs. Similarly the body itself becomes a bearer of signs, some legible, some esoteric. Masquerade becomes a mode of inscription, by which the trauma of injury and its effects are written negatively in metaphor. It is as if the intensity of the trauma brings with it a need to transfer the body from the register of image to that of pictography. Thus faces are read as masks, and ornaments as emblems and attributes. This discourse of the body is itself inscribed with a kind of codex of nature and cosmos, in which sun and moon, plant and animal, are pictograms. At the same time this pictographic effect de-eroticises the imagery.

Hayden Herrera, writing about Frida Kahlo, writes of 'her nearly beautiful face in the mirror'.[32] The aptness of 'nearly' carries with it a covert recognition of the overt ruin seen in *The Broken Column* against which beauty has been constructed as a defence. It is the artifice, the masquerade, which produces the uneasy feeling of slight mismatch between ostensible features and ostensible subject.

Tina Modotti, on the other hand, suffered from the inscription of beauty on her body by others. It is somehow appropriate that while Frida Kahlo is remembered for her jewellery and her extravagant costumes, Tina Modotti is remembered as one of the first women in Mexico to wear jeans.

It is the discourse of the body, together with its political and psychoanalytic implications, which provides a continuity for us with Mexico between the wars. The history of art, as Viktor Shklovsky observed, proceeds by knight's moves, through the oblique and unexpected rather than the linear and predictable. If the art of Frida Kahlo and Tina Modotti has appeared to be detached from the mainstream, this by no means entails any loss of value. In many ways their work may be more relevant than the central traditions of modernism, at a time when, in the light of feminism, the history of art is being revalued and remade.

Notes

1. André Breton, 'Frida Kahlo de Rivera', in *Surrealism and Painting* (New York: Harper and Row, 1972).
2. Trotsky arrived in Mexico on 9 January 1937. He was met at the port of Tampico by Frida Kahlo, and stayed with her in the 'Blue House' until May 1939.
3. 'Las Fotos de Tina Modotti, El Anecdotismo Revolucionario', *30/30*, 10 (1929).
4. See Florence Arquin, *Diego Rivera: The Shaping of an Artist, 1889–1921* (Oklahoma: Oklahoma University Press, 1971). Rivera was born in 1886.
5. See Dickran Tashjian, *Skyscraper Primitives* (Middletown: Weslyan University Press, 1975), and Catherine Turrill, 'Marius de Zayas', in *Avant-garde Painting and Sculpture in America 1910–25*, catalogue, Delaware Art Museum, 1975.
6. Alfred Barr Jr became the first Director of the Museum of Modern Art in New York in the year following his visit to Moscow in 1927–8. René d'Harnoncourt was his successor in this position.
7. 'The Crisis of the Easel Picture' (1948), in Clement Greenberg, *Art and Culture* (Boston: Beacon Press, 1961).

8. Porfirio Díaz was the last pre-revolutionary President of Mexico, whose régime extended from 1876 to 1911.

9. See Marevna [Vorobëv], *Life in Two Worlds* (New York: Abelard-Schulman, 1962) and *Life with the Painters of La Ruche* (London: Constable, 1972).

10. See, for instance, the periodical *Heresies*, New York, from 1977, which still provides the principal forum for debate on women's art and feminist aesthetics.

11. See the periodical *m/f*, London, from 1978, for a continuing debate on 'the discourse of the body'.

12. For a recent political analysis of the Mexican revolution, see Donald C. Hodges and Ross Gandy, *Mexico 1910–1976: Reform or Revolution?* (London: Zed Press, 1979).

13. 'El Ateneo de la Juventud' (The Athenaeum of Youth) was an intellectual society founded in 1909 with the purpose of reforming Mexican culture. See Carlos Monsivais, 'Notas sobre la Cultura Mexicana en el Siglo XX' in *Historia General de Mexico*, vol. 4 (Mexico, 1976).

14. Sheila Rowbotham, Lynne Segal and Hilary Wainright, *Beyond the Fragments* (London: Merlin Press, 1981). For another approach, see Elizabeth Fox-Genovese, 'The Personal is Not Political Enough', *Marxist Perspectives*, 8 (Winter 1979–80).

15. In *Old Mistresses* (London: Routledge and Kegan Paul, 1981), Roszika Parker and Griselda Pollock argue that this secondary organisation of masculine/feminine antinomy into social and cultural spheres dates from the Victorian period, and comment, 'for women artists have not acted outside cultural history, as many commentators seem to believe, but rather they have been impelled to act within it from a place other than that occupied by men'.

16. Walter Benjamin, 'Louis-Philippe or the Interior', *Charles Baudelaire: Lyric Poet in the Era of High Capitalism* (London: New Left Books, 1973).

17. Manuel Alvarez Bravo, quoted in Mildred Constantine, *Tina Modotti: A Fragile Life* (New York and London: Paddington Press, 1975).

18. See Hayden Herrera, 'Self-Portrait of Frida Kahlo as a Tehuana', in *Heresies*, 4 (1978–9).

19. See Bertram D. Wolfe, 'Rise of another Rivera', *Vogue* (1 November 1938).

20. See Jean Charlot, *An Artist and his Art*, vol. 2 (Honolulu: University of Hawaii Press, 1972).

21. See Gloria Kay Giffords, *Mexican Folk Retablos* (Tucson: Arizona University Press, 1974).

22. Anita Brenner, *Idols Behind Altars* (New York: Biblo and Tannen, 1976). This book contained photographs by Modotti and Weston.

23. Hayden Herrera, *Frida Kahlo* (New York: Harper and Row, 1982).

24. *The Daybooks of Edward Weston*, vol. 1 (Millerton, New York: Aperture, 1961).

25. See the magazine *Forma*, ed. Gabriel Fernandez Ledesma, 10 (Mexico, 1927).

26. See Carleton Beals, *Mexican Maze* (Philadelphia: J. P. Lippincott, 1931).

27. For this period see *Photography/Politics: One* (London: Commedia, 1979) and John Willett, *The New Society: Art and Politics in the Weimar Period 1917–33* (London: Thames and Hudson, 1978).

28. Walter Benjamin, 'The Work of Art in the Age of Mechanical Reproduction', *Illuminations* (London: Fontana, 1970).

29. The metaphor of the 'stricken deer' has a tradition in Mexican poetry. See, for instance, 'Verses Expressing the Feelings of a Lover' by Sor Juana Inez de La Cruz (Juana de Asbaje 1651–95):

If thou seest the wounded stag
that hastens down the mountain-side,
seeking, stricken, in icy stream
ease for its hurt,
and thirsting plunges in the crystal waters,
not in ease, in pain it mirrors me.

Translated by Samuel Beckett in Octavio Paz (ed.), *Anthology of Mexican Poetry* (London: Calder and Boyars, 1959). On the theory of the emblem, and Sor Juana's practice of it, see Robert J. Clements, *Picta Poesis* (Rome, 1960).
30. Letter from Tina Modotti to Edward Weston, quoted in Constantine, *Tina Modotti: A Fragile Life*, p. 175.
31. *The Daybooks of Edward Weston*, vol. 2, p. 32.
32. Herrera, in *Frida Kahlo*, 1982.

Part IV

Avant-Garde

10

Film, Feminism and the Avant-Garde*

* Written as a lecture for the series 'Women and Literature' organised by the Oxford Women's Studies Committee in 1978 and published in the anthology of the series Mary Jacobus (ed.), *Women Writing and Writing about Women*.

It is not until recently that any conjuncture has been possible between feminism and film. Women's political consciousness, under the impetus of the Women's Movement, has now turned critically towards cinema and, in spite of its brief time span, cinema now has a history that can be analysed from a feminist point of view. For the first time, the consciousness is there, and the body of work is sufficient. The heterogeneity of the cinema as an institution is reflected in its first encounter with feminism. There have been campaigns against sexism within the industry, analyses of sexism in representation, use of film for propaganda purposes and debates about culture politics. 'Woman and film' and 'woman in film' have only existed as critical concepts for roughly a decade. A first phase of thought has, it seems, been achieved. It is now possible to make some tentative assessments of feminist film criticism, find some perspective on the past and discuss directions for the future.

The collision between feminism and film is part of a wider explosive meeting between feminism and patriarchal culture. From early on, the Women's Movement called attention to the political significance of culture: to women's absence from the creation of dominant art and literature as an integral aspect of oppression. Out of this insight, other debates on politics and aesthetics acquired new life. It was (not exclusively, but to an important extent) feminism that gave a new urgency to the politics of culture and focused attention on connections between oppression and command of language. Largely excluded from creative traditions, subjected to patriarchal ideology within literature, popular arts and visual representation, women had to formulate an opposition to cultural sexism and discover a means of expression that broke with an art that had depended, for its existence, on an exclusively masculine concept of creativity.

What would women's cultural practice be like? What would art and literature within an ideology that did not oppress women be like? Debate has swirled and spiralled around these questions. On the one hand, there is a desire to explore the suppressed meaning of femininity, to assert a women's language as a slap in the face for patriarchy, a polemic and pleasure in self-discovery combined. On the other hand, there is a

111

drive to forge an aesthetic that attacks language and representation, not as something naturally linked with the male, but rather as something that soaks up dominant ideology, as a sponge soaks up water.

It is at this point that a crucial problem has to be faced. Can the new be discovered, like a gold-mine in a garden? Or does the new grow only out of the work of confrontation that is done? Does the very act of opposing traditional aesthetics and questioning male-dominated language generate a new language and carry an aesthetic with it? It is at this point that feminists have recently come to see the modernist avant-garde as relevant to their own struggle to develop a radical approach to art. At the moment this is still a wary approach, given the hesitations feminists necessarily feel towards any aspect of male-dominated culture. But the avant-garde poses certain questions which consciously confront traditional practice, often with a political moti-vation, working on ways to alter modes of representation and expecta-tions in consumption. These questions arise similarly for women, motivated by a history of oppression and longing for change. However, the path leading even to this point of view is twisted. In this essay I want to trace the turning-points, moments of reassessment and outside influences, to show how feminist film practice has come to be interested in – and have almost an objective alliance with – the radical avant-garde.

As a preamble, before dealing specifically with cinema, I want to outline the main arguments about women's place in past culture. Behind all the arguments lies a fascination with the unspoken history of women that has become mysterious because unrecorded by male chroniclers and overlooked by male historians. And there is a corresponding need to fantasise a tradition, a line of work, a feminine cultural context, however tenuous, as a homage to the trivialisation endured by women in the past.

First of all, particularly in the early days of the Women's Movement, but still present, there is a hope that women have, in fact, produced more in mainstream culture than has even been recognised. Research discovered at least some handfuls of women artists and writers whose work had been overlooked and undervalued. Secondly, in contrast to this rediscovered presence is the emphasis on absence, the insistence on the part of some feminists that a few outstanding, exceptional women do not properly alleviate the overall picture of discrimination. Thirdly, in proportion to women's exclusion from cultural participation, their image has been stolen and their bodies exploited. Finally, there has been an important revival of interest in minor arts and crafts, where, allocated their place in the division of labour, women 'embroider' their daily work, also drawing attention to the way that women have worked together, without claims to authorship or genius. A clash arises here between a celebration of the past and a guideline for the future. There is a difference between an interest in women's traditions – the individual or group achievements which women have to their credit, despite a hostile environment – and a belief in a feminine sensibility, tied to the domestic and then freed only into a similar orientation in art.

These general issues have found their place in debates between women about film. I want to trace the way in which these debates developed and how each line of argument both advanced and blocked the growth of feminist film culture. Feminists then had to become more ambitious, more demanding. It is these developments that I will discuss in the second part of my essay as 'The Search for a Theory' and 'The Search for a Practice', describing the alliances and influences which have worked together to produce an aesthetic that is still only in its infancy.

In 1972 *Women and Film*, the first journal of feminist film criticism, came out in California, and the first two women's film festivals were organised (in New York and in Edinburgh). These events were a response in film terms to the early attention paid by the Women's Movement to the politics of representation. A rough history of women in the cinema soon started to emerge.

RESEARCHING THE PAST

These early days of research into women's place in film history quickly established the fact that women had been excluded from the production and making of films, possibly in proportion to their notorious exploitation as sexual objects on the screen. The women's film festivals showed the results of painstaking research: surprise finds and lost women directors could be counted on the fingers of very few hands. Overall, the history of the cinema presented a particularly depressing picture of discrimination and marginalisation of women. In the very early days of one-reelers, before the film industry attracted big money, some women did direct films in Hollywood. The coming of the studio system, and, even more so, economic reorganisation with the introduction of sound, involved large-scale investment from banks and the electronics industry. Money and studio hierarchy closed the ranks so completely that Dorothy Arzner and Ida Lupino were literally the only women to direct films regularly in Hollywood until the 1970s. Both found their way up through acceptable women's jobs: Arzner was an editor, Lupino an actress. They are the exceptions that prove the rule. The work of women directors in the pioneering days has been largely lost. There is little left of the films of Lois Weber and Alice Guy, the outstanding women directors of the pre-First World War period. Leni Riefenstahl, the maker of Fascist documentaries in the 1930s, is ironically the only woman director whose name is a household word. Leontine Sagan, the brilliant director of

Mädchen in Uniform (Germany, 1931) is still forgotten, in spite of the interest her film aroused in the women's festivals. In Europe in the 1950s, in film industries impoverished and disorganised by the war and overshadowed by American imports, a few women began to make films: Mai Zetterling, once again actress turned director; Agnes Varda, photographer; and, in Eastern Europe, Marta Meszaros and Vera Chytilova. And then there was the avant-garde tradition. Here, outside the distrust of women endemic in commercial cinema, marginalised within a marginal sphere of cinema, women had more impact. At least they were recorded and remembered. Germaine Dulac appears in the history books, if only through Artaud's denunciation of *The Seashell and the Clergyman*. Maya Deren's pioneering work in the United States during the 1940s had earned her the title 'Mother of the Avant-garde'. But both directors' intermingling of cinematic movement and interior consciousness interested feminists and avant-gardistes alike. And it was this tradition that appeared to feed most dynamically into women's contemporary work.

Behind the work of research that went into these festivals, there lay a hope that, once rediscovered, films made by women would reveal a coherent aesthetic. The experience of oppression, awareness of women's exploitation in image, would act as a unifying element for women directors, however different their origins. Careful analysis would show how the struggles associated with being female under male domination found an expression that unified across diversity of all kinds. Certainly, the films made by women were predominantly about women, whether through choice or as another aspect or marginalisation. But it began to look increasingly doubtful whether a unified tradition could be traced, except on the superficial level of women as content. Claire Johnston and Pam Cook in their study of Dorothy Arzner took the question further, arguing that Arzner managed to throw the male assumptions and codes dominant in Hollywood into crisis, subverting them and opening up their contradictions.

In general the woman in Arzner's films determines her own identity through transgression and desire. Unlike most other Hollywood directors . . . in Arzner's work the discourse of the woman . . . is what gives the system of the text its structural coherence while at the same time rendering the discourse of the male fragmented and incoherent. The central female protagonists react against and thus transgress the male discourse which entraps them. These women do not sweep aside the existing order and found a new female order of language. Rather, they assert their own discourse in the face of the male one, by breaking it up, subverting it, and in a sense, re-writing it.[1]

This argument took the debate beyond a simple hope for a unified tradition into a careful, detailed analysis of the language and codes used by a woman director alone in an otherwise exclusively male world. Such work became a crucial advance in feminist film criticism, the first bricks towards building a theory. Claire Johnston continues: 'The need for oppressed people to write their own history cannot be overstressed. Memory, an understanding of struggles of the past and a sense of one's own history constitute a vital dynamic in any struggle.'

The Attack on Sexism

Certain stylistic conventions have grown up hand in hand with narrative cinema. The language of form should not intrude or overshadow the free flow of the story and must allow content to come to the fore. The first steps of feminist film criticism accepted these conventions, concentrating on the sexist *content* of cinematic narrative and exploitation of women as *images*. This was indeed a necessary polemic (similar politically to campaigns against sexism in advertising or role-indoctrination in children's books), exposing and protesting against the way in which active and passive roles in film narrative are divided along sex lines. At this point (the early issues of *Woman and Film*, the special women's issues of *The Velvet Light Trap* (Fall 1972) and *Take One* (February 1972)) the main demand was to replace one female role-model by another, stronger and more independent. Or to find images of women that were realistic and relevant to women's real-life experience. Both these demands assume that identification is the fundamental problem for cinema, and that feminist films would offer alternatives – the optimistic in fantasy, or the pessimistic in reality – lived out through the protagonists on the screen.

The importance of denouncing sexism is undoubted. But, as these demands are directed primarily at commercial and popular cinema, they also involve a confrontation with the sexist nature of the industry itself and its discrimination against women. Hollywood's immediate response to the Women's Movement was a retreat into what Molly Haskell in *From Reverence to Rape* describes as 'the buddy movie', showing how far these campaigns would still need to travel from the late 1960s and early 1970s.[2] The commercial cinema was not going to change overnight in either of its fundamental attitudes to women. Furthermore, a change in content alone, based on reversal of sex-roles, could do no more than reproduce the conventions established by male-dominated exploitative production with a new twist, and this twist could itself easily degenerate into a fetishistic male fantasy about fascinating, phallic women. However, the tradition of the melodrama, the old Hollywood genre of women's problems and family traumas, has re-emerged, providing vehicles for the women stars – always a necessary precondition for a Hollywood film concerned with women to become a bankable commodity.

First Feminist Films

The conditions in which it was first possible for women to make films arose through economic and technical changes that allowed a cinema to develop with an alternative economic base to the 35mm commercial product. So far as women were affected, these changes allowed them to enter the world of cinema in considerably greater numbers than the previous drop in the ocean. Looking at the production side of the cinema industry, there seems to be a negative correlation between the size of the investment and the participation of women. The larger the amount, the less likely was a woman to be trusted with it. Shirley Clarke describes her experience in Hollywood in an interview in *Take One*:

> I didn't have any means of getting any money. It may have to do with the fact that people with money do not talk about money to women. That's one of the things that showed up in my Hollywood dealings. Everyone said 'Fantastic. Do something for us. But don't expect much. Being a woman it's going to be difficult'. So when I got out there they had a man who was going to be my producer. And he was going to tell me how to make my film. Men just don't like to talk to women about money – that's all.[3]

The first glimmer of an alternative world came, hardly noticed, in the 1940s. Maya Deren made *Meshes of the Afternoon* in 1941 with 16mm equipment and no sound. After the war, 16mm equipment that had been used for wartime newsreels came onto the second-hand market in the United States and provided the basis for what came to be called the Underground Cinema. These developments opened up film-making to people outside the industry, and allowed not one but several new cinemas to be born. The equipment is smaller, cheaper in itself, in stock and laboratory costs. But it was not until the early 1960s, with the invention of Coutant's Eclair camera in France and the Nagra tape recorder in Switzerland that synchronised sound could be recorded with ease. In cultural terms these developments produced two distinct cross-fertilisations. Film became available as a medium for artists, both in the visual arts and dance. In the 1960s film could be used by political activists for propaganda and campaign films. The particular association of 16mm with *cinéma-vérité* gave it the appearance of an instrument of truth itself, grasping the real, unmediated by ideology. Film seemed to be freed from its historic enslavement to the commercial product.

Looking back at feminist film criticism and festivals in the early 1970s, it is obvious that the first unified wave of films produced by women came directly out of the Woman's Movement, a mixture of consciousness-raising and propaganda. Film was used to record women talking and then to direct discussion, so that the women on film could interact with the experiences and ideas of women at a meeting. There was a particular heady excitement to these films. For the first time ever, films were being made exclusively by women, about women and feminist politics, for other women. Susan Rice in the first issue of *Women and Film* comments on Kate Millett's film *Three Lives*:

> *Three Lives* is a Women's Liberation Cinema Production, and it is the only feature film I know of that not only takes women as its subject-matter, but was produced, directed, shot, recorded, lit, and edited by women. What makes this more than a stunt is the intimacy that this female crew seems to have elicited from its subjects. The element I find most compelling about the film is that it captures the tone and quality of relationships and significant conversation between women. If the film were to fail on every other level, this would stand as a note-worthy achievement.[4]

Or Dora Kaplan in the next issue writes of 'This new movement of women making political films politically' that

> This commitment to educate, change consciousness, and sensibility showed itself to be unalienated; that is, carried over to the process of film making itself; a film crew working collectively without hierarchy and specialization; a film crew working on an equal basis with the 'subject' in decision-making and production; and a film crew recognizing the distribution of the product to be an integral part of the process.[5]

Although it is hard to overestimate the vigour and immediacy of some of these films, they are closely tied to the ideology of consciousness-raising and agitation around particular feminist issues. This is their strength; their weakness lies in limitations of the *cinéma-vérité* tradition. While as documents they can have an immediate political use, their aesthetics are bound by a concept of film as a transparent medium, reproducing rather than questioning, a project which reduces the camera to a magical instrument. There lies behind this a further assumption, that the camera, by its very nature and the good intentions of its operator, can grasp essential truths and by registering typical shared experiences can create political unity through the process of identifi-cation. The politics are thus restricted to emotion and the cinema stays trapped in the old endless search for the other self on the screen.

Summary

Up to this point, I have used feminist film criticism around 1972 to mark a particular stage of conscious development and to show a need for a theoretical leap forward. But no leap forward could be conceived without this first spring-board: awareness of sexist exploitation and cultural oppression, and the resurrection of women who had struggled to make movies in the past. However, the way forward seemed blocked. The answers offered in this period did not match the needs of a feminist film culture. Demands for identification, for women's films that played on identification processes, still stayed subservient both to pre-existing cinematic formal traditions redolent of sexual exploitation and to the cinema of male domination. Any changes within the industry could only result from long-term agitation and activity on the part of women wanting to work within it, and from outside, gradual erosion through shifts in ideology. As a 16mm cinema took off and discrimination still prevailed in the industry, it became obvious that the independent sector would see the birth of a specifically feminist film-making practice. What would this cinema be like?

Desire to break with the past is rational and passionate. It is both an instinctual retreat from forms associated with oppression and a conscious drive to find uncontaminated ground on which to build a feminist aesthetics. Aesthetic and theoretical questions posed by mapping this new ground then widen the gap with the past. Is it then enough to break with sexist content alone? The dominant cinema has privileged content, whether in fiction or documentary, to subordinate the formal cinematic process itself. Identification between spectator and screen-protagonist closes up remaining or necessary gaps between form and content. (For instance, Hitchcock reconciles his extravagant and unusual use of cinema with the demands of convention, involving the spectator through suspense.) In order to construct a new language of cinema, therefore, a break in this all-pervasive artistic unity appeared to be a priority. At the same time a pre-digested, fully grown, alternative cinematic language could not be expected to fall neatly from the sky at the moment of need. Such an expectation assumes that women's cinema had a developed tradition winding through the overt history of cinema like an unseen thread, or that the very fact of being a feminist and making a film would in itself be an answer. Neither proposition could hold up. The first ignores the extent of past oppression, the second asserts that individual intention transcends the language and aesthetics of cinema. A language must have a collective existence, otherwise pervasive forms of expression return willy-nilly, penetrating any intuitive rapport between spectator and creator, at best a matter of hit and miss.

Thus the first constructive steps towards feminist film culture have begun to turn in the direction of the matter of film language itself, probing dislocation between cinematic form and represented material, and investigating various means of splitting open the closed space between screen and spectator. As woman's place in past cinematic representation has been mystified, at once a linchpin of visual pleasure and an affirmation of male dominance, so feminists now have become fascinated with the mysteries of cinematic representation itself, hidden by means of the sexualised female fantasy form: a tearing of the veil, but no ready-made answers lie behind it. The absence of answers, combined with fascination with the cinematic process, point towards the development of a feminist formalism. Politically, a feminist formalism is based on rejection of the past and on giving priority to challenging the spectator's place in cinema. From an aesthetic point of view the space and time of realist or illusionist aesthetics have immense limitations: they cannot satisfy the complex shifts feminist imagery desires. Splits in the cinematic sign allow ideas to interact with fiction and thought with fantasy. At the same time there is a pleasure in *tabula rasa*. Structures become visible and the bare bones of the cinematic process force themselves forward. Finally, from a theoretical point of view, it is essential to analyse and understand the working of cinematic language, before claims can be made for a new language of cinema.

At the end of May 1978, three women from the collective of the only English-language journal of feminist film theory – *Camera Obscura* (published in Berkeley, California) – presented their work at the London Film-makers' Co-op, for discussion with English film-makers (men and women) and feminists interested in the cinema. The three had been associate editors of *Women and Film*, the pioneering magazine of feminist film criticism. They broke with *Women and Film* on the grounds that feminism had to move beyond the first spring-board – the basic critique of sexism and the affirmation of women's lost tradition – and search for new images. The new journal, *Camera Obscura*, is conceived on two linked fronts. First, to investigate the mechanisms by which meaning is produced in film:

It is important to know where to locate ideology and patriarchy within the mode of representation in order to intervene and transform society, to define a praxis for change. Crucial to the feminist struggle is an awareness that any theory of how to change consciousness requires a notion of how consciousness is formed, of what change is and how it occurs.

And then the journal takes particular texts, so far only films made by women, as 'contributing to the development of a feminist counter-cinema, both by having as their central concern a feminist problematic, and by operating specific challenges to cinematic codes and narrative conventions of illusionist cinema'.[6]

A new theory and a new practice. I was struck at the Co-op weekend by the similarity between the *Camera Obscura* analysis and the thoughts I was developing for this essay. I was also struck by the historic conjuncture between feminist film theory, the *Camera Obscura* presentation, and the Co-op, home of avant-gardist film practice. This was a meeting, I felt, that could not until recently have taken place. It seemed to be a concrete indication, or mutual recognition, of a growing two-way traffic. On the part of feminist theorists, there is growing awareness of the avant-garde tradition; and on the part of the avant-garde, among both men and women film-makers, a sense of the relevance of the feminist challenge.

THE SEARCH FOR A THEORY

Both film theory and feminism, united by a common interest in the politics of images and problems of aesthetic language, have been influenced by recent intellectual debates around the split nature of the sign (semiotics) and the eruption of the unconscious in representation (psychoanalysis). There has also been a definite influence from Louis Althusser's Marxist philosophy, especially his essay 'Ideology and Ideological State Apparatuses'.[7]

The importance for the workings of bourgeois ideology which Althusser attributes to identification processes, imaginary representation of the subject and the illusion of reality, gave a new sense of political seriousness to aesthetic debates among avant-garde film-makers and film theorists. The realist aesthetics used means to entrap the spectator similar to those of bourgeois ideology itself. One could not, therefore, confront the other. Pam Cook (in her essay on Dorothy Arzner) makes the point that the system of representations generated by the classic Hollywood cinema fixes the spectator in a specific closed relationship to it, obliterating the possibility of experiencing contradiction.[8] This kind of argument fed into a reinforced anti-realism, providing the ground for theoretical links between avant-gardists opposing illusionism and political film-makers opposing bourgeois ideology. Furthermore the debate continued around the nature of the cinematic apparatus: how to liberate the destiny of the photographic process from simply recording, in keeping with the natural perspective vision of the human eye. Formalism provided an answer: foregrounding the cinematic process privileging the signifier, disrupts aesthetic unity and forces the spectator's attention on the means of production of meaning. *Camera Obscura* (in the first editorial) pointed out that

> Like the Camera Obscura, the cinematic apparatus is not ideologically neutral, but reproduces specific ideological predispositions: codes of movement, of iconic representation and perspective. The notion that 'reality' can be reflected in film negates any awareness of the intervention, the mediation of the cinematic apparatus. The impression of reality in the cinema is not due to its capacity for verisimilitude, its ability to reproduce faithfully a copy of an object, but rather to the complex process of the basic cinematic apparatus itself, which in its totality includes the spectator.[9]

From a feminist point of view, one crucial area of struggle is with or in ideology. Patriarchal ideology is made up of assumptions, 'truths' about the meaning of sexual difference, women's place in society, the mystery of femininity and so on. From this political point of view, feminist film theory has followed the aesthetic debate. However, ideology – whether bourgeois or patriarchal – is not a blanket-like or eternal totality and it is crucial for feminists to be aware of contradictions within it.

The twentieth century has seen the growth of oppositional aesthetics, under various avant-garde banners and movements. Although here too women have played only a marginal part, a search for theory cannot overlook the kind of questioning and confrontations that underlie other radical aesthetic movements.

I want to mention only one aspect of relations between semiotics and the avant-garde that affects women. Julia Kristeva, in her work on modernist poetics, has linked the crisis that produced the language of modernism with 'the feminine'.[10] She sees femininity as the repressed in the patriarchal order and as standing in a problematic relation to it. Tradition is transgressed by an eruption of linguistic excess, involving pleasure and 'the feminine' directly opposed to the logical language and repression endemic to patriarchy. A problem remains: woman, in these terms, only stands for what has been repressed, and it is the male poet's relation to femininity that erupts in his use of poetic language. The next step would, from a feminist point of view, have to move beyond *woman* unspeaking, a signifier of the 'other' of patriarchy, to a point where *women* can speak themselves, beyond a definition of 'femininity' assigned by patriarchy, to a poetic language made also by women and their understanding. But Kristeva's important point is this: transgression is played out through language itself. The break with the past has to work through the means of meaning-making itself, subverting its norms and refusing its otherwise imperturbable totality. Here, by extension, the importance of the independent film-making sector for feminism appears fully: it is outside the constraints of commercial cinema, in debate with the language of counter-cinema, that feminist experimentation can take place. Semiotics foregrounds language and emphasises both the crucial importance of the signifier (for a long time overlooked and subordinated to the signified) and the dual nature of the sign, thus suggesting the aesthetic mileage that can be gained by play on separation between its two aspects. For feminists this split has a triple attraction: aesthetic fascination with discontinuities; pleasure from disrupting the traditional unity of the sign; and theoretical advance from investigating language and the production of meaning.

One crucial contribution made by Freudian psychoanalysis is to pinpoint femininity as problematic for a society ordered by masculine dominance. Female sexuality, and also the feminine in male sexuality, hover as difficult and potentially uncontainable elements, repressed or erupting into neurotic symptoms. Here again there is a split, insisted on by Freud, between an appearance (whether a symptom, a habit or a slip) and the meaning behind it. In positing an unconscious the workings of which could not find direct conscious expression, Freud showed how, psychoanalytically, things can seldom be what they seem. Thus the image of woman in patriarchal representation refers primarily to connotations within the male unconscious, to its fears and fantasies. As Claire Johnston says in her study of women in the films of Raoul Walsh:

> For the male hero the female protagonist becomes an agent within the text of the film whereby his hidden secret can be brought to light, for it is in woman that his lack is located. She represents at one and the same time, the distant memory of maternal plenitude and the fetishized object of his fantasy of castration – a phallic replacement and thus a threat.[11]

I have argued elsewhere ('Visual Pleasure and Narrative Cinema') that psychoanalysis can be used to reveal the way in which conventions of narrative cinema are tailored to dominant masculine desire – that voyeuristic pleasure is built into the way a spectator reads film.

> The place of the look defines cinema, the possibility of varying it and exposing it. This is what makes cinema quite different from, say, strip-tease, theatre, shows, and so on. Going far beyond highlighting a woman's to-be-looked-at-ness, the cinema builds the way she is to be looked at into the spectacle itself.[12]

Polemically, this proposition leads on to the necessity, for counter-cinema, of exposing the force of pleasure inherent in the cinematic experience in so far as it is organised around male erotic privilege and built on an imbalance between male/female, active/passive.

THE SEARCH FOR A PRACTICE

The disparate elements which I have drawn together under the heading 'The Search for a Theory' do not add up to a coherent whole. I have concentrated, furthermore, on those influences on feminist film theory that have implications for film-making practice, influences which all point towards both a desire and a need for rupture with closed, homogeneous forms of representation. Psychoanalysis dissolves the veneer of surface meanings: semiotics focuses on the split nature of the sign and on language itself as a site for change; confrontation with ideology brings up the issue of identification, of how a text 'places' a spectator. Now I want to outline influences from the avant-garde tradition and the ways in which feminist film-making practice has taken a position in relation to them.

Throughout this essay, I have referred to the persistent difficulty of articulating the means by which an aesthetic break can find formal expression. How does an independent aesthetic evolve out of confrontation with a dominant one? An important aspect of avant-garde aesthetics is negation: a work is formed, or driven to find a position, by the very code of the dominant tradition that is being opposed. These works have then to be read, and achieve meaning, in the reflected light of the aesthetics they negate. One aspect of the problems implicit in formulating a new aesthetics from scratch is thus circumvented. Traditional forms are known and recognised, and the spectator can recognise and read their negation. In cinematic terms traditional illusionist aesthetics have privileged the signified, organising a text so that its mechanics would attract minimal notice. A crucial and influential response within avant-garde aesthetics has been pioneered by the New American Cinema of the 1960s, which stresses the place of the signifier, illuminating the complexity of the cinematic process (as Annette Michelson puts it in the introduction to *New Forms in Film*, 'the assertion of the still photographic frame composing the strip, the assertion through the flicker of the medium as projection of light, the assertion of the nature of projection through the use of sound. . . .').[13]

This emphasis on the importance of the signifier has thrown the place of the signified into crisis. For instance, Peter Gidal, a leading avant-garde film-maker in England, has rejected all content and narrative, both in his own work and as an aesthetic principle. In the introduction to *Structural Film Anthology*, he writes: 'The Structuralist/Materialist film must minimize the content in its overpowering, imagistically seductive sense, in an attempt to get through this miasmic area of "experience" and proceed with film as film'.[14]

For feminist film-makers, the way these arguments elevate the signifier is important. There is a link with those aspects of feminist film theory that demand a return to *tabula rasa* and question how meaning is made. But women cannot be satisfied with an aesthetics that restricts counter-cinema to work on form alone. Feminism is bound to its politics; its experimentation cannot exclude work on content. Peter Wollen (in his article 'The Two Avant-Gardes') traces a line of development where the demand for a new politics inseparably links problems of form and content. Going back to Eisenstein and Vertov, influenced by Brecht, re-emerging with the late work of Godard, this tradition has broken down rigid demarcations between fact and fiction and laid a foundation for experimentation with narrative.[15]

It is hard, as yet, to speak of a feminist film-making practice. Women film-makers are still few and far between, and influences on them are not necessarily coherent. Rather than generalising, it is preferable to exemplify tendencies and movements among women film-makers. For instance Annabel Nicolson (a long-standing member of the London Co-op) has used the old tradition of women's applied arts to experiment with film as material. In her expanded piece *Reel Time* (1973), she brings out the relationship between the projector and a sewing machine, running loops of film depicting herself sewing film through the sewing machine, then runs it through the projector until the film tears and starts to slip. Joyce Wieland in her first film *Handtinting* (made in New York in the 1960s) carried over her previous experiments with quilting into film, puncturing the strip with needles and dyeing the celluloid. There is also an aspect of her work which is miniature, home-movie scale: she describes *Rat Life and Diet in North America* as 'a film made at my kitchen table' and, using her pet gerbils as characters, she creates a narrative version of a domestic still life.[16]

Yvonne Rainer turned to film-making from dance (Maya Deren and Shirley Clarke also started their careers as dancers – one role in the arts where women are less likely to suffer discrimination and oppression). Rainer has done crucially important work with narrative, exploring its radical possibilities. She describes her way of working:

A novelist might well laugh at my makeshift dallying with story-telling. For me the story is an empty frame on which to hang images and thoughts which need support. I feel no obligation to flesh out this armature with credible details of time and place. . . . I was much more concerned with interweaving psychological and formal content, i.e., with images being filled up or emptied by readings or their absence, with text and image being illustrated to various degrees . . . .

This made for a situation where the story came and went, sometimes disappearing altogether as the extreme prolongation of certain sound-less images . . . I accumulate stuff from my own writing, paragraphs, sentences, scraps of paper, stills from previous films, photos. Ulti-mately the process of sorting out forces me to organise it and make the parts cohere in some kind of fashion.[17]

Rainer shifts her story-telling and gives an ironic commentary on its development by means of written titles, interrupting the flow of images, using cliché in words and in situations, dwelling on emotion and performance and women's relation to them as traditional modes of expression. As a logical conclusion, perhaps, to this combination of interests, melodrama is invoked, but also, other forms of communication considered special to women (diaries, letters, intimate conversations and confidences), all distanced by an ironic handling of familiar self-doubts and self-questioning.

In my own films (co-directed with Peter Wollen), *Penthesilea* (1974) and *Riddles of the Sphinx* (1977), and also in Chantal Akerman's films, there is a meeting between the melodramatic tradition and psychoanalysis. Akerman's *Jeanne Dielman*, for example, shows the life of a woman over three days, dwelling minutely on daily repetition and domestic details. Once her routine is thrown off course, slight slips accumulate, leading almost imperceptibly to a cataclysmic eruption at the end. And then Akerman's *News from Home* uses letters from an anxious mother to her daughter read as sound-track over long static shots of New York on the image-track, separating sound and image to create action. *Riddles of the Sphinx* deals with dilemmas of motherhood lived within patriarchal society; the story of a woman (first married, in the home, then separated and working) with a two-year-old daughter is embedded in the centre of other approaches to the subject, direct or visual or poetic. What recurs overall is a constant return to woman, not indeed as a visual image, but as a subject of inquiry, a content which cannot be considered within the aesthetic lines laid down by traditional cinematic practice. Pleasure and involvement are not the result of identification, narrative tension or eroticised femininity, but arise from surprising and excessive use of the camera, unfamiliar framing of scenes and the human body, the demands made on the spectator to put together disparate elements. The story, the visual themes and the ideas are not in coherent conjunction with one another, and ask to be read in terms of developing relations between feminism and experimental film and psychoanalysis.

I began by pointing out how, in the brief history of film, feminism has only recently had any impact at all. Even now, the sphere in which the impact has been felt is extremely restricted. Recent technological developments allow the growth of film outside the industry, but without solid economic foundations. The future directions of 16mm and of experimental film are uncertain, but the conjunction between their growth and the historic eruption of feminist politics is unprecedented in the history of the arts. Here, at last, the demands of women can have a determining effect on aesthetics, as the work of feminist film theorists and film-makers gains strength and influence within the experimental sphere.

Notes

1. Pam Cook and Claire Johnston, 'Dorothy Arzner: Critical Strategies', in Claire Johnston (ed.), *Dorothy Arzner, Towards a Feminist Cinema* (London: British Film Institute, 1975).
2. Molly Haskell, *From Reverence to Rape: The Treatment of Women in the Movies* (Chicago: University of Chicago Press, 1987) p. 362.
3. Shirley Clarke, 'Image and Images', *Take One*, III, 2 (1972).
4. Susan Rice, 'Three Lives', *Women and Film*, I, 1 (1972).
5. Dora Kaplan, 'Selected Short Subjects', *Women and Film*, I, 2 (1972).
6. 'Feminism and Film; Critical Approaches', *Camera Obscura*, 1 (1976).
7. Louis Althusser, 'Ideology and Ideological State Apparatuses', *Lenin and Philosophy and Other Essays* (London: New Left Books, 1971).
8. Claire Johnston paraphrasing Pam Cook, 'Approaching the Work of Dorothy Arzner', Johnston, *Dorothy Arzner*, p. 2.
9. 'Feminism and Film; Critical Approaches', *Camera Obscura*, 1 (1976).
10. Julia Kristeva, 'Signifying Practice and Means of Production', *Edinburgh '76 Magazine; Psychoanalysis, Cinema and Avant-Garde* (1976).
11. Claire Johnston, 'The Place of Women in the Cinema of Raoul Walsh', in P. Hardy (ed.), *Raoul Walsh* (Edinburgh, 1974) p. 45.
12. Laura Mulvey, 'Visual Pleasure and Narrative Cinema', *Screen*, XVI, 3 (1975).
13. Annette Michelsa, 'Film and the Radical Aspiration', *New Forms in Film* (Montreux, 1974), p. 15.
14. Peter Crital, 'Theory and Definition of the Structural/Materialist Film', *Structural Film Anthology* (London: British Film Institute, 1976).
15. Peter Wollen, 'The Two Avant-Gardes', *Studio International*, 190, 1978 (November/December 1975).
16. 'Kay Armatage Interviews Joyce Wieland', *Take One*, XIII, 2 (1972).
17. 'Yvonne Rainer: Interview', *Camera Obscura*, 1 (1976).

11

Dialogue with Spectatorship: Barbara Kruger and Victor Burgin*

* Written as a review of 'We Won't Play Nature to Your Culture' held at the ICA gallery and of 'Hotel Latone' for *Creative Camera* in 1983.

Barbara Kruger's exhibition *We Won't Play Nature to Your Culture* and Victor Burgin's book *Hotel Latone* are such different kinds of work that at first it seems almost arbitrary to discuss them together, or just a simple exploitation of the fact that both use words and photographs in juxtaposition. Kruger's enormous enlargements of found photographs are cropped and manipulated for rhetorical effect, then slashed across with words that evoke the pain and anger of sexual oppression. The words are sometimes a silent cry of personal pain, sometimes a slogan of political anger. The images are elusive, like the last fragment of a dream that stays in the memory. These two elements, word and image, are bound together by frames painted bright red. The size is important, echoing the persistent theme of power relations in the works themselves, leaving the spectator both overwhelmed and exhilarated as he or she is faced with a series of possible relations with the image on the wall. To look at the works in a catalogue is an experience of loss. The blown-up, grainy texture of the actual works seems to disintegrate the images from within, and adds to their mystery. Just as the scale of the Kruger work is significant, so it seems suitable that *Hotel Latone* should have a book format (although it originated as an exhibition in Calais in 1982). The photographs are precise and clear so that the reader, or looker rather, has to scan the images and reflect on their smallest detail. It is possible to turn the pages, follow the story's given sequence and then flip back or forward to discover a pattern or repetition. The images and the text put themselves at the reader's disposal, and need time, in their strangeness, to be thought about. It is a more obviously private experience than that of a gallery. *Hotel Latone* is in three, unmarked, parts and tells a story of impossible desire. Burgin makes narrative and visual use of condensation and displacement (Freud's terms for the mechanisms used by the unconscious to evade repression) and draws on myth to expand his frames of reference. He can thus interweave the vicissitudes of the individual psyche with collective fantasy and with the mechanics of his own creative process.

127

Burgin and Kruger share a concern with spectatorship and the act of looking, the point at which the psychodynamics of voyeurism and the power relations of masculinity and femininity can affect a work of art. Both artists use language, in particular personal pronouns, to make visible and explicit the process of exchange between an art object and its spectator. This mode of address positions the subject and affirms identity. Burgin treats sexual identity as a trap, a destiny not set in motion by biology but by the construction of sexual difference through the Oedipus complex. Kruger emphasises the ambivalence of sexual identity. Both artists make important contributions to the aesthetics of sexual politics or, rather, they use sexual scenarios to attack patriarchal politics. Behind this project lies the conjunction between feminism and psychoanalysis that had such a sweeping influence over the 1970s avant-garde. Work on, and with, theory became an element within artistic practice, influenced the negative aesthetics of the time, and generated notoriously difficult art work that seemed to need special commitment or privileged knowledge in order to be understood. Pleasure as a factor in art went into crisis.

We Won't Play Nature to Your Culture and *Hotel Latone* mark a new departure, a different kind of challenge to the spectator, a twist to the spectator's 'work' on the text. Emotion and reverie are central themes in the content of the works but also are the essential means of understanding and deciphering them. This is not a backward move into subjectivity or intuition, but a structured exchange between text reader and the collective fantasy that has produced text and reader alike. Collective fantasy is generated by a collective unconscious, not the Jungian collective unconscious, but a pool of raw material common to all who share a similar induction into sexual difference, experiences of castration anxiety, the Oedipus complex and, indeed, the psychic drives. Collective unconscious is what myth grows from, the raw material of repression and its return in popular fantasy and narrative. Myth, with its ritual and safeguarding function, transforms this experience of pain and desire and reconciles it with terms that can fit social reality.

The Kruger and Burgin works are about desire and sexual difference and our understanding (or misunderstanding) of both under patriarchy. Kruger starts with sexual oppression but goes beyond to arrive at the point encapsulated by Luce Irigaray: 'What I desire and what I am waiting for, is what men will do and say if their sexuality gets freed from the empire of phallocentrism'. Burgin's *Hotel Latone* seems to be feeling a way to an answer, examining the male unconscious from within the point of view of 'masculinity'. He opens up a void that is concealed by the masquerade of masculinity under patriarchy. Looking at *We Won't Play Nature to Your Culture* and *Hotel Latone*, it is possible to feel that the old 'difficult' concepts no longer need difficult presentation. Psychoanalytic discourse has become the source of fascinating images that are about the psychic life of the mind and about the power of images, but these images must also produce reverie and flashes of recognition similar to the experience of looking at a *trompe-l'oeil* or just grasping a *déjà vu*. The reading process is not easy or intuitive but it is not didactic either.

Barbara Kruger's works in *We Won't Play Nature to Your Culture* can be viewed or read on various levels. They have an immediate, emotional impact. But they can also be taken, more slowly, as a complex comment on the place of scenario and representation in male–female relations under patriarchy. She builds on the feminist analysis of representation as political, and on feminist appropriation of psychoanalytical theory as a means of understanding oppression. However, her images go further, both in language and visual material. The obvious vulnerability of the would-be resistant female complements a rigid, and therefore brittle, male control. Patriarchy freezes woman into representation and, in doing so, fossilises man. Woman's vulnerability recurs as a motif a number of times, in essence in 'I can't look at you and breathe at the same time' which combines woman's exclusion from active looking with a grainy texture (that of the water and the photographic surface). The female figure swims backstroke, exposed and defenceless against imminent disintegration. 'Your gaze hits the side of my face' shows the reverse side of the problem. Here the threat of destruction is emphasised by a statue's mask-like perfection and its smooth, white surface. An exterior, like a shell (both self-protective and exhibitionist), shields the object of gaze ineffectively from an act of aggression. Voyeurism slips into sadism, but the female profile remains inert. In these two images the act of articulation, the words themselves, seem to hold the moment of disintegration at bay, for a split second at least. And the photograph's inherent stillness reflects the way that time stands still at a moment of fear.

'I am your slice of life' and 'I am your almost nothing' evoke another kind of disintegration, a retreat into a cliché that ironically restates masochistic self-denial in love. Like the photograph itself, cliché freezes a scenario. Kruger reproduces the cliché-metaphor literally and sur-prisingly in the image. The texture, the pierced surface, the delicately dissolving hair evoke the pain of self-effacement. The tension in 'We won't play nature to your culture' and 'I will not become what I mean to you' is rather different. Here the elements in the image contradict each other, as the visuals actually do represent a 'becoming' and a 'playing'. The moment held in suspense is like a flash of resistance, but none the less impotent. This time the impotence is due to generalised, socialised forces at work in which femininity is assigned a place, willy-nilly. The cliché text again is a resistance and this time the language of the oppressor is undermined by the negative.

Although woman is conventionally fetishised into cultural material (verbal, visual) and this semiotic fact is a starting-point for Kruger's work, it is not its finishing-point. The images do not describe or show. They elicit a response from the spectator that is emotional in addition to intellectual recognition of a political discourse. The image/word relationship is a montage or collision; one does not illustrate the other. In a series centred around the sadistic, violent aspects of patriarchy, the word/image relationship is more literal. Her analysis of power ('You transform power into pose') emphasises cultural authority, and its destructiveness ('You divide and rule', 'Your manias become science', 'You have searched and destroyed'). The cliché phrases are brought to life through anger and accusation but the spectator is not forced to dream.

At this point the work would seem to reproduce a personal and political dichotomy equivalent to male and female spheres: public/private and emotion/politics. This could be a reiteration of the feminist rhetoric that was so necessary to establish woman's articulation of oppression, but there are crucial fissures that break up the ground between these two opposing worlds. 'Keep us at a distance' and 'We are the failure of ritual cleansing' suggest that the oppressed are also a threat. Woman cannot be completely colonised and man is not completely in control. Male power has its own vulnerability in 'Your property is a rumour of power' and 'Your life is a perpetual insomnia'. It is as though man, in exercising patriarchal power and freezing woman into spectacle, has also turned himself into a masquerade that can crack. And this brings in its wake an empty, frightening sexuality. Here the images regain a complexity and resonance, a sense of loss due to the rigidity of the masculine and feminine opposition.

Numbness, inability to feel, pervade the images while the accompanying words carry accusation from the political into the personal sphere which, this time, is masculine ('You are seduced by the sex appeal of the inorganic', 'You delight in the loss of others', 'Your pleasure is spasmodic and shortlived', and 'You re-enact the dance of insertion and wounding'). In these works the words have grown and dominate the visual text, but the poignancy of juxtaposition is as vivid as in those that evoke feminine complicity and resistance. The images are once again an incitement to dream, desire and rebel against loss. Power is a trap that alienates, both into the making of history and transforming the other into pose, but is almost nothing in personal terms.

Hotel Latone uses travel as a metaphor for the movements of the unconscious. The book starts in a hotel. This is a literal 'displacement' of the characters that evokes the Freudian concept of displacement, which Burgin appropriates both as a formal device and a theme. Like a dream, the text and the photographs represent the way that repressed material struggles to find expression by latching onto objects, images, words, anything that seems to allow it to speak. This displacement is a means of articulating the unspeakable, but its language is distorted and symbolic. Displacement is crucial for the mechanism of fetishistic denial, also an important theme in *Hotel Latone*. The third photograph is of female feet in high-heeled shoes, the classic fetish object sought by the gaze that wants to know but refuses to accept female 'castration'. The book associates fetishistic fixing with the look. The text 'In December everything is frozen, petrified for all time' is alongside a photograph of a man standing still in the street, staring fixedly off image. A woman stepping off the pavement behind him is caught in mid-movement, bringing to mind Burgin's previous writing on the relationship between the photograph and fetishism. Thus, fetishism and the look, as well as being central to the content of the book, reflect back on photography itself. Condensation of theme, theory and form again echoes the workings of the unconscious.

Condensation is the term used to describe a point in a dream which is overdetermined by several meanings or references, like a pun. But because it acts as a point of intersection, a nodal point, it can spark apparently random lines of association or thought, that then generate new movements or developments in a story-line. In *Hotel Latone* the story-line develops with abrupt changes of time and place that are reminiscent of the dream work. The man in the street photograph is followed immediately by 'In that empty cabin, in those silent woods' alongside the interior of a hunting lodge. The connotations evoked by the photograph's strange space and *mise en scène* make it into an image of the male mind. This, in turn, is accompanied by 'Silent and all-encompassing woods which press against the window-panes' alongside a photograph of two men. The posture and look of one at the other expresses repressed homosexual desire. The following page 'As in a fairy tale' shifts the angle of the shot in the hunting lodge to frame the trophies on the wall. Once again the theme of a fetish object returns, this time represented by the dead animals and inanimate litter of objects that figure the stuff that inhabits the male unconscious.

The second section of the book, still using the mechanisms of condensation and displacement, revolves around castration anxiety. Here one text and accompanying photograph are literally displaced and separated one from the other by two pages. The photograph itself is now represented as an object lying on a table top. The motifs running through this section are associated with the ease with which masculinity masquerading as phallic power can crack and collapse, especially when faced with a role reversal of the socially demanded 'masculine' and 'feminine' positions as 'active' and 'passive'. An active woman is a threat. Phaedra's tragic and destructive love for Hippolytus, the passive object of her desiring gaze, is mentioned here as a point of reference. Next, a photograph of broken Greek columns and a headless statue of a woman appears alongside 'The effort of holding the camera to her eye in the noon heat is causing perspiration to run into the hollow of the eye-piece', emphasising the perverse activity and unaccustomed effort for a woman to be in this position of active looker.

The final section of the book uses the Latona myth, once again as a point of condensation. The Latona fountain in Versailles is the nodal point, starting off a line of thought around fetishisation of woman as representation. It is as though masculinity in crisis, or under threat, was forced necessarily to turn the threatening object, woman, into stone, 'petrified for all time'. The sculpture, like photography, has frozen movement and gesture. But another element is brought into play by the Latona myth. (This throws light retrospectively on Phaedra, who, as Hippolytus's stepmother, transgressed the incest taboo.) To quote Bachofen's *Myth, Religion and Mother Right*:

> Matriarchal is the Lycian Apollo, whose mother is Latona queen of the swamp bottom, and who dwells in the land of his birth only during the six dead winter months; patriarchal is the Hellenistic god exalted to metaphysical purity, who rules over Delos during the six life-giving summer months.

(Latona's other child, Artemis, is the protector of the Amazons and virginity.) Iconographically, Latona represents the mother as an image of loss. Loss of pre-Oedipal oneness with the mother and the woman's body as source of castration anxiety effect a split between male desire and its object, that is then fixed and frozen in woman as image, safe and possessable.

> He had not previously noticed the image. It reminded him of a passage from Sade, where the heroine is posed on a pedestal surrounded by a moat. Her admirer can cause the pedestal to turn by means of a remote control: he may look but he has no means of approaching her.

In the end the woman recognises this scenario, sadly, and the fact that she herself has, by now, little or nothing to do with male desire. The crisis of sexual difference, with castration at its core, leaves male and female out of sync. They cannot be symmetrical or complement one another. The book ends with photographs of birth, 'condensing' a number of themes. Birth is the first moment of placing 'a boy' or 'a girl'. The last page has the same text as the first, thus using the birth image to suggest the cyclical, endless repetition of human drama. But the birth scene is also a means of revealing the ultimate point of horror: the mother's genitals (the Medusa's head).

I have described and given a fragmentary, partial reading of aspects of *We Won't Play Nature to Your Culture* and *Hotel Latone* that struck me forcibly and moved me. This raises the question of reading and the validity of a reading. I decoded the images by allowing myself to day-dream about them rather than interpret them. This brings back the issue of text and reader exchange through the shared fears and fantasies of the collective unconscious. I would like to use Bunuel's *Notes on the Making of 'Un chien andalou'* in this context:

The sources from which the film draws its inspiration are those of poetry, freed from its ballast of reason and tradition. Its aim is to provoke in the spectator instinctive reactions of attraction and repulsion. *Un chien andalou* would not have existed if the movement called surrealist had not existed. For its 'ideology', its psychic motivation and the systematic use of the poetic image as an arm to overthrow accepted notions, correspond to the characteristics of all authentically surrealist work. This film has no intention of attracting or pleasing the spectator; indeed, on the contrary, it attacks him, to the degree that he belongs to a society with which surrealism is at war . . .

The producer–director of the film, Bunuel, wrote the scenario in collaboration with the painter Dali. For it, both took their point of view from a dream image, which, in its turn, probed others by the same process until the whole took form as a continuity. It should be noted that when an idea appeared the collaborators discarded it immediately if it was derived from a remembrance, or from their cultural pattern, or if, simply, it had a conscious association from an earlier idea. They accepted only those representations as valid which, though they moved them profoundly, had no possible explanation . . . NOTHING in the film, SYMBOLISES ANYTHING. The only method of investigation of the symbols would be, perhaps, psycho-analysis.

Although *Un chien andalou,* and particularly its surrealist framework, is in many ways unlike the works discussed here, Bunuel's statement brings up relevant ideas that can be expanded and adapted. The combination of emotion and structure allows individual reverie to coexist with group or collective unconscious, to produce a poetics within the rigour of psychoanalytic theory. In Freudian terms this process would be similar to that of the Oedipal drama as a generalised scenario through which everyone negotiates their trajectory; or, on a linguistic plane, a *langue* which allows each speech act to be an individual *parole*.

In *Un chien andalou* one is confronted with a series of reverie-producing images, that, according to the passion or repression of particular spectators, can produce different responses. There is no correct reading. A process of disturbance (or, as Eisenstein put it, 'shocks', or 'montage of attractions') is programmed into the work, but its effect is not predetermined. The starting-point is curiosity. A mysterious image sets up an enigma which offers pleasure through the very process of decoding. Solving a riddle is as basic a source of aesthetic pleasure as spectatorship, but the pleasure is intellectual rather than visual. At this point in time, when the pleasures of spectatorship seem hopelessly compromised by the interface between sexual difference and the component instincts of sexuality (as Freud describes in *Three Essays on Sexuality*) enigma offers a new point of departure. This process carries the spectator into his/her psychic structure. The image itself only 'works' if its mystery or enigma generates introspection, or, indeed, an equally telling resistance. Decipherment is demanded, clues are offered, but the reveries and associations of ideas are specific to the individual. However, the shared psychic structures that trigger off the individual response bring the pleasures and anxieties of reverie back inexorably to problems of repression and desire as shared and social.

A reverie-generating image must avoid idiolect and the various pitfalls offered, in this context at least, by artistic self-expression. The spectator is not invited to share the artist's insights, dreams or experiences (as, for instance, in Cocteau's *Le Sang d'un poète* or Maya Deren's *Meshes of the Afternoon* which have an aesthetic and cultural importance of a different kind). This relation between image and reverie is closer to that of popular culture, Hitchcock's movies, for instance, or fairy stories. But there is an important political difference between the avant-garde and the popular. The popular can disturb, bring difficult material to the fore, cause returns of the repressed, but tends to reconcile contradiction in the last resort. Both the popular and this kind of avant-garde privilege 'trigger' images over artistic expression and establish a terrain in which terrors and fascinations produced by taboos, repressions and complexes find material and concrete form in art, story-telling or any other suitable form of representation. The teller and the listener are separated by skill perhaps, but dream the same dreams and share the same dreads. A 'poetics of psychoanalysis' is important here. The 'trigger' images say more than can ever be put into either descriptive words or realist imagery. The unconscious too, due to censorship or repression, cannot 'speak' itself literally or rationally, and the achievement in this kind of art is to make a poetics of the 'unspeakable'. This was Bunuel's aim and he also recognised its political implications. The post-feminist art has taken the surrealist project into a new politics. The individual dreamers are confronted with the structures of patriarchy as they are brought into touch with their own psychic patterns. The starting-point is political.

The emphasis that both artists place on sight brings up another important interface between aesthetics and psychoanalysis: the special qualities associated with photography. Vision, pleasure in looking as a component instinct of sexuality (the area of interest to Kruger and Burgin) bear no relation to seeing as the means of perceiving the real world. Sight as a drive attaches itself to pleasure-giving, or anxiety-alleviation. Objects become symptoms, referring back to the psyche, as it robs them of their true nature as material things and gives them a new meaning and significance. Women have always been the favourite objects at the receiving end of this magical transformation process. In its history, photography has been usually associated with sight as perception of the real, a record of material existence. Kruger and Burgin free the photograph from its command over historic time and space. Its indexicality now refers to things which, although real and concrete, are not actually visible. Much more than still photography, the cinema, with its devotion to fiction and the fantastic, has used the indexical aspect of photography to slip in and out of the visible world and find concrete images for those realities of emotion that cannot be seen, while being often excessively felt.

The cinema has materialised fears, anxieties and desires that inhabit our minds and the world about us like a modern version of the medieval spirit world, stalking our lives as unseen presence. The cinema absorbed photographic play with tricks and narrative fiction that had amused the nineteenth century, leaving still photography pure but perhaps denuded. Méliès, for instance, was introduced to the magical potential inherent in film by the successful genre of ghost photography. In making Méliès a patron saint, the surrealists recognised the link between his project to materialise the world of fairy stories, spirits and primitive science fiction and their project to materialise another invisible world: that of the Freudian unconscious. The use Burgin makes of still photographs in *Hotel Latone* revives this project. At the same time he brings photography back to narrative and to the tableau, a privileged or overdetermined moment in a longer story. Kruger's use of photography emphasises the frozen moment of a scenario in a different manner that has been discussed very productively by Craig Owens in *The Medusa Effect*.

These aspects of the works that extend or push against the limits of the ascetic aesthetics of the 1970s, in particular the 'poetics of psychoanalysis' and 'dematerialisation' of photography, are assisted by language. Both *We Won't Play Nature to Your Culture* and *Hotel Latone* exploit ambivalence in language, especially the essential ambivalence that belongs to shifters of time, place and person. Burgin uses the indeterminate 'they', 'that', 'she', 'he', mostly as mechanisms on which to pivot the story into different directions, as carriers of condensation. In Kruger the personal pronouns have an important significance. While the fact that the artist/narrator is a woman suggests at first glance a straight construction of identity – 'I' = woman and 'you' = man – the intrinsic ambivalence of the shifter breaks down both stable subject position and secure sexual identity. Whatever the implications contained by the connotative elements in the image may be, a 'you' is an address and the addressee is the viewer, male or female. This carries the masochistic and exhibitionist motifs in the sexual scenarios further; the spectator is necessarily in a masculine position as looker-on and looker-in and looker-at. 'He' controls as voyeur, whatever 'his' sex. But the 'I' also demands identity and as the looker 'you' are addressed as you read the text, the 'he' among the spectators can be transformed by an identification with the first person, and the 'she' among the spectators can then identify with the feminine position given by the image. But rather than establishing, once again, the active–passive dichotomy that echoes masculine–feminine as a binary opposition, Kruger's use of language breaks down that dualistic topology to explore, not a space in between the two, but a non-space in which one term is freed from its function of defining the other.

Kruger takes her images beyond demand and refuses the 'desire and wait for' in Irigaray's ironic and laconic comment. Simultaneously, Burgin's *Hotel Latone* represents an unease, an exasperation with the traps of male sexuality 'within the empire of phallocratism' and the politics that accompany it. In retreating far back, exploring the mechanics of the 'masculine' unconscious, this strategy opens up new ground, an alternative to the sexuality that can only challenge itself by reversal.

12

'Magnificent Obsession': An Introduction to the Work of Five Photographers*

* Written as the catalogue text for the exhibition 'Magnificent Obsession' held at the ARC Gallery, Toronto, and the Optica Gallery, Montreal, in 1985.

This is an exhibition of photography that shatters preconceptions of what a photograph is or should be. The fantasy of a privileged insight that tears the mask away from perceived reality gives way to another reality, that of the mask itself and the reality of fantasy. Photography is generally assumed to be primarily anchored to the visible. The pleasurable paradox, familiar to the cinema, that the photographic image can be organised to express an abstract idea, an argument, the interior world of desire and imagination, seems strange to still photography.

The cinema is a medium of sequence, event and fiction. Expectations of the still image, on the other hand, have grown from an aesthetic of transparency, autonomy and homogeneity within the single whole. It is clear, at first glance, that the aesthetics of the works on exhibition here are derived from opposition to general expectation and have grown from counter-strategy. They break the rules. All use words, not as caption but as a parallel to the image, to defy autonomy; all are stylised to de-naturalise transparency; all use series to break out of the confines imposed by the autonomous single image.

These five artists studied together at the Polytechnic of Central London, Britain, in the 1970s, the period when a conjuncture between feminist politics, psychoanalytic theory and deconstructive aesthetics produced radical avant-garde across the visual arts. Feminism established representation as a terrain for political struggle and questions about images of women necessarily split over to raise wider issues about the image and authenticity. Psychoanalysis provided the language and concepts to expand the sexual politics of representation to include, for instance, desire, the look and fetishism. The photograph, in particular, lost its innocent one-to-one relation to reality. Perhaps, in retrospect, the inclusion of theory within practice could be taken as both a mainspring and a hallmark of the British radical avant-garde of the 1970s, producing, as a result, works that were considered as 'difficult' as the theory that informed them. Theory forced a rupture with the established aesthetic conventions of the autonomous image but it also provided a framework for an alternative aesthetic. So, for instance, by including psychoanalytic theory, Victor Burgin, Mary Kelly or I, in the films that I made with Peter Wollen, established the possibility of a word/image juxtaposition that could become infinitely more flexible and varied.

These photographs are the work of a next generation, no longer strictly bound by the confrontational aesthetics of the 1970s. The formal influences are there, there is a continuity of interest and concern but there are important and marked differences, particularly with respect to realism and pleasure. It is as though the long, hard battle against the transparency of realism and the spectator pleasure inscribed by tradition and convention (of which the use of women's image is emblematic) has broken down and reached the end of the road. Out of the débris a language and imagery can emerge that are no longer primarily concerned with an either/or dichotomy. But there is no spirit of compromise or even synthesis here. The values and desires of this group have developed out of the process of working their original influences through, to the point of distance and displacement where 'pleasure' and 'realism' are material for irony and play. In this sense, the exhibition has an art-historical perspective, quite apart from the intrinsic interest of the individual work, in that it records the way a specific movement can grow, change and develop, avoiding the dangers of fossilised repetition and purism.

The work, however, still seems difficult, apparently demanding an initiated reading. Confrontational, negative aesthetics can draw on the act of opposing convention as a source of meaning and significance. The next step is harder. It is easier to oppose and deconstruct than to construct alternatives and to capture the spectator's imagination while maintaining a radical approach to spectatorship and address. Riddles and enigmas offer the spectator the lures and pleasures of decipherment, while demanding active participation and work in creating the text's meaning. These photographic series all revolve around clues, and clues to meanings, that form a mode of address that ask the spectator to find and follow them into an emotional or intellectual response. The play with enigma and riddle is an invitation to search for an entry point, through association and personal reverie, that may vary for each individual spectator. This is not to say that there is no precise line of argument laid down or programmed into the work by the artist, but the aesthetic strategies allow flexibility, detours of the imagination, oblique approaches to penetrate an intention which is not reducible to personal self-expression but revolves around collective, shared cultural interests and concerns.

An important clue is contained in the exhibition title. 'Magnificent Obsession' is named after Douglas Sirk's 1953 melodrama in which the heroine loses and regains her sight. The reference to vision makes an initial link with photography but there are further implications in the title. The word 'obsession' invokes the psychoanalytic underpinnings to photographic practice, so important to this movement. Victor Burgin has commented on the close relationship between the photograph and the fetish: 'The photograph, like the fetish, is the result of a look which has, instantaneously and forever, isolated, "frozen", a fragment of the spatio-temporal continuum'. Although these photographers have moved into series, out of the 'fragment', there is a sense that, in Karen Knorr's words: 'image-makers must accept compromise with fetishism'. The camera's almost natural function as instrument of the photographer's voyeuristic power, to be handed on to the spectator, provides both a point of resistance and departure for Geoff Miles's *The Trapper's Pleasure of the Text*. And there is also the characteristic obsession with meticulous details of image, print and finish. But whereas an awareness of photography's relation to processes originating in the unconscious and the instincts inflects the work in the direction of theory and self-reflexivity, the accompanying word 'magnificent' clearly rejects the austerity and asceticism in favour of a grandeur of visual scope, from the sheer size of Mark Lewis's prints to Oliver Richon's use of colour and front projection to Mitra Tabrizian's *film noir* lighting.

The title 'Magnificent Obsession' places the show squarely in juxtaposition to the melodrama as a genre, throwing new light on the aesthetics of photography as well as challenging the critical orthodoxy that the photograph is essentially objective. The photograph's stillness is usually related to a moment in time recorded by the shutter, and the rays of light. The aesthetics of melodrama also give great weight to the frozen moment, the moment at which emotion exceeds expression in language and erupts into gesture, heightened by *mise en scène*. Fassbinder, in his remakes of the Sirkian melodramas, would occasionally hold a scene in tableau, in the manner of the nineteenth-century theatrical melodrama, where gesture, music and staging played a crucial role, decisively separating the genre from literary theatre. The photographs in this show formalise their 'stillness' in relation to these melodramatic codes. The moment caught is dramatic rather than natural. Miles and Lewis use the further reference to gesture and stasis by incorporating a statue and shop-window dummy into the image. Tabrizian and Richon use the look itself as the point that holds time in check. In *Country Life* Knorr substitutes objects for gestures that evoke the perpetual masquerade of aristocratic living. Peter Brooks has said of the melodrama:

In the gap of the language code, the grandiose melodramatic gesture is a gesturing towards a tenor that is both grandiose and ineffable. Consequently it is adequate to speak of decoding such a gesture; we must rather decipher it, follow its directions, re-name its indications in our translations.

The image, then, triggers the spectator's stream of consciousness into an internal verbal interpretation. The same process is brought into play here, as by its very nature the photograph is mute. These artists provide trigger images that provoke curiosity and reverie. The words do not supply the image with an explanation but add another level of discourse, equal to the others.

To decipher, the spectator must also 'read' *mise en scène*. There are moments when the scene as a whole, staging, characters, lighting, must share the weight of representing a meaning which is diffused because it is too delicate or too excessive to be conveyed in words. This visual representation of meaning, blatantly constructed and non-naturalistic, is strongly invoked here, with direct reference to Hollywood codes, in Mitra Tabrizian's *Correct Distance*. Roland Barthes, approaching the visual representation of meaning from another vantage-point, uses semiology to analyse the language of advertisements, which combines the codes of melodrama and the form of still photography. In placing themselves under the aegis of melodrama and also overtly acknowledging the influence of Barthes, the artists in this group have combined references to strands of popular culture in a surprising and innovative manner. It is important, at this point, to remember that this stylisation, reliance on *mise en scène*, and use of character is also the result of collective revulsion against a concept of the photograph's natural essence. André Bazin states in 'The Ontology of the Photographic Image':

> Photography affects us like a phenomenon in nature, like a flower or a snow-flake whose vegetable or earthly origins are an inseparable part of their beauty. . . . The aesthetic qualities of photography are to be sought in its power to lay bare the realities. . . . Only the impassive lens, stripping its object of all those ways of seeing it, those piled up preconceptions, that spiritual dust and grime with which my eyes have covered it, is able to present it in all its virginal purity to my attention and consequently to my love.

For this group, the photograph is a screen that blocks. It is not a transparent screen that carries the imprint of 'realities' and maintains the belief that something truly lies beyond. Following Mario Pernilo, Richon describes the theologies of representation to give the argument context:

> For the iconophile, the image is a good appearance which must reveal

and translate a profound reality: God. St Thomas Aquinas claimed that the respect paid to an image should equate the respect paid to the model. Against this, the iconoclast considers the image as a bad semblance which can only mask and distort the profound reality of God. Calvin condemned the use of icons because, among other things, they lessen our fear of the Divine, rendering his presence too familiar. Iconophiles and iconoclasts are obsessed with models, Origins and fascinated by Deep Meanings. They are both asking: what is behind the image, what is the meaning behind it, what is the image's behind. . . . What they will eventually find is precisely what they wish to disavow, that behind the veil of the surface there is nothing, the function of the veil being to hide nothingness: to put something in the place of nothing.

Fiction and fantasy undercut and replace authenticity. These images do not represent the world but reveal the symptoms of material repressed in the unconscious or ideology. The realities represented here are enacted because they are precisely not visible to the naked eye or lens. It is these aesthetic considerations that generate the gesture to narrative that marks all these works. Pronouns imply characters and, in sequence, they then evoke a fictional world or diegetic space. These works do not in fact tell stories as such. They materialise cultural worlds, redolent of myth and social fantasy, that are opened up for the spectator's curiosity and desire.

Mitra Tabrizian, through generic lighting, *mise en scène* and heightened gesture, evokes the codes, characters and conventions of Hollywood *film noir*. This 'world' conjures up the cinematic site of the *femme fatale*, who connotes woman as enigma, threatening active sexuality and androgyny. In the movies, the story must, in the last resort, distance itself and close off identification with this figure who is doomed to an ending of failure and probable death. The still image, however, can generate identification and represent enigma without recourse to narrative closure. The *femme fatale* acts as a trigger image for individual fantasy, free-floating and trans-sex, activated by the narrative codes but not contained by them. The world of *film noir* is also another world, an underworld, closer to repressed, unspoken desires than genres based on a rigid system of masculine/feminine binary opposition. The evocative figure of the *femme fatale* has reappeared in contemporary advertising which has recycled her independence and allure to appeal to modern woman's fantasy of sexual and economic freedom. In deconstructing this 'post-feminist' imagery, Tabrizian draws attention both to the roots of this particular glamour in the psychoanalytic sense – the magical attraction, for both sexes, displayed by the phallic or androgynous woman – and to the present formal traits in advertising photography: irony, intertextuality and nostalgia.

Karen Knorr transforms the social, documentary reality of aristocratic high-life into a personified fantasy that suggests a world as remote and contained as a fiction. Codes, cultural tradition, gesture, objects and settings are clearly enunciated in the milieu itself to define and distinguish a special élite status, and more significantly, a tradition. Tradition appears visibly and materially in a *mise en scène* which maintains the past alive in the present. The *Gentlemen* series emphasises this double presence. The club portraits are characters in their own right, and provide a context for the photographed portraits. *Country Life*, more obliquely than *Correct Distance*, also brings a narrative genre into play. The detective novel was born at the same time as photography and is equally tied to obsession with material evidence as clues. In this series, possessions are evidence of mastery and clues to the nature of the masters. The spectator is drawn into observing behind the closed walls inhabited by a privileged élite, whose privilege is precisely maintained in isolation, the mark of real and actual political and economic ascendancy. At the same time, the photographs suggest a more immediate suspended narrative. Significant events may have just taken place. Once again, the spectator is offered a closed world for fantasy and curiosity.

Olivier Richon's 'world' of the Orient is also closely tied to the origins of photography. The juxtaposition between nineteenth-century academic painting then and the photograph now depicts the relation between the two as a phantasmatically recreated myth. The moment when academic painting appeared stylistically as the precursor of photography is doubled with another point of mythic origin: that of Ancient Egypt and the Holy Land as the cradle of civilisation. Richon traces the nineteenth-century obsession with this 'paradise lost', the pivotal point at which pre-cultural innocence turned into civilisation. He then superimposes another 'paradise lost', the pivotal point at which the last moment of illusionistic innocence was transformed by photography. A painting, existing as something unique in itself, marked the loss of the scene it represented. The photograph, available to endless reproduction, marks the loss of the painting's unique aura. The British Museum and the heroic (or anti-heroic) names invoked conjure up another fantasy world: the means by which a myth of origins is narrated and perpetuated by preserving traces and relics from the past. As Champollian deciphered the hieroglyphics on the Rosetta Stone, and de Lesseps, as engineer, excavated the Suez Canal, Disraeli, the politician, absorbed both into the traditions of Western Civilisation so that its descendants could move freely from the Museum to the Mother Country to travel back in time and tour the exotic Orient. There they could enjoy and witness a way of life that belonged to the Bible in all its innocence and beauty, another 'paradise lost' to the advanced civilisation of the industrial revolution.

Mark Lewis and Geoff Miles are both Canadians and have returned to live and work in their own country. They both use Canadian landscape and mythology as a frame of reference in their work, as a commonly recognised 'pool' of aesthetic and theoretical source material for investigation and reverie. 'Canada' here can be taken to provide the sphere or diegetic 'world' equivalent to those discussed above. (And indeed, Miles's *The Trapper's Pleasure of the Text* juxtaposes the photographer's practice with the mythic origins of Canadian national identity, positing, in a manner similar to Richon, that the photograph has a close link with the birth of myth and the myth of birth.) But here the historical and cultural perspective is more immediate. The question of Canadian national identity is political in the most direct sense of the word, and it brings the political together with cultural and ideological issues immediately and inevitably.

For the Canada delineated by multinationals, international finance, US economic and political imperialism, national identity is a point of resistance, defining the border fortifications against exterior colonial penetration. Here nationalism can perform the political function familiar in third world countries. For the Canada of different cultural groups with a rich range of tradition and diverse but not necessarily contradictory aspirations, this constructed national identity poses a threat to interior heterogeneity. Miles's series works as an indictment of the way in which Canadian national identity has actually been constructed as male, Anglo-Saxon and committed to the principles of 'free trade' and private enterprise. He extends the argument, interweaving image and text, to an indictment of the compromised position of photography itself. Within this exposition of the social, sexual and economic politics of photography, Miles examines the ancient tradition that once again generates a new mythology and conceals the workings of ideology: the nature/culture opposition. It is here that the 'Trapper' becomes the pivotal point of the narrative and line of argument.

The Trapper image condenses the photographer's activity with that of the original white Canadian adventurer. Both are out to capture the objects they stalk; both, then, retain remnants of the original, now lost to life; both act as the precursor of a complex system: the colonising state and its representation of national identity in everyday life. The Trapper as metaphor also illuminates the indexical nature of photography that typically links (fossilised by the mechanical process of light hitting celluloid) the object to the image. At the same time the metaphor ironises and parodies the way that photographic aesthetics have apotheosised the decisive moment (the kill) and consequently the 'Trapper' himself as hero. Miles also comments on the psychoanalytic implications of this power relationship, so that the Trapper's prey is transformed, by the end of the series, into the sexualised image of woman. The quotations from Roland Barthes's *The Pleasure of the Text* place this work in a particular theoretical frame of reference. For Barthes, 'myth' is the false construction of history that conceals contradiction, and photographic images, due to their innate plausibility, are ideally suited means to this end. Miles draws attention to this aspect of photography and ironises its invisibility by his use of the nature/culture opposition, juxtaposing the theme of nature within culture with the photograph's own construction of nature through a cultural practice.

Mark Lewis uses the landscape and mythology as a terrain on which to project the hero's image and examine the particular construction of masculinity that this image evokes. There is a revealing parallel here with Tabrizian's work on the *femme fatale*. Just as she sees the masquerade of femininity as an image representing a desire for a strong female sexuality, Lewis sees the masquerade of masculinity as an image that represses the male body and its lived sexuality. The reference to the Amazons in one of the works in the series *Another Love Story* is an important clue to this perspective on the hero. Greek mythology is the origin of heroic myths and sagas in which the hero of the myth is himself mythologised. At the same time, the Amazons as strong, wild women represent what masculinity must repress under the polarised opposite 'femininity' but men none the less desire. Tabrizian conjures up that fantasy woman, using dramatic lighting to create the fictional scene of desire. Lewis, on the other hand, photographs the day-to-day currency of the masculine image, using a variety of models to bring out an emptiness that both evokes the fragility and vulnerability of the masculine masquerade and the hero's vulnerability to his own masochistic desire for death at the hands of, in the arms of, the phallic woman – a point of fantasy rebirth and regeneration for male sexuality.

Both Tabrizian and Lewis are working with the sexual politics of representation in a new way, moving beyond a deconstruction of the active/passive dichotomy, to envisaging a sexuality that is not posited on binary opposition but can risk the desire of androgyny. For Lewis, the hero depends on a certain landscape in which he can travel and adventure freely. The photographs document the persistent representation of the Canadian landscape within the Canadian cityscape, affirming a national heritage that actually lies beyond the reach of ordinary citizens. But the landscape triggers a series of mythological identifications, in which the wilderness comes to personify the feminine – a fantasy territory which the nation explores as hero, as masculine. The Canadian landscape invites reverie and the creation of stories and images in which the gap between ordinary life and adventure may be momentarily forgotten: the day-dreamer becomes hero. By placing the hero's masculinity in crisis, Lewis challenges the dreamer's sexual politics and the Canadian's national identity.

Both Mark Lewis and Mitra Tabrizian started off as documentary photographers with a strong political commitment to realism. A shift in concern towards sexual politics, under the influence of feminism and psychoanalysis, has produced an equivalent shift in style and approach to the photographic image; the latter is now freed to convey an invisible reality, dream, myth and fantasy. But there is an important difference between the two that illustrates the heterogeneity of the work in this group. Lewis, and Miles too, are photographing in their native city, deeply involved with the development and the problems of their own culture. Canadian culture is not yet a closed book. The historical anomalies that Canada has grown from make contradictions visible. Uniform national identity is challenged by a pride in heterogeneity and difference. It is significant that Lewis and Miles have returned to Canada from London. There is a strong contrast here with the other three members of the group, also expatriate in London but still living and working there. Knorr is a US citizen who has never lived in her own country but was brought up initially in Puerto Rico and then in Britain; Richon is Swiss; Tabrizian is Iranian. All three are in a state of crisis with their own national identity and cultural traditions.

Richon and Tabrizian come from 'iconoclast' cultures. For both Calvinism and Islam, the image is a source of deep suspicion and repression. It is then fitting, perhaps, that Richon and Tabrizian represent the 'iconophile' extreme of the group. Richon's use of lush colour, characters and sexual drama as an undertow running through his images takes him far from the austerity, asceticism and commitment to 'use value' that is the hallmark of Puritanism. For Tabrizian there is another dimension. Coming from a culture in which women's sexuality is denied visibly, she approaches feminist questions about sexuality and images of women from under the pall of Islam. So in this context images that connote female sexuality are exhilarating and exciting, in contrast to those of Western society in which the sexualised image of woman is the currency of oppression. Once again, there is a lushness and excess in the image itself, the material textures turned into light and shade. Arriving in London during the 1970s she could discover discourses – psychoanalysis and sexual politics of feminism – that made it possible to articulate these issues in a way that was precisely impossible in Iran. For British feminists, the question of women's oppression led straight to the question of representation. But for Tabrizian there is an underlying contradiction: in Iran, women's oppression occupies a different order of reality: 'Here I work on the minute nuances of psychoanalytic theory, while in Iran prostitutes are executed'.

For Richon, the journey to London was also an escape from his social and cultural origins. Switzerland lacks a coherent national identity, divided as it is between three languages and many dialects. Bourgeois life is consequently dedicated particularly to the coherent construction of a class identity through a highly regulated, repressed and ritualised experience of everyday life. As francophone Swiss, Richon felt an enormous attraction to French culture that threatened to sweep up and overwhelm him. Moving to Britain at a point when French theory was at maximum influence allowed him to return to French culture by a 'knight's move'.

Karen Knorr came to London from the privileged no man's land of international trade. In the United States, experience of national culture is very much an experience of daily life – the acquisition or rejection of current mythologies. An expatriate American may have little sense of 'American-ness', but rather, an unusual consciousness of hybrid immigrant origins (in Knorr's case: Norwegian, Russian, French and Polish, in addition to which she grew up speaking German and Spanish rather than English) that are normally buried behind the invisible assumption of national identity. The experience of capitalism at first hand in Latin America and Europe also give US economic imperialism an unusual degree of visibility. Knorr chronicles a world in decay. Its stiffness and rigidity seem to try to hold this inevitable process in check. But it is also a man's world. Behind Knorr's portraits there is an underlying pleasure in role reversal, turning upside-down a natural order of things so that the woman outsider acquires, through the act of photography, power over the powerful.

These comments on the cultural origins and national identities of the artists are not intended, by any means, to 'explain' their work. There is, however, an important interface, often overlooked in recent art theory, between personal desire, chances or accidents of individual biography and the forces of history that exert a powerful influence on someone's decision to become an artist and on the kind of work that is then produced. There is also an element of curiosity. Why, as Thornton Wilder wondered in *The Bridge of San Luis Rey*, did these five people end up linked together? An explanation is provided, perhaps, by the aesthetic climate of Britain in the 1970s, in which refusal of cultural and national traditions and a pleasure in heterogeneity were the guiding principles of innovation and experiment. British culture was itself very much in crisis. The 1960s had seen a massive growth of interest in French theory (initiated by the *New Left Review*), both Marxist and psychoanalytic, and also in US popular culture, movies and music. Both these were essentially antithetical to the 'great tradition' of British culture which came to be seen as complacently chauvinistic in both the national and sexual senses of the word. It is to this background, under the catalyst of feminism, that I owe my own starting-point. There is an additional personal element in my pleasure in introducing this exhibition. It allows me, as a Canadian living and working in Britain, to make links between my two cultures and brings me face to face with my own fantasy of origins in the Canadian wilderness.

13

Impending Time: Mary Kelly's *Corpus**

* Written as the catalogue text for 'Corpus' held at the Riverside Studios, London, and at Kettle's Yard Gallery, Cambridge, in 1986.

Corpus, the first section of Mary Kelly's large project *Interim*, stirs up feelings that cannot quite be pinned down into words, images that are on the verge of being discovered and ideas that might be on the tip of a collective tongue. This sensation is due to the exhibition's subject matter and to its visual presentation. Both are allied to the debates and experiments around women's relation to language and images that drew feminist aesthetics into 'alliance' with avant-garde aesthetics during the 1970s. Mary Kelly's work as an artist and theorist, and my own work as a film-maker and theorist, are identified with this movement; and we both gained a cultural identity and framework from its existence. But our common political origins go back further, to the early days of the Women's Movement in 1970. It is for this reason that writing the introduction to this catalogue means more to me than the pleasure of discussing and celebrating the work of an artist I admire, and consider to have great political and poetic significance.

Paradoxically, our shared experience in the Women's Movement gives the exhibition a meaning for me that goes beyond the immediate level of commitment to feminist politics and aesthetics. The fact that now, from the perspective of 1986, we can look back to a common origin and involvement in a movement that has necessarily acquired a history, raises questions about how passing time becomes history and, then, questions about the political aspects of our concepts of time. And these speculations find an echo in the content of the exhibition: the crisis of the female body at a certain age, and the formal aspects of the exhibition: the crisis of an avant-garde at a certain age.

At first glance, *Corpus* might seem to be about endings. Woman's beauty is like a *memento mori*, suggesting by its very perfection the inevitability of human decay. In a similar fashion, an avant-garde must be synonymous with innovation, validated by a gloss of novelty, and is thus stalked from its very inception by a threat of entropy and obsolescence. My own tendency, in the early to mid-1980s, was to acquiesce in the death of the avant-garde. The conjuncture between radical politics and radical aesthetics that had been so important in the 1970s seemed to have outlived its usefulness. It should give way to the demands of time, following the same destiny as a woman who loses her ability to desire as she accepts the world's surface estimation of her desirability.

At second glance, *Corpus* specifically resists such a fatalistic closing-off of an epoch into an ending. The exhibition is not about the woman aged, but about an *Interim*, an intermediate time during which the 'something' that might be pending can be transformed by changed understanding and perspectives so that it can be opened up to un-expected eventualities. Time is put 'on hold', as it were, and stretched out for minute horizontal examination, not as a Canute-like resistance to the fact of passing time, but as a means of analysing the images and mythologies that predestine and constrain our experience of lived time. Similarly, Mary Kelly's aesthetic position seems to have avoided the avant-garde's proclivity to swing like a pendulum between the Scylla of purism on the margins and the Charybdis of recuperation at the centre. She also seems to have transcended the 1970s paranoia about visual pleasure. Although there are numerous references to theory, and particularly the notoriously difficult psychoanalytic theory, there are other means of entry into understanding and enjoying the work. It is itself unashamedly beautiful and satisfying to the spectator. Without losing principle or intellectual vigour, poetry and visual experience are now immediate, giving hope for an avant-garde that can live beyond the founding moment of negative aesthetics. There is something opportune about this exhibition, as though Mary Kelly had, with a sixth sense, suggested that in considering the crisis of the woman's body as a construction in discourse, the avant-garde needs to face its position in historical time and the critical, art-historical constructions that overlay its presence as a movement.

Quite apart from the problems raised by an avant-garde's 'natural' life span, the transition from the 1970s to the 1980s has been particularly difficult. In retrospect the 1970s have a self-contained identity. Feminist art and theory were born and became self-aware, articulate, political and aesthetic projects for the first time. There was an important coincidence between this transformative moment and a widespread reaction against the aesthetics of realism, echoing many aspects of feminist positions on representation and imagery. In the wider social and economic sphere, the 1970s and 1980s are divided, with the effects of Thatcherism aggravating recession, unemployment, poverty, industrial crisis. It might seem more appropriate, faced with the exigencies of this situation, to turn away from the specialised issues of the 1970s avant-garde to the real social and economic problems at hand. But there is something to be learnt, perhaps, from that other difficult and disastrous transition from the 1920s to the 1930s, when the politics of representation and concern with questions such as the representation of the unconscious fell from priority to irrelevance in the face of political and economic turmoil. Now it seems crucial not to abandon the feminist commitment to form and language as areas of struggle (since from a feminist perspective representation must be a political issue) while also reassessing the relation between art and politics at a time of historical change. And the feminist use of psychoanalytic theory has established that there is a reality of the psyche and collective fantasy that cannot be ignored.

The aesthetics of heterogeneity that evolved during the 1970s allows different levels of discourse to be juxtaposed, fragmenting a cohesive view of the world, and of history as a single strand that progresses on a vertical axis through time. The knight's move, detour through the unconscious, lack of synchronisation, these are all strategies now associated with the post-modern that can also expand understanding of the relations between artistic practice and society. But there is a danger, that fascination with the image as such, with the simulacrum's self-sufficiency, might sever representation from its moorings to float on the surface of things in a passionate and relevant but isolated dialogue with itself. While *Corpus* is undoubtedly about problems of representation and images, it is also about material and historical reality. The woman's body is not presented simply as an item of discourse, but lived in time and sexuality and emotion. Mary Kelly uses heterogeneity as a means to arouse poetic curiosity, and there is rigorous uncertainty about the final answers to the issues she is raising.

There is also a problem of transition specific to this artist. The theme of time in *Corpus* can throw light back on to her previous work, *Post-partum Document*, and the difficulties of moving on from there. Complicated and demanding, simultaneously monumental and as intricately woven as a tapestry, *Post-partum Document* epitomises the theoretical asceticism of its time. Kelly documented, from her own experience, the space of motherhood between birth and onset of the child's Oedipus complex. The trajectory through the Oedipus complex ends with a child's quasi-understanding of its place in the historical dimension and its first inklings of the continuous, progressive nature of conscious visualisation of time. In contrast, the mother and child's dyadic relation is based on the experience of space in a continuous present tense.

Infancy is a perpetual present. This could be linked with the small child's extraordinary memory – which is not a memory but a continuous actuality. So too, because of the Oedipus and Castration complexes, only humans have yesterdays. As far as we can tell neither animals nor pre-Oedipal human infants divide time into past, present and future. Time for them would seem to be nearer to spatial relationships: here, there; come, gone; horizontal, punctuated dura-tion rather than a vertical, temporal perspective.[1]

In addition to making the crucial distinction between temporal and spatial relations, this point suggests that our understanding of time is generally dependent on a construction of images in space, such as a linear verticality as opposed to horizontal punctuating points. In recent work on narrative structure, it has been usual to describe the cause/effect temporal linearity of a story as a *horizontal* line of development. In the difficulty of grasping the idea of the passing of time, it is interesting to consider how significant the visualisation of the process can be, and how limited our conceptual vocabulary seems when it is needed. Within the aesthetic dimension, Maya Deren, in a famous symposium held in New York in 1963, tried to use the images of horizontal and vertical to distinguish between her conception of poetry and narrative:

> The distinction of poetry is its construction (what I mean by a poetic structure), and the poetic construct arises from the fact, if you will, that it is a vertical investigation of a situation, in that it probes the ramifications of the moment, and is concerned in a sense, not with what is occurring, but what it feels like and what it means . . . Now it may also include action, but its attack is what I would call a vertical attack, and this may be a little bit clearer if you contrast it to what I would call the horizontal attack of drama which is concerned with the development, let us say within a very small situation from feeling to feeling.

It is not particularly important that Deren and Mitchell use their images of space/time differently. It is important that they both evoke an imaginative space (poetry on the one hand and fantasy on the other) that exists alongside or outside an image of sequential linearity, which only has space to acknowledge its inexorable movement into the future. (There is surely a place between these two quotations for Julia Kristeva's concept of the semiotic, in which she links the rhythms and patterns of poetry to the heterogeneity, the non-linearity, of the pre-Oedipal.) Juliet Mitchell later comments:

> The great theorists of the nineteenth-century tradition – Darwin, Marx and Freud – explain the present by the past. The dominant sociological phenomenologies of the twentieth century in which Klein participated study lateral, horizontal, not vertical relationships.

Feminist theory has mapped out another dimension to the 'lateral', by drawing attention to the area of contact between the unconscious and its manifestation in collective fantasy, that is, roughly speaking, popular culture and its representations. Freud, too, saw layers and levels to the human psyche in which time is intricated and fossilised in the space of the unconscious. But the scars and traces that emerge symptomatically in language, images and symbolisations, as well as cultural phenomena, were to him, primarily, a means of using the past to interpret and cure the individual in the present. Feminism, on the other hand, as a political movement must endeavour to unravel, to question, to reinvent the terrain of popular fantasy in which women's secondary status is sealed by the collective psyche.

Interim focuses more on this area than does *Post-partum Document*, especially in its reference to the discourses of advertising and popular medicine. In *Post-partum Document* an implicit narrative drive runs through the work, a line of development organised around the child's phase-by-phase progress towards the Oedipus complex. The artist/narrator/theorist Mary Kelly knows in advance that, at the end of the story, the mother Mary Kelly will have to accept the narrative's resolution and give place to the future in the Name of the Father. (As Lynne Tillman has pointed out to me: theory itself seems to occupy the place of the third term, an epitomised paternal presence.) On the other hand, almost at odds wth this narrative drive, is a different depiction of time. *Post-partum Document* takes place within minute modifications of real time as Mary Kelly used life's own dimension, the actual growth and development of her own child, to generate the different sections of the work. So the self-doubt, the questions, uncertainties and anxieties of the mother's every day hold the vertical linearity of time in suspense, spreading out into strands that branch alongside and in juxtaposition to each other. These conflicting concepts of time, space and narrative are grounded in the mother's own contradictory desire. Her memorabilia are incorporated in the exhibition like a weight, or force of inertia, that tries to withstand the passage of time, but also like a sign of recognition that these memories will one day make a link with the past, across the Oedipal resolution and the end of the story. But the end of the story brings a strange reversal of roles in its wake. The artist/narrator/theorist has seen the mother's melodrama through to the end, but has in the process written herself out of existence. Monika Gagnon has pointed out that one of the final panels reads:

$$\frac{\text{(What will I do?)}}{\text{S}}$$

poignantly foreseeing the gap left by the end of the work as well as the loss of the dyad.

Whereas *Post-partum Document* had to accept narrative closure, *Corpus* makes an important contribution to opening out the question of endings, both in the word and image panels. One of the fascinating aspects of this work is its refusal to be pinned down or categorised. Although the written texts are not arranged as conventional stories, they contain many references to story-telling, swerving from anecdote and recounting 'personal experiences' to the fantastic world of fairy stories. The reader has to move from the register of real life and its unattainable desires to that of the imagination where those desires can be 'lived out' in fantasy. In film, feminists have, by and large, refused to follow extreme modernist repudiation of narrative. Stories, myths and legends belong to the structure of our collective fantasy and cannot be ignored. But narrative also raises quite complex issues for feminism, particularly to do with the active/passive, male/female distribution of functions within a story and also the question of endings, of resolution of the story-line. Vladimir Propp has theorised the relation between character and narrative function in folk-tales. The hero's trials and tribulations have a specific, stable point of departure and move through a series of discrete points, a transformative process until he emerges triumphant into a new stability at the end, a moment of heroic transcendence and narrative resolution.

Mary Kelly builds on the history of debate and experiment that now exists as a body of work in this area, using it as a spring-board and reference point. Her central protagonist is drawn more from the melodrama, the women's genre, which centres on a heroine victim, and produces a particular kind of identification, based on sympathy rather than idealisation. The overwhelming odds and real, unresolvable problems that the victim protagonist faces can only find a satisfactory 'ending' by unlikely, privileged good fortune, a means of escape. This is the kind of narrative closure that Douglas Sirk cites as the *'deus ex machina'* or 'tying the story together with pink ribbons'. The artifice is clear to the spectator/reader. Mary Kelly draws unerringly on this tradition when she ends her series of written texts in Disneyland and 'they lived happily ever after'. She brings together the Proppian structure and its recognition of the importance of endings with the melodrama's ironic undermining of them. Both the fairy story and the melodrama depend on transition from a state of misfortune to happiness. The misfortune is characteristically grounded in recognisable conditions of oppression, the world's injustice to those without power. The state of happiness is manifestly really only to be achieved through collective imagination. *Corpus* is both documentary and fantasy. Alongside the references to fairy tales, the discourses of advertising, popular medicine and romantic fiction is the presence of the tape-recorder. The stories vividly reflect women's real dilemmas and the handwritten texts are reminiscent of a diary, but they are also images, textures, traces of the body in an emblematic sense.

At another level this combination of the real with fantasy refers to the analytic process itself, with its illusive double register which refers both to an individual's experience of real events and the invisible processes of the unconscious. References to psychoanalysis as a discourse and a history run through the whole work. The images, arranged in five sets of three, are named after the poses that Charcot identified as expressing the symptoms of sexual desperation in his hysterical female patients, and thus sets up two different historical traditions. First there is the history of psychoanalysis and its founding conversion from the study of the physical symptom (Charcot) to the study of word and language (Freud). Then there is also the history of psychoanalysis within feminism, and its origins in an intuitive fascination with hysteria as specific to women and their sexual oppression under patriarchy. (Freud's case-history 'Dora' is a pivotal point for both these histories and Mary Kelly refers to Dora's relation to her mother in the final set of texts.) Both psychoanalysis and feminism desire to be transformative. In terms of narrative, they would belong to the middle section of a story where change, adventures and traumas are acknowledged, within a time structure but one that questions the inevitability of closure and reso-lution, the stable point at the end of a 'correct line' of development.

Corpus is made up of a series of pieces, each arranged in a triptych, each triptych organised around a woman's garment. The first two images in each triptych are closely linked together in a binary opposition. The first represents masquerade, the glossy finish of Hitchcock's blonde heroines, also the pervasive female presence in advertising which condenses women's relation to commodity consumption with the rep-resentation of woman's body as commodity. The second image tears off the mask to reveal a hidden disorder, representing the body's vulnerability, its wounds, as it were, and its actual uncontrollable symptoms. In the garments, their arrangement and their relation to women's speech/writing and still unspeakable desire, *Corpus* achieves a very fine balance between the iconoclastic repression of the body during the 1970s which led to woman becoming unrepresentable and a recognition that such a reaction against the exploitation of women in images could lead to a repression of the discourse of the body and sexuality altogether. But it is wrong to overemphasise the dependent relations of the first two images. The presence of the third breaks into the neat duality that constructs our mythologies into polarisations such as public/private, inside/outside, voyeurism/exhibitionism, mother/whore, masculinity/feminity and so on. The third image, with its explicit sexual reference to a discourse of perversion, opens up the question, beyond the balance between surface attraction, desirability, and inner physical and emotional feeling to the problem of female sexual desire. Mary Kelly implies that desire cannot be expressed without an image that can represent it. This third panel, then, speaks to the future, to the common need to redefine women's relation to their image, beyond the question of male appropriation of their image for masculine pleasure, to discover a feminine desire and understand female sexuality. The question, the gap, therefore, is addressed to 'us'.

Note

1. Juliet Mitchell, 'Introduction' to *The Selected Melanie Klein* (Harmondsworth: Penguin, 1986).

Part V

Boundaries

14

Changes: Thoughts on Myth, Narrative and Historical Experience*

* Presented as a paper at the conference 'New Narrative Cinema and the Future of Film Theory' organised by the Department of Communications, Simon Fraser University, Vancouver, in 1983 and published in *Discourse* in 1985 and *History Workshop Journal* in 1987.

ENDINGS

My work as a film-maker and film-theorist is grounded in the 1970s, particularly in the meeting between feminist politics, psychoanalytic theory and avant-garde aesthetics that had such influence then. After the 1983 election and into 1984, I began to feel that work I considered to be ongoing, in the present tense, had shifted into the past to become identified with the previous decade. My formative experiences, desires and failures that had to do with cultural struggle seemed gradually to be relegated to a closed epoch. The avant-garde was over. The Women's Movement no longer existed as an organisation, in spite of the widespread influence of feminism. And the changed political and economic climate marked the 1980s off from the 1970s. It was tempting to accept a kind of natural entropy: that eras just did come to an end. But then, the sense of *historical* closure recalled the distrust of *narrative* closure that had always been a point of principle for the feminist avant-garde. Once a movement can be reviewed retrospectively its story can be told, but *how* it should be told could still be considered. It seemed as though narrative patterns and expectations of endings had become inextricably intertwined in history as in fiction. We had argued in the 1970s that narrative closure resolves contradiction and stabilises the energy for change generated by a story-line. The same factors seemed to colour my perception of the rhythms and patterns of history. An ending would offer a way out of responsibility, as though one could be indemnified by regret for once-upon-a-time acts of struggle in phrases such as 'the end of an era'. Changes could seem to just happen, the product of a single narrative line under which the minutiae of political struggle were lost. Heterogeneity, discordance and lack of synchronisation between strands of history could be unified.

FROM PARABOLAS TO NARRATIVE

It is out of the question to generalise . . . all the same, the typical
pattern of a sharp rise followed by an abrupt fall can very easily be
imagined as the probable profile in the pre-industrial economy,
reflecting the brief hour of glory of some city's industry or a passing
boom in exports, over almost as quickly as last year's fashions; or
competing industries of which one regularly ousts the other; or the
perpetual migration of industries which seem to rise from the ashes
as they leave their country of origin . . .

All this is quite natural in a period when economies consisted of
sectors somewhat disconnected from each other. What is surprising,
on the other hand, is that in Walter G. Hofman's book *British Industry*
1700–1900 one finds the same kind of parabola.

This must all mean something, but it is not to say we have found
the explanation. The really difficult task is to detect the link between
the particular industry studied and the *economic context surrounding it*
upon which its own career depends.[1]

Parabolic patterns can be applied to the modern avant-garde; a sudden,
marked rise into visibility, followed by a downward trend and declining
energy, 'over almost as quickly as last year's fashions'. The way that
parabolic patterns attract narrativisation became clearly exemplified as
the consolidated triumph of Thatcherism was tested by the miners'
strike. The strike led me to question the political relevance of my own
work; but some of the principles lying behind avant-garde aesthetics
and theory seemed applicable to this very different context.

Daily depiction on television turned the strike, in effect, into a 'social
drama',[2] moulding events around personality, individualised conflict,
and serial-type narrative sequence. Narration is not the same in Downing
Street as it is on the picket line, and the roles of villain and victim vary
in another set of polarisations. Like the Frankenstein monster,[3] the
miners struggled for control of their own story and, like the monster,
were cast simultaneously as evil and tragic. At the climactic moment of
the struggle inevitably comes *victory* or *defeat*, immediately preceding an
ending; and it is in the interests of the one who loses, whether cast as
villain or victim, to keep the story open and alive, to resist resolution
and closure, to insist that change can continue to happen and take on
the surrounding context and its contradictions. But the 'end of an era'
opposition conjures up a phantasmagoric polarisation between past and
future in which the catastrophic present and the complex processes of
class struggle are repressed.

The Conservative government attempted to cash in on the economic
parabola, the decline of the old industries, closing down the pits to

signal (politically, economically, historically) the 'end of an era', closing off the macro-story of the labour movement, the trade-union movement, even the industrial working class itself. The 'end of an era' was orchestrated around a rhetoric of binary oppositions or polarisations, concealing the processes of history behind the seemingly natural and eternal connotations of technical and economic progress. The old world would give way to a new world, the electronic would replace the mechanical, international would replace national investment, finance capital would overtake industry, the free market would shake off the restraints imposed by labour organisation and, above all, solidarity. This ending could become enshrined in popular mythology by clothing complex political and economic factors in the binarism of a modern/archaic opposition.

POLARISATIONS I: BINARY PATTERNS AND DECONSTRUCTION

This problem of dealing with difference without constituting an opposition may just be what feminism is all about (might be what psychoanalysis is all about). Difference produces great anxiety. Polarisation, which is the theatrical representation of difference, tames and binds that anxiety. The classic example is sexual difference, which is represented as polar opposition (active–passive, energy–matter, and all the other polar oppositions that share the trait of taming the anxiety that specific differences provoke).[4]

My own work with film theory has been deeply influenced by binary modes of thought. I began to consider the tension between this influence and my desire for change. The problems were epitomised by the place that an article I had written in 1973 (published 1975) had come to occupy in film theoretical orthodoxy. 'Visual Pleasure and Narrative Cinema'[5] was written in the polemical spirit that belongs properly to the early confrontational moments of a movement. The great problem is then to see how to move to 'something new', from creative confrontation to creativity. There had been an enormous sense of excitement in exploring patriarchal myths, analysing images of sexual difference, trying to extract the meanings that lay behind the images of women in popular culture, revealing the 'taming and binding' that seemed to have organised representations of difference for nearly as long as our culture can remember. For all this, the binary mode of thought provided a necessary, dynamic analytical tool. Feminist film criticism took on images as a political issue, exposing the power relations concealed behind the phoney balance between masculine and feminine, drawing attention to the patterns of otherness that flesh out the raw nerve of sexual difference in popular culture and mythology (public vs. private space, nomadic vs. stable, sun vs. moon, mind vs. body, the law vs. the sexual, creator of culture vs. closeness to nature, etc.).

When I wrote 'Visual Pleasure and Narrative Cinema', I was fascinated by the various overlaps and interconnections between the conditions of spectatorship in the cinema and the representations (in story and image) of sexual difference on the screen. The spectacle offers itself to the active gaze of the spectator, but is split, itself, into active or passive elements along the lines demanded by socially established connotations of masculinity and femininity. My argument was influenced by Freud, and looking back, it seems no accident that I drew above all on 'Three Essays on Sexuality' and 'Instincts and their Vicissitudes'.[6] That is, I privileged the Freudian theory of drives as organised around active/passive pairings (named by Freud, metaphorically, as masculine/feminine) giving rise to the sexual instincts: sadism/masochism, voyeurism/exhibitionism. In analysing sexual difference in popular narrative cinema, it seemed as though Freud's metaphoric naming, designed to express the ambivalence within the individual psyche, was doomed to reflect the actual conditions under which masculinity and femininity are depicted and socially understood. I argued that the spectator's position, active and voyeuristic, is inscribed as 'masculine' and, through various narrative and cinematic devices, the woman's body exists as the erotic, spectacular and exhibitionist 'other', so that the male protagonist on screen can occupy the active role of advancing the story-line. There is a sense in which this argument, important as it is for analysing the existing state of things, hinders the possibility of change and remains caught ultimately within its own dualistic terms. The polarisation only allows an 'either/or'. As the two terms (masculine/feminine, voyeuristic/exhibitionist, active/passive) remain dependent on each other for meaning, their only possible movement is into inversion. They cannot be shifted easily into a new phase or new significance. There can be no space in between or space outside such a pairing.

The article wanted to provoke the question, 'So what next, then?' Change seemed to be just around the corner in the mid-1970s, and an article written in a polemical spirit and above all, to precipitate change, loses significance outside historical context and integrated into the timeless body of film theory. To articulate the relationship between cultural forms and women's oppression, to use psychoanalysis in discussing and exposing this relationship, both of these must precipitate a next phase, that will shift the terms and connotations that cluster around representations of sexual difference. But the either/or binary pattern seemed to leave the argument trapped within its own conceptual frame of reference, unable to advance politically into a new terrain or suggest an alternative theory of spectatorship in the cinema.

POLARISATIONS II: CONCEPTUAL TOPOLOGY

Outside and inside form a dialectic of division, the obvious geometry of which blinds us as soon as we bring it into play in metaphorical domains. . . . Unless one is careful, it is made the basis of all images that govern all thoughts of positive and negative . . . . Thus profound metaphysics is rooted in an implicit geometry that confers spatiality upon thought: if a metaphysician could not draw, what would he think? Open and closed, for him, are thoughts . . . . And so, simple geometrical opposition becomes tinged with aggressivity. Formal opposition is incapable of remaining calm. It is obsessed by myth.[7]

It is as though the very invisibility of abstract ideas attracts a material, metaphoric form. The interest lies in whether the forms of this 'conceptual topology', as I have called it, might affect the formulation of the ideas themselves and their ultimate destiny. Is it possible that the way in which ideas are visualised can, at a certain point, block the process that brings thought into a dialectical relationship with history? I still stand by my 'Visual Pleasure' article, but it belongs to a particular moment in the history of our particular movement. I feel now that its 'conceptual topology' contributed in some way to blocking advance, although it certainly provoked very rigorous responses that went far beyond its original parameters. But when I looked back at the article after some time, the spatial patterning of ideas caught my attention, how they acquire a metaphorical substance and how this 'conceptual topology' then relates to its historical context. This is the question of *how* ideas are formulated in relation to *when*, the moment in the life span of a political or aesthetic movement that is, itself, subject to a parabolic curve. Just as feminist avant-garde aesthetics has argued that representations must make their formal structures visible (foregrounding signifiers, for instance), so perhaps should the transparency of history and abstract ideas be questioned to reveal their material underpinnings. Then, it could be easier to decipher the constraints that lead to entropy and endings, to build from one historical context to another without the endless loss inherent in the 'tradition of the new'.

POLARISATIONS III: NEGATIVE AESTHETICS

More and more radically Godard has developed a counter-cinema whose values are counterposed to those of orthodox cinema. . . . My approach is to take seven of the values of the old cinema, Hollywood-Mosfilm, as Godard would put it, and contrast these with their (revolutionary, materialist) counterparts and contraries. In a sense, the seven deadly sins of the cinema against the seven cardinal virtues.[8]

'Visual Pleasure and Narrative Cinema' was written as a polemic, a challenge to dominant cinematic codes. There was a sense of excitement in this negational stance that compensated for such an attack on a form of cinema, the Hollywood studio system movies, that I loved and that had taught me about cinematic pleasure. A similar kind of excitement compensated for the 'difficultness' of the films I made with Peter Wollen, that could be described as a return to zero, or an aesthetic 'scorched earth policy'. Our first film *Penthesilea* was devised very much within this intellectual and aesthetic spirit. We broke with the codes and conventions of editing that articulate a flowing, homogeneous, coherent fictional time, space and point of view, using long 'chapters' made up of sequence shots. The camera strategy combined with the lack of editing was intended to negate possible and expected shifts in look, in order to foreground the 'work' involved in cinematic spectatorship, and undercut the looker/looked-at dichotomy that fixes visual pleasure. These strategies, however, depend on acknowledging the dominant codes in the very act of negation itself; it could only be through an audience's knowledge of the dominant that the avant-garde could acquire meaning and significance. A negative aesthetic can produce an inversion of the meanings and pleasures it confronts, but it risks remaining locked in a dialogue with its adversary. Counter-aesthetics, too, can harden into a system of dualistic opposition. But it is also important to acknowledge that negative aesthetics can act as a motor force in the early phases of a movement, initiating and expressing the desire for change.

NEGATION AND SEXUAL DIFFERENCE: WOMAN IS 'NOT MAN'

Woman is therefore placed 'beyond' (beyond the phallus). That 'beyond' refers at once to her most total mystification as absolute Other (and hence nothing other but other), and to a *question*, the question of her own *jouissance*, of her greater or lesser access to the residue of the dialectic to which she is so constantly subjected. The problem is that once the notion of 'woman' has been so relentlessly exposed as a fantasy, then any such question becomes an almost impossible one to pose.

Lacan's reference to woman as Other needs, therefore, to be seen as an attempt to hold apart two moments which are in constant danger of collapsing into each other – that which assigns woman to the negative place of its own (phallic) system, and that which asks the question as to whether women might, as a very effect of that assignation, break against and beyond that system itself. For Lacan, that break is always within language, it is the break of the subject *in* language. The concept of *jouissance* (what escapes in sexuality) and the concept of *significance* (what shifts within language) are inseparable.[9]

Jacques Lacan's ideas and theories of psychoanalysis swept through the extreme theoretical wings of both film and feminism in the mid- to late 1970s. His influence broadened and advanced ways of conceptualising sexual difference, emphasising the fictional, constructed nature of masculinity and femininity, the results of social and symbolic, not biological, imperatives. From a political point of view, this position has an immediate attraction for feminists: once anatomy is no longer destiny, women's oppression and exploitation can become contingent rather than necessary. The Lacanian account of the Oedipus complex pivots on the relation of the Father to law, culture and symbolisation, so motherhood under patriarchy gains an important psychoanalytic dimension. But, in the last resort, the theory and the politics remain in tension. The Lacanian representation of sexual difference (defined by the presence or absence of the Phallus) leaves woman in a negative relation, defined as 'not-man', and trapped within a theory that brilliantly describes the power relationships of patriarchy but acknowledges no need for escape.

The Lacanian 'symbolic order', ruled by the Name of the Father, defines the areas of circulation and exchange through which society expresses relations in conceptual, that is, symbolic, terms beyond the natural and the experiential. Language, the universal, most sophisticated means of symbolic articulation, seals this process. Lacan mapped his concept of the symbolic on to Freud's concept of the Oedipal trajectory: access to the symbolic order is achieved by crossing the frontier, out of the imaginary, the dyadic world of mother and child, into recognition of the Father's Name and his Law. That is, out of a body-based, maternal relationship into one created by social exchange, culture and legal taboos (of which the first, of course, is the incest taboo).

The Oedipus complex is described as a trajectory, a journey or a process. But the doubts, the dust churned up by adventures on the way, the contradictions, are stabilised around a resolution in which the temporal process is split into a spatial opposition, structured around mother/father – a mythic condensation with mother as past and father as future – that suppresses a possible dialectical relationship between the two. In this scheme, any attempt at an exploration of the maternal relationship and its fantasies must appear as a retreat into the body, as a rejection of the symbolic and the Word, into a Utopian quest for a natural femininity, outside the 'tragic and beneficial' experience of castration. But motherhood is overdetermined, the site of imbrication

between body and psyche and society. Myth flourishes at the point
where the social and psychoanalytic overlap, redolent of fascination and
anxiety and generating both creative energy (stories, images) and the
'taming and binding' process through which collective contact with the
unconscious is masked. (Feminist film theory and criticism about
Hollywood cinema has recognised and analysed this paradox.) The
question is whether it is possible to open up the sphere of the pre-
Oedipal, to transform its silence through language and politics. 'What
escapes in sexuality' must take us back to the Women's Movement in
the early 1970s, when the woman's body and motherhood were political
issues, in terms of language and representation but also as a site of
oppression and thus organisation for struggle. There is a danger that
this dimension can be quite simply repressed, so that the relation
between *jouissance* and women's oppression becomes again subject to
nature, an eternal Idea, outside human investigation. It is here, perhaps,
that poetic curiosity, the desire of an avant-garde ('what shifts within
language') can contribute as much as convinced theoretical certainty.
The destabilising force of negative aesthetics acts as an initial break and
starting-point. But desire for an alternative language or symbolic system
becomes particularly difficult in relation to the pre-Oedipal, as the child's
psychic reality seems inextricably caught up with myths of motherhood.
The child's pre- or extra-verbal symbolisations, outside articulated
language, can become metonymically associated with the cultural marginalisation of the woman's sphere, epitomised by motherhood and its
silence. The individual psyche's complicated and ambivalent journey
loses a past and begins its history in language around the terms
established by patriarchal value and mythology. The castration complex,
initiated by curiosity and questions, is closed by anxiety and polarisations.

SOCIAL OPPRESSION AND THE MYTH OF 'OTHERNESS'

In passing from history to nature, myth acts economically: it abolishes
the complexity of human acts, it gives them the simplicity of essences,
it does away with all dialectics, with any going back on what is
immediately visible, it organises a world which is without contradiction
because it is without depth, a world which is open and wallowing in
the evident, it establishes a blissful clarity: things appear to mean
something by themselves.[10]

One way to discover the attributes and self-definition of a 'high culture'
is through its opposite, the low culture that represents what the
dominant is not. Feminism has drawn attention to the way that women

have been presented in a negative relation to creativity and artistic practices.[11] But this polarisation around access to culture is not particular to sex oppression. The mind/body opposition is characteristic of other oppositions of dominance (black/white, colonised/conqueror, peasant/noble, bourgeois/worker) and in each case the oppressed are linked to nature (the body) and the dominant to culture (and the mind). Whatever actual cultural deprivation and economic exploitation may give the myth a historical foundation, it is there to organise 'the complexity of human acts'.

It cannot be easy to move from oppression and its mythologies to resistance in history. A detour through a no man's land or threshold area of counter-myth and symbolisation is necessary. There is an analogy here with the unstable, heterogeneous discourse of Julia Kristeva's semiotic that the symbolic cannot contain within its own order. The pre-Oedipal, rather than an alternative or opposite state to the post-Oedipal, is in *transition* to articulated language: its gestures, signs and symbols have meaning but do not achieve the full sense of language. The lost memory of the mother's body is similar to other metaphors of a buried past, or a lost history, that contribute to the rhetoric of oppressed people, in a colonial, class or even sexual context. When Fr Miguel Hidalgo called on the people of Mexico to revolt against Spanish rule in 1810, he used the image of Our Lady of Guadalupe as the emblem of the uprising and signal for revolt. She had appeared to a poor Indian in a vision near the site that had once been sacred to the Aztec mother goddess, Tonantzin.[12] Guadalupe not only cared for the interests of the poorest people in Mexico, but also forged a link with the pre-Columbian, Indian religion that had been so savagely suppressed by the Spanish conquest. The image of the Black Virgin condenses the metonymic chain that links the 'lower orders', the despised race, to the land, the body, nature, motherhood, the lost past, the pre-Oedipal as Golden Age, the metaphors and emblems that belong to desire rather than reason. This is not to argue that any direct analogy between the loss of the mother and the sense of loss experienced in colonisation exists either in historical or psychoanalytic terms, but rather to emphasise the intermeshing of the two in the rhetoric of the oppressed. It is a rhetoric that takes on the low side of the polar opposition, in order to turn the world upside-down, and stake out *the right to imagine* another.

Kristeva's concept of the semiotic was influenced by Mikhail Bakhtin's work on medieval carnival,[13] For Bakhtin, carnival's strength arose out of its place in class culture: a transgressive space, but acknowledged and permitted by the Law, through which the resentments and envy of class hatred could be acted out in ritual and metaphor. Carnival gloried in the peasant side of the cultural connotations associated with the peasant/noble opposition, the lower part of the body, its functions, the earth, the cycles of nature. Carnival inverted the normal experience of daily life, celebrating pleasure and excess in food, drink and sex. Hardship and morals could thus both be mocked. Bakhtin emphasises that the festival also kept alive an ancient tradition that had little place in medieval 'high' culture: the tradition of the comic (the genres of laughter Umberto Eco describes in *The Name of the Rose* as frowned on by the Church as transgressive).

TRANSGRESSION AND THE LAW

If you think that the heterogeneous, polyvalent world is a separate structure in its own right, the law is disruptable. The Carnival can be held on the church steps. But if this is not the case, if the carnival and the church do not exist independently of each other, the pre-Oedipal and the Oedipal are not separate discrete states – if, instead, the Oedipal with the castration complex is what defines the pre-Oedipal, then the only way you can challenge the church is from within an alternative symbolic universe. You cannot choose the imaginary, the semiotic, the carnival as an alternative to the law. It is set up by the law precisely in its own ludic space, its area of imaginary alternative, but not as a symbolic alternative. So that, politically speaking, it is only the symbolic, a new symbolism, a new law, that can challenge the dominant law.[14]

This passage sets out very distinctly the difficulty of envisaging change from within the conceptual framework of a polarised mythology. It is also crucial to this structure that the carnivalesque ludic space, in which the Law allows its own injustice to be represented in a period of controlled disorder, is constructed primarily around rituals of inversion that can very easily be reversed back into 'order' at the end of the day. The problem seems reminiscent of my difficulties with my 'Visual Pleasure' article. Apart from inversion, shifts in position are hard to envisage. And should the system be challenged by 'a new symbolism, a new law', it is equally hard to envisage where that new 'symbolic' would come from. Perhaps the image of carnival can be used to move out of the immediate issues at stake here, the problem of the politics of the Oedipus complex, its relation to women, language and the symbolic order, to extend the argument to the problem of the politics of myth, its relationship to change, language and historical experience. As I argued in relation to the strategies of the avant-garde, a negation or inversion of dominant codes and conventions can fossilise into a dualistic opposition or it can provide a spring-board, a means of testing out the terms of a dialect, an unformed language that can then develop in its own signifying space.

A spatial structure of inversions is crucial to the symbolic language of carnival, but there is also another, alternative, structure that exists in time, in the process of ritualised change from one state to another, from everyday norm to the licence of disorder and back again. This tripartite structure allows cultural forms and rituals to be used to express disruptive desire, both the desire repressed by a symbolic order and the Law as such, and the desire of the oppressed for change. In this sense it is integrative and arguably conservative, providing, in the last resort, a social safety-valve for the forces of disorder. Disruption is followed by restoration of a *status quo*, in a manner that is reminiscent of narrative patterns. But, more important, the gestures, emblems and metaphors of carnivalesque ritual can provide an almost invisible breeding ground for a language of protest and resistance. Inversion has a central place in the history of transgression within the law, but it is neither the only ritual of carnival, nor is it necessarily simply reversible back into the order of everyday.

I want to argue that the image of the disorderly woman did not always function to keep women in their place. On the contrary, it was a multivalent image that could operate, first, to widen the behavioural options for women within and even outside marriage, and second, to sanction riot and political disobedience for both men and women in a society that allowed the lower orders few formal means of protest. Play with the unruly woman is partly a chance for temporary release from traditional and stable hierarchy; but it is also part of the conflict over the basic distribution of power in a society. The woman-on-top might even facilitate innovation in historical theory and political behaviour.[15]

NARRATIVE AND CHANGE I: ORDER AND DISORDER

One attribute of myth, according to Barthes, is to impose stasis on history and conceal contradiction. The structure of myth, according to Lévi-Strauss, is primarily spatial rather than temporal, organised around thematic bundles and binary oppositions. Propp emphasises the linearity of the folk-tale, its transformative processes linked like a chain from function to function. From the point of view of envisaging an imaginative framework that can provide a model for conceptualising and offering patterns and expectations to the chaotic experiences of life and history, it is this aspect of story-telling that I want to emphasise here, with the significance of narrative closure still under question.

Gerald Prince gives the following definition of a minimal narrative as having three phases:

> A minimal story consists of three conjoined events. The first and third are stative, the second is active. Furthermore, the third is the inverse of the first. Finally, the three events are conjoined by three conjunctive features, in such a way that (a) the first event precedes the second in time and the second precedes the third, and (b) the second event causes the third.[16]

This definition establishes on a formal and structural level that the opening and closing states of a narrative are static, not subject to change, while the middle section is active and is marked by its difference from the other two. In an article 'Oedipus: Time and Structure in Narrative Form', Terence Turner fills out this basic structure, to give an ideological inflection to the relationship between stasis and event in narrative. He describes the *active* section of narrative as *disruptive* of a given *status quo*:

> The story is bounded at both ends by an implicit or explicit assertion of synchronic order. The narrative itself, however, represents a complex mediation of this order, necessitated by the eruption of conflict and confusion . . . of the original synchronic order.[17]

In the middle section, the drama and pleasure consist in the eruption of events that disorders the laws of everyday normality. Turner argues that the desire and excess that characterise the middle phase of narrative represent a collectively acknowledged, but unspeakable, conflict with the codes of law that define and contain the normal course of life. This phase celebrates transgressive desire and organises it into a stylised cultural form: narrative. Just as the middle section erupts into action with disorder, so the end must integrate disorder back into stability. The rule of law closes in the space for transgression and disruption.

Turner also argues that this kind of narrative can tell the story of a transitional phase in which social and/or economic change needs to be given the ideological force of order and be integrated into a new expectation of everyday normality. Both he and Propp cite the Oedipus story in this context. There is here, perhaps, some visible link between the parabolic curves of history and economic forces, cited by Braudel, and the structure of stories that must represent, symbolically, moments of social transformation, absorbing the abnormal back into a sense of an order that is altered but still recognisably subject to the law.

NARRATIVE AND CHANGE II: LIMINALITY

Arnold van Gennep analyses the structure of rites of passage also in terms of a tripartite system. These rituals guide an individual through the transitional moments of life, marking the disruption and difficulty of change and the reintegration back into the ordered life of a community. There are rites of separation that initiate the process and put the person concerned into a state of privilege or crisis outside the norms of everyday existence. These are followed by transitional rites, during which the person is in a liminal relation to the world, in a no man's land, that may well be marked literally by a particular relationship to place ('transitional periods that require a certain autonomy'). These rites are followed by those of reincorporation.[18]

The literal representation of transition as movement through a threshold, from one space to another, has a very different mythic connotation from that of a binary opposition. Here it is the possibility of change that is celebrated, and the alteration of status implies movement on a linear model, rather than opposition on a polar model. There is a strong suggestion of *liminality* in the middle phase of a story, very often actually marked by literal movement in space, a journey, an adventure, but certainly by extraordinary events in which the rules and expectations of ordinary existence are left in suspense. Propp's analysis of narrative establishes that a story begins with the disruption of a stable state by 'an act of villainy', that separates out the next phase of the story into crisis and privilege, the hero's exceptional status and his tribulations. Peter Wollen has applied Propp's analysis of narrative structure to Hitchcock's movies; but he has also commented:

> It is appropriate to begin to write about Hitchcock by quoting Buchan: 'Now I saw how thin is the protection of civilisation. An accident and a bogus ambulance – a false charge and a bogus arrest – there were a dozen ways of spiriting one out of this gay and bustling world'.[19]

Hitchcock's heroes are plunged into a world turned upside-down, in which identity and even name become uncertain, in which the logical expectations of everyday life are reversed in a nightmare universe that also celebrates the pleasure and excitement of liminality. But journeys end with safe returns . . . .

Although a folk-tale may well deal with social transition, as the hero leaves home to seek his fortune, the symmetry between beginning and end is important. The home that is left at the opening of a story is matched by another home established at the end (as Terence Turner says: 'bounded at both ends by synchronic order') while the shift from poverty to riches evokes the relation of inversion between the first and third states in Prince's minimal story and a return, with stability, to binarism. Significantly, these stories also represent another transition, from immature sexuality to marriage and manhood. Marriage represents the ritual function of reincorporation back into the ordered state of society but also the individual's new status within society.

NARRATIVE AND CHANGE III: FESTIVALS OF THE OPPRESSED

Edmund Leach has used van Gennep's tripartite phasing of rites of passage in his analysis of carnival. Similarly, a carnival would start with events marking it off from normal life and, particularly, time. It would then proceed to the privileged, liminal phase, with its particular rituals of inversion, and conclude with the process of reincorporation into the normal cycles of life and time. In principle this pattern would be inescapably subject to the Law, as Juliet Mitchell argues for the 'ludic space'. The example of the failed uprising that concluded with the carnival at Romans in 1580, although it confirms an aspect of her argument, also offers another, more complex dimension to the metaphor.

In his brilliant and tragic book *Carnival at Romans*[20] Emmanuel Le Roy Ladurie emphasises the crucial place occupied by the rites of inversion in restoring order in the face of popular revolt. Because these rites depended on a concept of order, temporarily inverted, their reversal in the final phases of the carnival provided the means to restore the dominance of the ruling class. Just as the people had pushed the licence of carnival beyond its normal limits in the middle phase, to express popular unrest and discontent, so the world was turned right side up again with a savage suppression of the revolt. Although the ritual and the narrative structure favoured closure (and the interests of the ruling class) the experience at Romans had another, historical dimension. As intense class conflict and specific struggles had built up during some time preceding carnival, the festival was no longer either a politically neutral expression of individual desire finding collective expression within the law's ludic space, nor was it any longer simply the safety-valve through which class resentment could be graphically acted out and neutralised. The rites of carnival provided a people on the threshold of political consciousness with a liminal moment outside the time and space of the dominant order. Furthermore, carnival provided the people with a primitive but ready-made language of gesture, metaphor, emblem and symbolism at a moment when control over the abstraction of political concepts lagged behind the first inklings of political consciousness. Ladurie says:

Carnival was not merely a satiric and purely temporal reversal of the dual social order, finally intended to justify the *status quo* in an objectively conservative manner. It would be more accurate to say it was a satirical, lyrical, epic-learning experience for highly diversified groups. It was a way to action, perhaps; modifying the society as a whole in the direction of social justice and political progress.

Perhaps it is significant that the next important phase in the peasants' struggle for rights moved into the courts and progress was achieved within the language of lawyer's rationality and control over the processes of the law.

It is clearly impossible to generalise. But the relation between desire, desire for political change and access to language to articulate these desires must be of interest to feminists influenced by psychoanalytic theory. It is also important to see how collective cultural events can act as a spearhead for more organised politics. But to transcend to something beyond a safety-valve for discontent, the political and historical context is crucial. In contemporary society, similar patterns may be perceived in the 'rituals of resistance' associated with sub-cultures. A group can mark out its claim to liminal existence through clothes, music, emblematic loyalty, and so on. In a study of the zoot-suit riots in Los Angeles in the 1940s, Stuart Cosgrove distinguishes between the different levels of catharsis or epic-learning experience involved in a contemporary version of carnivalesque confrontation:

> The zoot-suit was simultaneously the garb of the victim and the attacker, the persecuted, the 'sinister' clown and the grotesque dandy. But the central opposition was between the style of the delinquent and the disinherited. To wear a zoot-suit was to risk the repressive intolerance of war-time society and to invite the attention of the police, the parent generation and the uniformed members of the armed forces. For many pachuchos the zoot-suit riots were simply high times in Los Angeles when they were momentarily in control of the streets; for others it was a realisation that they were outcasts in a society that was not of their making. . . . The zoot-suit riots were not political riots in the strictest sense, but for many participants they were an entry into the language of politics, an inarticulate rejection of the straight world and its organisation.[21]

COLLECTIVE FANTASY: THE POLITICS OF THE UNCONSCIOUS

In the framework of class and political structure this specific character (moments of crisis, of breaking points in the cycle of nature or in the life of society and man) could be realised without distortion only in Carnival and similar market place festivals. They were the second life of the people, who for a time entered the utopian realm of community, freedom and abundance. . . . As opposed to the official feast, one might say that carnival celebrated a temporary liberation from the prevailing myth and from the established order; it marked the suspension of all hierarchical rank, privileges and norms of prohibitions. Carnival was the true feast of time, the feast of becoming, change and renewal. It was hostile to all that was immortalised and completed.[22]

Rather than as a model, an alternative to the Law, I am using carnival as an image to give shape and form to the tension that exists between a conceptual topology that draws its metaphors from space and one that draws its metaphors from time. In the imagery of carnival, the binary, the rituals of inversion, are tied to the spatial, the polarised; and their reversal closes the liminal phase of the festival. It is this liminal phase that suggests imagery of change, transformation and liberation, the burrowing of the old mole rather than the eagle soaring in the sky.

The Oedipus complex shares some of the features of the tripartite narrative of ritual structure. If the dyadic relationship between mother and child corresponds to the initial stative phase, then disrupted by the Oedipal moment, its journey populated by desires, anxieties and contradictions, then the third phase would correspond to resolution and closure around the Law of the Father and his symbolic order. In Freud's version, the Oedipal experience is never perfected, but always remains partial, likely to be deviant and probably never to be completed, especially in the case of women. Rather than dismiss the pre-Oedipal on a binary model, this area between silence and speech, the terrain in which desire almost finds expression, should be taken seriously by feminist psychoanalytic theory, not on the grounds that it presents an alternative symbolic order, but that its imagery, and metaphor, and gesture could provide the basis for change *only* through the fact of feminism's existence as a political context, the expression of revolt against a patriarchal symbolic. That is, the psychoanalytic has to try to take on the political and the historical problems raised by change.

Freud recognised that the actual process of disrupting the dyad, transmission of the incest taboo, submission to the father's prohibition, could not be equivalent for male and female if organised around the castration complex. The non-equivalence also implies an imbalance of power, as Althusser acknowledges in his essay 'Freud and Lacan': 'the Oedipal phase is centred and arranged wholly around the signifier *phallus*: the emblem of the Father, the emblem of right, of the Law, the fantasy image of all Right.' According to Lacan, and also to Freud's basic model, the problem for the small boy is a simple one of transition, in which he accepts that he will grow up to inherit the 'Right' without any need to switch the gender of his object of desire. The little girl, on the other hand, has to move into masquerade and inversion. In the boy's case, integration and closure are comparatively easily achieved; in the girl's case, as Freud reiterates, they are endlessly postponed. Although each individual lives out the Oedipal trajectory personally and uniquely, patterns of experience, affective structures, language and signs are shared. The problems, contradictions and irreconcilable demands made by the acquisition of sexual identity, family structures and historical conditions surface in collectively held desires, obsessions and anxieties. This is the shared, social dimension of the unconscious, of the kind that Freud referred to in *Jokes and the Unconscious*, which erupts symptomatically in popular culture, whether folk-tales, carnival or the movies. These are temporal forms, narrative forms. If narrative, with the help of avant-garde principles, can be conceived around ending that is not closure, and the state of liminality as politically significant, it can question the symbolic, and enable myth and symbols to be constantly revalued. A feminist perspective should insist on the possibility of change without closure, drawing by analogy on the female Oedipus complex, the crucible out of which sexual identity does not emerge as pure gold.

DEPARTURES

'Pleasure becomes a serious matter in the context of innovative change' (Victor Turner).

Notes

With thanks to Ronan Bennett and Kaja Silverman.

A previous version of this article appeared in *Discourse*, no. 7, Berkeley, Spring 1985.

1. Fernand Braudel, *Civilisation and Capitalism. Volume 2, The Wheels of Commerce* (London: Fontana, 1985). I chose this particular passage because it uses the word *parabola*, rather than the word *cycle*. For Braudel's discussion of secula and Kondratieff cycles see *Civilisation and Capitalism. Volume 3, The Perspective on the World* (London: Fontana, 1984).
2. Victor Turner, *Dramas, Fields, and Metaphors, Symbolic Action in Human Society* (Ithaca: Cornell University Press, 1974).
3. The analogy between the Frankenstein monster and the industrial working class is suggested by Franco Moretti's essay in *Signs Taken for Wonders* (London: Verso, 1983).

4. Jane Gallop, *Feminism and Psychoanalysis* (London: Macmillan, 1982).
5. Laura Mulvey, 'Visual Pleasure and Narrative Cinema', *Screen*, xvi, 3 (1975).
6. Sigmund Freud, 'Instincts and Their Vicissitudes', *The Standard Edition* (London: The Hogarth Press, 1962), vol. 14; 'Three Essays on Sexuality', *The Standard Edition*, vol. 7.
7. Gaston Bachelard, *The Poetics of Space* (New York: The Orion Press, 1964).
8. Peter Wollen, *Godard and Counter Cinema: Vent d'Est, Readings and Writings*, (London: Verso, 1983).
9. Jacqueline Rose, *Feminine Sexuality, Jacques Lacan and the Ecole Freudienne*, co-edited with Juliet Mitchell (London: Macmillan, 1982).
10. Roland Barthes, *Mythologies* (London: Cape, 1972).
11. 'Women are presented negatively, as lacking in creativity, with nothing significant to contribute, and as having no influence on the course of art. Paradoxically, to negate them women have to be acknowledged; they are mentioned in order to be categorised, set apart and marginalised.' This is 'one of the major elements in of the construction of the hegemony of men in cultural practices, in art'. Rozsika Parker and Griselda Pollock, *Old Mistresses* (London: Routledge & Kegan Paul, 1981).
12. The relationship between the old and new religion is described by Anita Brenner in *Idols Behind Altars* (New York: Biblio and Tannen, 1976): 'Every time the friars razed a teocali they had a church built there with. They buried idols and planted crosses. And again the Indians though this time surely not so innocent, did precisely the same thing. Says Geronimo, rather upset by this discovery: "The friars had many crosses made for them and placed in all the gates and entrances to villages and upon some high hills . . . [The Indians] would put their idols under or behind the cross, making believe they adored the cross, but adoring really the figure of the demon they had hidden there." '
13. Mikhail Bakhtin, *Rabelais and his World* (Cambridge, Mass.: MIT, 1968).
14. Juliet Mitchell, 'Psychoanalysis, Narrative and Femininity', in *Woman, the Longest Revolution* (London: Virago, 1984).
15. Natalie Zemon Davis, *Society and Culture in Early Modern France* (Stanford University Press, 1975).
16. Gerald Prince, *A Grammar of Stories* (The Hague: Mouton, 1973).
17. Terence Turner, 'Time and Structure in Narrative Form', *Forms of Symbolic Action*, Proceedings of the 1969 annual spring meeting of the American Ethnological Society.
18. Arnold van Gennep, *The Rites of Passage* (London: Routledge & Kegan Paul, 1960). Van Gennep's concept of liminality is very usefully developed by Victor Turner, *Dramas, Fields and Metaphors*.
19. Peter Wollen: 'Hitchock's Vision', *Cinema*, 1, 3 (1969).
20. Emmanuel Le Roy Ladurie, *Carnival at Romans* (Harmondsworth: Penguin, 1981).
21. Stuart Cosgrove: 'The Zoot Suit: Style Warfare', *History Workshop Journal*, 18 (1984).
22. Mikhail Bakhtin, *Rabelais and his World* (Cambridge, Mass.: MIT, 1968).

15

The Oedipus Myth: Beyond the Riddles of the Sphinx*

* Based on research for a series of seminars held at the Department of Cinema Studies, New York University, in 1986 and presented as a lecture in the series 'Psychoanalysis and Popular Culture' held at the ICA in 1987.

Riddles of the Sphinx was made in 1976–7. The film used the Sphinx as an emblem through which to hang a question mark over the Oedipus complex, to investigate the extent to which it represents a riddle for women committed to Freudian theory but still determined to think about psychoanlysis radically or, as I have said before, with poetic licence. *Riddles of the Sphinx* and *Penthesilea,* our previous film, used ancient Greece to invoke a mythic point of origin for Western civilisation, that had been reiterated by high culture throughout our history. Both the history of the Oedipus Complex and the history of antiquity suggest a movement from an earlier 'maternal' stage to a later 'paternal' or 'patriarchal' order. For me, as someone whose interest in psychoanalytic theory was a direct off-shoot of fascination with the origins of women's oppression, this dual temporality was exciting. Perhaps there was an original moment in the chronology of our civilisation that was repeated in the chronology of each individual consciousness. Leaving aside the temptation to make speculative connections and an analogy between the earlier culture of mother goddesses and the pre-Oedipal, the idea of a founding moment of civilisation, repeated in consciousness, suggested that it might be possible to modify or change the terms on which civilisation is founded within the psyche and thus challenge the origins of patriarchal power through psychoanalytic politics and theory.

These Utopian dreams now belong to more than ten years ago. In the meantime, the relation between feminism and psychoanalysis has become infinitely more complex and less instrumental. But some primitive attraction to the fantasy of origins, a Gordian knot that would suddenly unravel, persisted for me. My interest then concentrated on breaking down the binarism of the before/after opposition, by considering the Oedipus story as a passage through time, a journey that could metaphorically open out or stretch the Oedipal trajectory through significant details and through its formal, narrational, properties.

In 1986–7, I returned to the Oedipus story.[1] My intention was to consider the story in the light of different disciplines and from different angles. Whereas in *Riddles of the Sphinx,* our intention had been to shift

177

narrative perspective to the mother in the Oedipal triangle, this time my intention was rather to discover things that the story itself suggested through its mode of telling and then through the theoretical work on narrative that could be brought to bear on its narrative structures; and to consider whether the signifiers of narration were linked to its signified, whether, that is, certain kinds of material demanded certain modes of telling. The first part of the paper (in two sections) is about the core Oedipus story. Then there is a digression about the metaphors of space and time that negotiate shifts between the poetics of psychoanalysis and narrativity. The final part (also in two sections) stretches out the core of the Oedipus story to the moment of his death and the pre-history before his birth.

OEDIPUS: THE CORE STORY

Freud re-tells the Oedipus myth in the following manner:

> Oedipus, son of Laius, king of Thebes, and of Jocasta, was exposed as an infant because an oracle had warned Laius that the still unborn infant would be his father's murderer. The child was rescued and grew up as a prince in an alien court, until, in doubt as to his origin, he too questioned the oracle and was warned to avoid his home since he was destined to murder his father and take his mother in marriage. On the road leading away from what he believed to be his home, he met King Laius and slew him in a sudden quarrel. He came next to Thebes and solved the riddle set him by the Sphinx who barred his way. Out of gratitude the Thebans made him their king and gave him Jocasta's hand in marriage. He reigned long in peace and honour and she, who unknown to him, was his mother, bore him two sons and two daughters. Then, at last a plague broke out and the Thebans made inquiry once more of the oracle. It is at this point that the Sophocles tragedy opens. The messenger brings back the reply that the plague will cease when the murderer of Laius has been driven from the land.
>
> But he, where is he? Where shall now be read
> The fading record of this ancient guilt?
>
> The action of this play consists of nothing other than the process of revealing, with cunning delays and ever mounting excitement – a process that can be likened to the work of psychoanalysis – that Oedipus himself is the murderer of Laius, but further that he is the son of the murdered man and of Jocasta. Appalled by the abomination

which he himself has unwittingly perpetrated, Oedipus blinds himself and forsakes his home. The oracle has been fulfilled.[2]

From a structural point of view, the story, as it is told above, is separated into two parts according to two codes of narration. This formal division implies that the story is a hybrid; or rather, its hybrid form indicates that it has come into being across transitional material that cannot be contained within a unified narrational system. It functions as a pivot. Roland Barthes, in *S/Z*, analyses the codes of narrative and distinguishes two as irreversible in time, propelling the story forward point by point, from its beginning to its end. The proairetic is the code of action. It governs events in sequence, on a cause and effect basis. It is, in Barthes's words, the voice of empirics. The hermeneutic is the code of enquiry. It sets up an enigma, formulates the questions that ensue and holds an answer in suspense until the moment of its solution. It is, again in Barthes's words, the voice of truth. Whereas the proairetic code functions on a single, linear temporal level, the hermeneutic folds back on the past and contains two levels of temporality. Although the two codes are very commonly interwoven, the chronological split in the Oedipus story according to these two codes is striking.

1 The Proairetic Code

The structure of the first part of the story conforms in broad outline to Vladimir Propp's analysis of a type of folk narrative in *The Morphology of the Folktale*. The dramatis personae perform a series of fixed and given actions as the hero travels along the course of a journey from home, arriving unknown at a new and future home where he performs a difficult task (for instance, he rescues the people or the princess from a monster or a dragon). He is then rewarded with the kingdom and the hand of the princess in marriage. His actions, and those of the helpers or enemies that he meets on the way, take the story forward within a chronologically linear time. The linearity of the narrative is reflected in the linearity of the journey as it moves through time and space; the journey space of the road the hero takes also represents a passage through time, from departure to arrival. Thus the formal aspect of the story is materialised in its serial events and its imagery or *mise en scène*. The journey also represents a social space. The hero is transformed from one status to another, as though the story reflected, in narrative form, a rite of passage. The hero, Oedipus, leaves the security of his home in Corinth as an exceptional but untried young man, to encounter hurdles and cross boundaries as an adventurer in a liminal space and without recognised name or identity. His journey takes him out of youth into maturity, out of anonymity into recognition, from unmarried to married status, from lone individual in doubt as to his name and parentage into the possession of property and power. The spatial metaphor of the journey as transition is joined by the spatial metaphor of the social pyramid: the hero ascends the apex and becomes king.

Freud recounts a similar series of events in his essay 'On Creative Writing and Day-dreaming', in which he condenses the 'erotic and ambitious' aspirations of the ego (as hero of the psyche) with the presence of the invulnerable hero of popular fiction. The day-dream also tells of a transition in space and time and social status, but in Freud's example the hero's upward mobility takes place in an urban, bourgeois milieu.

> He is given a job, finds favour with his new employer, makes himself indispensable in the business, is taken into the employer's family, marries the charming young daughter of the house, and then becomes a director of the business, first as his employer's partner and then as his successor.

In this fantasy, the dreamer has regained what he possessed in his happy childhood, the protecting house, the loving parents, the first objects of his affectionate feelings. 'It seems to me, that through this revealing characteristic of invulnerability, we can immediately recognise His Majesty the Ego, the hero alike of every day-dream and every story.'[3]

(Perhaps Dick Whittington mediates between the peasant hero of the Proppian folk-tale and Freud's bourgeois scenario.) However, the Oedipus story has a different twist. Oedipus arrives at Thebes only apparently as an unknown outsider. With a deeper symmetry, he has arrived at his own true home, and, instead of inheriting through marriage and from his father-in-law, he inherits the kingdom to which he is patrilineally entitled. At the simplest level, the folk tale pattern celebrates a transition to maturity similar to that of a rite of passage; on another level it reflects day-dreams of social aspiration in a society in which wide separation of wealth and power divide the propertied from the dispossessed. Both levels together condense family relations and property relations, as though the word 'possession' were a key that could turn either way between the psychoanalytic and the social.

Concentrating on the 'ambitious and erotic' aspects of the day-dreaming ego's consciousness, Freud overlooks the Oedipal, unconscious aspects of his paradigm day-dream. The hero recognises by leaving home that to 'become the father' he must avoid his own Oedipal set-up, which invites rivalry and desire, but particularly rivalry with the father. If the journey then represents escape into exogamous kinship relations, *kingship* and possession bring back a memory of Oedipal rivalry. With its Oedipal twist, the repressed returns. The day-dreaming ego's consciousness is faced with the ultimate horror, and hope beyond expression, that the poor parents you leave will return in the form of the king or king substitute and his daughter who are waiting for you to rescue them at the end of your journey. There are also echoes here of the social complexity of family romance. In a footnote about his own Revolutionary Dream[4] Freud notes: 'A prince is known as the father of his country; the father is the oldest, first, and for children the only authority. And, indeed, the whole rebellious content of the dream, with its *lèse-majesté* and its derision of higher authorities went back to rebellion against my father.' This quotation carries the question of property and social status, the desire to *become* the father by avoiding conflict with him, to possibly radical undertones to Oedipal rivalry. The son is the dispossessed and thus liable to identify with rebellion against the possessing powers that be,[5] an aspect, perhaps, of the short term radicalism of youth.

For Propp, the Oedipus story is a symptom of a social and historical transition that determines the transitional or hybrid content of the narrative material itself. The early folk-tale structure is a reflection of an ancient marriage pattern.

> The usual order of events in the fairy tale reflects matrilocal marriage, the entry of the bridegroom into the bride's family . . . Now let us see what happens to Oedipus. Just like the fairy tale hero, he is sent away from home. But after his upbringing he does not go to the country of his future wife. Rather, unbeknownst to himself, he returns to the home of his father. As a hero of the new patriarchal order he heads for his father's family, the family where he belongs, rather than his wife's family. This shift in Oedipus' destination represents a turning-point in the history of the tale. At this point Oedipus diverges from the fairy tale and forms a new offshoot, a new tale within the framework of the same compositional scheme.[6]

Propp then points out that Oedipus goes through the same three adventures as the fairy tale hero. He kills the old king, he solves the riddle of the Sphinx and rids the city of distress, he receives the hand of the queen.

> According to patriarchal ideas, the heir could not ascend the throne during the life time of the old king . . . Under the matriarchal system, on the contrary, the heir appears as the daughter's husband first, and then the old king is removed, or as the fairy tale has it, shares the kingdom with his son-in-law. Hence in the fairy tale the proclamation

comes from the old king himself, while in the Oedipus it comes from the citizens of Thebes who have lost their king.

In Propp's terms, the change of sequence whereby the old king is killed, by his own son, before the difficult task is performed, is one mark of the transitional, historical nature of the Oedipus story. Writing in the Soviet Union, as a scholar of folk tale and anthropology, Propp was looking for a historical materialist explanation of the Oedipus story. But he, too, comes up with a story of *origins*, the origin of patriarchal inheritance. And it is revealing that he is *only* interested in the part of the story that is under the aegis of the proairetic code.

In Freudian terms, Propp's explanation takes the story inexorably back, in its transitional mode, to father–son rivalry and the incest taboo which lie at the core of the Oedipus complex. The question of property and inheritance is of primary importance to Propp, confirming the story's grounding in the social. But the father's attempt at infanticide has disordered the true line of inheritance, and opened up the way for incest to return by an oblique route, the old folk tale pattern. Heroism and apotheosis through achievements coalesce with blood legitimacy, so that the hero is bound to commit incest in order to reclaim his patrimony in this hybrid or pivotal story. Although Propp's emphasis on the matrilocal is clearly at several moves from Bachofen's *Mutterrecht* or Engel's *Origins of Private Property and the Family*, there is a residual, suggestive link with forms of social organisation in which patriarchy was not supremely in command. The misty, forgotten epochs of time and mythology in which things might have been other for women return as a ghostly presence. Propp's interpretation acknowledges the coming of an era in which the exchange of women as signifier of relations between men takes on a new inflection in relation to property and inheritance. Teresa de Lauretis,[7] in her powerful narrative and topological analysis of the Oedipus story (to which these observations are indebted) emphasises the essential masculinity of its folk-tale structure. The hero spans the space of the story and commands the action (the proairetic code). The feminine principle is static, represented either by the Sphinx or the Princess, Jocasta. She is a resistance, a boundary to be crossed, a space of enclosure. It is clear that the hero represents an active force of masculinity, or perhaps, the *rite de passage* of *mensch* and thus *man* as the universal point of reference under patriarchy, and the subject position is definitely that of the male child. However both the parent functions are *other*, that of the father as much as that of the mother. And in the Oedipus story, it is the father's response to the oracle's prophecy, 'your son shall kill you' that disorders the family structure and generates his son's future trajectory as hero and its tragic consequences. The social-historical problem of inheritance, the narrative structure of myth, and the trajectory of the individual psyche meet at a crossroads.

2   The Hermeneutic Code

At a particular point in his narration of the Oedipus story, Freud says: 'Here Sophocles' tragedy begins'. The aesthetics of Greek drama, its commitment to the unities of time, place and action as well as the constraints of performance, would all influence the placing of the first part of the myth within a containing formal structure. Sophocles folds the horizontal, chronologically linear materialisation of that narrative, realised in the spatial pattern of a journey (also a journey through time and a rite of passage through the social space and time of liminality) within another narrative code, the hermeneutic. However, this is not a simple story-teller's decision, or a purely formal device. The unravelling of the enigma is essential to the Oedipus story in its own right; and the formal narrational pattern that the hermeneutic code generates is a key to the ultimate meaning of the play. Not only does the old mystery of Oedipus's true parentage remain unsolved between the two parts of the story but a murder has been committed and the criminal must be revealed. The play proceeds to follow through a sequence of enigmas, in which the actions of the first part of the story are transformed into clues or bits of evidence out of which the truth will ultimately be disclosed. In this process Oedipus takes on the role of investigator. But it only gradually emerges that he is telling his own story, revealing, as detective hero, the hidden meaning behind his actions as the hero of the folk-tale.

The play opens with a generative enigma that activates all the subsequent inquiries. Thebes is inflicted with a plague and Oedipus undertakes to find out why. He is confident of his abilities; he has become king as a result of his intelligence, his riddle-solving powers. This fact, too, pre-figured his future and separates him from heroes who depend on physical strength to conquer a monster.

> But I came by. Oedipus the ignorant, I stopped the Sphinx!
> with no help from the birds, the flight of my own intelligence
> hit the mark.[8]

The oracle offers a clue to the mystery and sets up another. The murderer of Laius must be found.

> 'No! I'll start again – I'll bring it all to light myself!'[9]

At the beginning of the play Teiresias, the seer, gives the true answer to the murder mystery. Oedipus responds bitterly, in an excess of anger that speaks simultaneously of the necessity for delay within the hermeneutic code, the processes of resistance and negation in psychoanalysis, and the quick temper Oedipus inherited from his father. In order to re-assure him, Jocasta recounts the old prophecy, that Laius would be killed by his son, and describes the circumstances of his death 'where the three roads meet'. Oedipus recognises the description, and knows he is himself the murderer. From that moment on, he is not so much a regal, or legal, investigator as a man desperately seeking the truth of his own family origins and the meaning of his actions. But as the evidence accumulates inexorably, Oedipus still resists, bearing out Teiresias's warning:

> You with your precious eyes,
> you're blind to the corruption of your life,
> to the house you life in, those who love with –
> who *are* your parents? Do you know? All unknowing
> you are the scourge of your own flesh and blood. . . .[10]

After Jocasta's suicide he sees the meaning of his life for the first time, in all its unwitting horror and perversity. He blinds himself and leaves the city. The second part of the story thus strips away the folk-tale's happy ending; the hero's material apotheosis, marriage, power and property are revealed to be worthless illusions.

The second part of the story is thus necessarily posited on the code of mystery and investigation. The *locus classicus* of the hermeneutic code, the detective story, only developed formally as a genre comparatively recently. Oedipus, ahead of the genre, acts as a detective faced with a murder to solve, and the hybrid, two-part story acquires another formal duality, that of time.

According to Tzvestan Todorov, the detective story, and particularly its 'whodunit' mode, is always based on a double time structure. There are two stories to be told. The first precedes the opening of the narrative and is the story of the crime. This story is gradually unfolded in the course of the second which is the story of the investigation. The first story cannot be completed until the identity of the criminal is revealed by the process of detection. As Michel Butor, cited both by Todorov and by Peter Wollen, has his detective story writer say in *Passing Time*:

> The narrative superimposes two temporal levels: the days of investi-
> gation that begin with the crime, the days of drama that lead up to it.

The two levels of time entail a metaphysical shift from action to thought that is foreshadowed, in Oedipus's case, by the nature of his encounter with the riddling Sphinx, a monster, but one that can only be defeated by intelligence. The power of the hero's actions in the proairetically dominated folk-tale pattern is replaced by the power of the law. The struggle between hero and monster is replaced by a struggle between a criminal and the law's representative. The heroic adventure is replaced by the inexorable process of justice. The rite of passage is replaced by the theme of morality. And whereas the folk-tale type story is about the acquisition of power and property the second part of the story is about the acquisition of self-knowledge. The popular, oral, folk-tale tradition, with its emphasis on function (in Propp's terms) gives way to a literary genre that depends on the decipherment of clues and suspense for its mode of narration. Todorov describes the work done by narrational codes within detective fiction. Thus, he says, story A tells what really happened and story B tells how the narrator, and so the reader, gets to know about it. He invokes the distinction made by Russian formalist critics between story (fable) and plot (subject):

> In the story there is no inversion of time, actions follow their natural order; in the plot the author can present results before their causes, the end before the beginning.[11]

The plot consists of the orchestrated accumulation of evidence, of clues that have to be found and interpreted, remnants and traces of past action. Memory and the testimony of witnesses must play a crucial part in this process. In *Oedipus Rex*, Oedipus is shown to be a determined investigator, armed at first with the righteousness and the responsibilities of kingship. Later, as a desperate man in a position of power, he investigates with anger and cruelty, especially when his witnesses are poor and defenceless, like the shepherd who rescued him in his infancy. Class position plays ironically with our foreknowledge of Oedipus's own ultimate fate. But it is still the process of his investigation and his knowledge that control narrative development. The act of narration is inseparable from the detective form itself, and the writer, the ultimate literary narrator, controls the readers' knowledge or suspense through the process of the hero's investigation and discovery. It is here that the Oedipus story, once again, both works within a given narrative code and represents a twist, a deviation from a particular composition's scheme (Propp's term). In this case, the detective is himself the criminal. Propp argues that the shift in the chronology of functions in the Oedipus story transforms the tale into a transitional model within the folk-tale and the proairetic code; *Oedipus Rex* takes the detective genre into wider questions of the unconscious. What is at stake on this level of narration is not just the ability of an exceptional man to interpret clues and evidence, but the ability of man to understand the truth of his own history. As Freud says, the play unfolds 'like the process of psycho-analysis itself'. The relationship between the Oedipus myth and psycho-analysis, therefore, lies in its narrative methodology and the meta-physical implications of its narrative form, in addition to the overt content of the story (rivalry with the father and desire for the mother) that first attracted Freud's attention.

I have emphasised the popular, detective structure of the narrative pattern in *Oedipus Rex* rather than its place as literary tragedy to highlight the importance of clues, riddles and enigmas that link Oedipus figuratively with the clues, riddles and enigmas of the unconscious that psychoanalysis deciphers. Teiresias is also a seer, who deciphers riddles, and is linked as a hybrid, a hermaphrodite, with the Sphinx. Oedipus conquers the Sphinx in the final moments of his heroic story; she 'returns' in the shape of Teiresias at the opening of *Oedipus Rex*. Teiresias 'returns' in the image of the blind Oedipus 'seeing' the truth as he exiles himself from the city he won by his victory over the Sphinx. The folk-tale hero's journey is resolved in the material world with material success; the detective undertakes an investigation in pursuit of knowledge in the name of the Law; the hero of *Oedipus Rex* finds himself thrown into an inferno of self-discovery through which he will understand his origins, his fate and, ultimately, have the possibility of redemption. The hero's triumphant apotheosis, achieved with the answer 'man', turns sour and the detective's search for a criminal inaugurates a metaphysical journey. The literal space of the road has been replaced by an abstract journey into the self. The horizontal continuum of the proairetically based plot has changed direction into the self which then must precipitate an excavation into the past. The axis of exploration shifts between space and time. But time attracts figures of space: of the layering of history, on top, as it were, of the spatial layers of geological time.

BELOW THE SURFACE: TIME AND SPACE

Freud described the unconscious in terms of topology, using spatial figures and images to evoke the relation between a surface consciousness and the stuff of repression, hidden from consciousness, that could only be investigated or excavated obliquely. Signs and symptoms bear witness to the continuous presence of psychopathology, and to the working of the unconscious in the present tense, as a living monument to the past, the traumatic experiences of childhood. Things that are concealed from surface consciousness have roots in the past. It is perhaps at least of poetic interest that Freud's world, the second half of the nineteenth century, saw the growth of two cultural phenomena that both bear a relation to these two levels and to the structure of the Oedipus myth as we inherit it. These two phenomena are the development of archaeology and the development of the detective story as a popular literary genre. *The Moonstone* by Wilkie Collins, generally considered to be the first example of the detective genre, was published in 1868. During the 1860s Schliemann excavated Troy. (Freud was born in 1856.) Both the detective story and archaeology dig into lost or concealed worlds; in one case it is the mystery of an urban underworld that is revealed, in the other it is the lost cities of antiquity that are brought to light. The two tropes condense in the contemporary connotations of the Oedipus story and also suggest figures for the topology of the unconscious, a concealed layer in the psyche, and the process of investigation, psychoanalysis, which interprets them.

In his reminiscence of Freud, the Wolf Man says:

> Once we happened to speak of Conan Doyle and his creation Sherlock Holmes. I had thought Freud would have no use for this type of light reading matter and was surprised to find that he had read this author attentively. The fact that circumstantial evidence is useful in psychoanalysis when reconstructing a childhood history may explain Freud's interest in this type of literature.[12]

It is tempting to see the detective story as the myth or legend of the newly constituted industrial cities that had grown up *outside* order. The nether world of the city, seething with bars, prostitutes and criminals, also the uncontrollable presence of the working class, could provide a mythic terrain for scenarios of adventure and constitute a modern space of liminality similar to the no man's land through which the heroes of antiquity travelled. But whereas the ancient or the folk-tale heroes embarked on a linear journey outside the city space, the journey of the urban detective is a descent into a hidden world of what is repressed by bourgeois morality and respectability to decode and decipher signs and restore order through the process of reason. This sense of spatial *mise en scène* is familiar, too, in the Hollywood movie genre *film noir*, and suggests a link between such a descent into a nether world and the hero's rite of passage that condenses the liminal space of adventure and the abstract journey of self discovery:

> What [*film noir* screen-plays] share in adaptation to the screen is the tendency to organise the unfolding of an enigma as a single character's initiation into an alien world; they present a process of psychological upheaval that is manifest in verbal, behavioural, and physiological signs as well as in certain optical/perceptual changes projected onto the environment. It is the *process* of change, the transition, which constitutes the ground of film-noir narrative. Whether or not the 'first story' is suppressed in favour of a narrating investigator there is a

consistent stress on internal transformation – in all its ramifications – incited through participation in a criminal milieu, on the slippage of personal identity and its reassumption in an unintegrated form.[13]

Rites of passage, celebrated in narrative, find an appropriate diegesis, a contemporary scenario for self-discovery and transition. The Oedipus story brings together the two narrative forms to transform achievement through action into self-discovery. This evolution takes the Oedipus model out of a primary emphasis on its immediate content, patricide and incest, and raises formal questions about the way that the signifier of narration affects a story's signified. These images and processes of popular mythology relate, by analogy, to psychoanalysis. The topological space of the city, its dark, after-hours underworld, echoes Freud's topology of the psyche. The journey and its narration parallel the process by which unconscious material is transformed.

The Oedipus story emanated from Mycenae, a civilisation that could barely be discerned beyond the lost years of the Dark Ages (as those centuries would still have seemed to Freud's generation). In its apotheosis as *Oedipus Rex*, the myth became part of the literary legacy of classical, historical Greece, suspended between the timelessness of great literature and remoteness in a historical period that is taken to be the origins of Western civilisation. Freud is well known to have been fascinated to the point of obsession with the remnants of ancient civilisations. He collected antiquities and his visits to Rome and Athens were crucial experiences in his life. Again, the Wolf-Man tells us:

> In the weeks before the end of my analysis, we often spoke of the danger of the patient's feeling too close a tie to the therapist . . . In this connection, Freud was of the opinion that at the end of a treatment, a gift from the patient could contribute, as a symbolic act, to lessening his feeling of gratitude and consequent dependence on the physician. So we agreed that I would give Freud something as a remembrance. As I knew his love for archaeology, the gift I chose for him was a female Egyptian figure, with a mitre-shaped head-dress. Freud placed it on his desk. Twenty years later, looking through a magazine, I saw a picture of Freud at his desk. 'My' Egyptian immediately struck my eye, the figure which for me symbolised my analysis with Freud, who himself called me 'a piece of psycho-analysis'.[14]

Freud used the image provided by the burial of the ancient world as a metaphor for the topology of the unconscious and Pompeii, buried so suddenly by a volcanic eruption, provided him with a particularly vivid example. Analysing Jensen's story *Gradiva*, he was fascinated by the author's use of Pompeii to evoke both the repression and the preservation of childhood desire, its mis-recognition and ultimate excavation. In his notes on his analysis of the Rat Man he says:

> I then made some short observations on the psychological differences between the conscious and the unconscious, and the fact that what was conscious was subject to the process of wearing away, while what was unconscious was relatively unchanging. I illustrated my remarks by pointing at the antiquities standing about in my room. They were, in fact, only objects found in a tomb and their burial had been their preservation. The destruction of Pompeii was only beginning now that it had been dug up.[15]

The detective story is a narrative that carries the hero into another space, a nether world. Exploration of this space depends on a re-telling of events, the investigation of an immediate past that lies within the experience of the characters involved in the drama. This, as argued above, is also the narrative pattern of *Oedipus Rex*. Archaeology depends on the preservation of actual objects in time, and the fossilisation of these objects in a medium that preserves their reality intact. In semiological terms, its signs are indexical. They come to the surface as a challenge to the erosion of time and provide a point of contact with, and traces of, a remote and almost lost epoch. Detection, too, makes use of indexical signs in the traces and clues which have to be interpreted and read to make sense. This leads, once again, to the psychoanalytic process. Lacan takes the analogy with archaeology and its indexical traces one step further:

> [The unconscious] is the censored chapter. But the truth can be rediscovered: usually it has been written down elsewhere.
> Namely:
> – monuments: this is my body. The hysterical nucleus of a neurosis in which the hysterical symptom reveals the structure of a language. Deciphered like an inscription, which once recovered, can without serious loss be destroyed;
> – in archival documents: these are my childhood memories, just as impenetrable as are such documents when I do not know their provenance;
> – in semantic evolution: this corresponds to the stock of words and acceptations of my own particular vocabulary, as it does to my style of life and to my character;
> – in traditions, too, and even in the legends which in a heroicised form, bear my history:
> – and, lastly, in the traces that are inevitably preserved by the

distortions necessitated by linking the adulterated chapter to the
chapters surrounding it, and whose meaning will be established by
my exegesis.[16]

There is an interesting coincidence between the indexical signs cited
by Lacan and those cited by historians as the only means of retrieving
the culture of the Dark Ages of antiquity across cultural amnesia and a
total lack of historical records. These were the traces left by objects
recovered in archaeology, the dialects and forms of language that
persisted though geographically dispersed, and the legends that were
handed on orally through a period of time that had no written language.
The exegesis can only come into being in the final historical narration.
It is obviously this point that interests Lacan:

> What we teach the subject to recognise as his unconscious is his
> history – that is to say, we help him to perfect the present historicisation
> of the facts that have already determined a certain number of the
> historical turning-points in his existence.[17]

So, what is specific about Oedipus, the crucial issue that separates him
from the simple detectives of the whodunit, is the theme of internal
transformation which obliquely relates him to the modern, post-
psychoanalytic, heroes-in-crisis of the *film noir*. The story he investigates
is his own; he is the criminal in his detective story. The evidence and
clues he compiles all pile up against him but also allow him to see his
own history, to go through the process of recognition and understand
'the historical turning-points in his existence'.

Lacan then returns again to antiquity, to the Athenian drama which
he describes as: 'the original myths of the city state and the "material"
through which a nation today learns to read the symbol of destiny on
the march'. He moves away from the question of narration in an
individual analysis to collective fantasies narrated in culture. He has
thus traced a triple relationship: between fossilised indexical evidence
left as remnants of the past, the process of psychoanalysis that interprets
these traces (as practised in relation to individuals) and the collective
construction of history and mythology. In the shift from Freud to these
points of Lacan's, another shift is contained. That is, the shift between
the matter of the Oedipus story as it relates to the Oedipus complex
(the incestuous and murderous fantasies of a small child) and the
question of the structure of narration as a process of recognition both in
an individual analysis and, then, perhaps, in culture. For Lacan, of
course, this is above all an issue of the function of language and the
symbolic, which allows raw, indexical, material to be transformed into
words, to be narrated, and so transformed into something else. This

issue, too, makes a dramatic appearance in Sophocles's second Oedipus play.

BEYOND THE CORE STORY

1 The Ending: The Father's Legacy

After Oedipus left Thebes, the third traumatic departure of his life (he was expelled from Thebes as an infant; he left Corinth in search of his true parentage), he wandered in poverty and great mental and physical suffering, accompanied only by his daughter, Antigone. Sophocles starts the play *Oedipus at Colonus* at the moment when they arrive at a little wood, outside Athens, that is sacred to the Eumenides. Oedipus recognises the place where he is destined to die but is challenged by the local people who see his presence there as sacrilegious. Theseus, the king of Athens, is summoned while the people (the Chorus) question Oedipus and ask his name; it is he who is now subject to investigation and interrogation. When Oedipus finally speaks his name, the people react with the fear and terror combined with fascination that Freud noted in contemporary reactions to *Oedipus Rex*, and that he used as evidence for the universality of the Oedipus complex. Then Ismene arrives, with the news of another oracle, again the third in Oedipus's life (the first precipitated his expulsion from Thebes by his father and then, when it was repeated to him, determined his decision to avoid Corinth and travel from Delphi towards Thebes; it was the second that instructed him to find the murderer of Laius and which sets in motion the investigative process of *Oedipus Rex*). This time the oracle promises that Oedipus will achieve a special, transcendent power at the moment of his death, which he will be able to bestow on the people among whom he chooses to die. The Thebans, therefore, want him back, locked as they are in a war between the two sons, Polyneices besieging with a foreign army the city that is now under the control of Eteocles and their maternal uncle, Creon. The Chorus question Oedipus again. They want to hear his story, the most unspeakable story that they already know by hearsay. ('Your name, old stranger, echoes through the world.') As Oedipus tells the story, the events of his life are repeated for a third time, the events that he first enacted, then re-traced in investigation, he now recounts in his own words.[18] Theseus arrives and Oedipus promises to bestow the 'blessing' of his death on him and his people. Creon arrives and when Oedipus denounces him bitterly, he threatens the two girls until Theseus intervenes to rescue them. Polyneices then arrives also in search of his father's mysterious power and this time Oedipus curses both his sons. Theseus returns and is alone allowed to accompany Oedipus to the moment of his death. He dies in strange circumstances, leaving no body. Finally Antigone takes the decision to go back to Thebes to try to end the fratricidal war between her brothers.

The play has little complex action or narrative structure. It is about death, naming and inheritance. Thebes is falling into primal chaos, torn by fratricidal feud, outside history and lacking government. Athens is at the dawn of civilisation. There is, perhaps, an 'invention of tradition' aspect to Sophocles's last play, written when he was in his nineties, at the end of the glorious fourth century, at a moment when Athens was itself under siege during the Peloponnesian War. Theseus is considered to be the legendary founder of the Athenian state; he organised the legal system, established a constitution and abdicated from the kingship. Oedipus's choice in bestowing his 'blessing' on Athens, in preference to his own tragic city, takes on a particular cultural significance. From a Lacanian perspective, the story of Oedipus at Colonus can be interpreted as the story of the coming into being of the resolution of the Oedipus complex around the Name of the Father, the Law, and the Symbolic Order. Oedipus performed the different roles in the inter-generational drama out of phase by a generation. As a man, in the role of child, he acted out the Oedipal desire; then as child and father, he performs the act of symbolic castration, blinding himself and stripping himself of all power and possessions (usurped from his father). At Colonus, he arrives to meet his death purged and cleansed by suffering. At the end of *Oedipus Rex* he was polluted but now he has undergone yet another psychic metamorphosis:

> Don't reject me as you look into the horror
> of my face, these sockets raked and blind.
> I come as someone sacred, someone filled
> with piety and power.[19]

His power is no longer the material power of property and possessions or even the abstract power of the king as representative of the law who can solve mysteries in the Name of the Law. His power emanates from his unique identity as the emblematic embodiment of Oedipal desire; action transmuted by narration, the flesh, as it were, made Word. The Athenian legacy, personified by Theseus, confirms that the qualities of culture and civilisation that complement the incest taboo are there in Oedipus's gift of power. Realised by the old man, the child's experience is visibly born into culture and bequeathed to civilisation. This myth of origins, in which the incest taboo is an essential corollary to the law of social organisation, is central to both Lévi-Strauss's and Lacan's concepts of the origins of culture;

> The Oedipus is articulated in the forms of social institutions and
> of language of which the members themselves are unconscious –

unconscious as to their meaning and, above all, to their origin. The Oedipal unconscious is homologous with all these symbolic structures. The Oedipus is the drama of the social being who must become a subject and who can only do so by internalising the social rules, by entering on an equal footing into the register of the symbolic, of Culture and of language . . . a development which presupposes the transition from nature into culture . . . we can say that the Oedipus is the unconscious articulation of a human world of culture and language; it is the very structure of the unconscious forms of society.[20]

In an exquisitely mapped article, to which I cannot do justice here, Shoshana Felman argues a parallel development between *Oedipus Rex/Oedipus at Colonus* and *The Interpretation of Dreams/Beyond the Pleasure Principle*. In each case, the first work is about sexuality and Oedipal desire and the second is the compulsion to repeat and the death drive. It is the compulsion to repeat lived experience that generates symbolisation and consequently myth and narrative.

Oedipus *is born*, through the assumption of his death (of his radical self-expropriation) *into the life of his history*. *Oedipus at Colonus* is about the transformation of Oedipus' story into history: it does not tell the drama, it is *about the telling* and re-telling of the drama. It is, in other words, about the *historicisation* of Oedipus' destiny, through the *symbolisation* – the transformation into speech – of Oedipal desire.[21]

She also argues that there is a third transition in the sequence: the shift from Freud to Lacan in the history of the psychoanalytic movement. All these transitions represent a transmutation of Oedipal desire in which the place of the object of desire is taken by questions of language and symbolisation. (Lacan: 'What we teach the subject to recognise as his unconscious in his history'.) Shoshana Felman argues that the generative force of psychoanalysis is characterised by the compulsion to repeat, itself characteristic of the death drive. In analysis, the analysand repeats, in words and narrative, lived experience and past events: 'What is then, psychoanalysis if not, precisely a life-usage of the death instinct – a practical productive usage of the compulsion to repeat . . .'.

Peter Brooks has used *Beyond the Pleasure Principle* most illuminatingly to discuss the impact of the compulsion to repeat and the death drive on narrative. Repetition offers mastery over a state of loss and anxiety (as Freud noticed in his famous example of the game that he interpreted as a child's symbolisation, by means of a toy, of his mother's absence and imagined return):

An event gains meaning by its repetition, which is both a recall of an

earlier moment and a variation on it . . . Repetition creates a return
in the text, a doubling back. We cannot say whether this is a return
to, or a return of: for instance, a return to origins or a return of the
repressed.[22]

And:

We have a curious situation in which two principles of forward
movement operate upon one another so as to create a retard . . . This
might be consubstantial with the fact that a repetition can take
us both backward and forward because these terms have become
reversible: the end is a time before the beginning.[23]

The Oedipus story is punctuated with foretellings, tellings and re-
tellings: the oracles foretell, Teiresias tells, at the beginning of *Oedipus
Rex*, the story that Oedipus then has to piece together for himself, and
that he then re-tells to the Chorus at Colonus. The story itself existed
as a myth before its literary re-working by Sophocles, so it would have
been well known to the Athenian audience to whom the play would
have necessarily seemed a re-telling. The story has since been used and
re-told many times. Lévi-Strauss makes this point: 'Not only Sophocles
but Freud himself should be included among the recorded versions of
the Oedipus myth on a par with earlier or seemingly more authentic
versions'.[24] In the light of Lévi-Strauss's interpretation of the Oedipus
myth as about belief in the autochthonous origins of man, he strangely
omits the hero's 'rebirth' in the wilderness, shared with many other
heroes such as Romulus, Moses, and Cyrus and commented on by
Freud in 'Moses and Monotheism'. The significance of the act of telling
and of narrational patterns in the Oedipus story confirms the importance,
dismissed by structuralism, of narrative in myth. Terence Turner has
criticised Lévi-Strauss's analysis of the Oedipus myth to draw attention
to and reinstate the contribution of temporal structures ('the syntactic
structures of narrative sequence') to the meaning of myth, alongside
the component elements, the 'bundles' that are central to Lévi-Strauss's
structural analysis.

Myths do indeed provide synchronic models of diachronic processes,
but they do this directly at the level of organisation as temporal
sequences, through the correspondence between their sequential
patterns and aspects of the diachronic processes they 'model'. The
unique mythical relationship between synchrony and diachrony,
between historical events and timeless structure, must be sought in
the way myth itself patterns time in the syntactic structure of its
narrative; that is, in Lévi-Strauss' own words 'in the story which it
tells'.[25]

He brings out the link between narrative sequence as a structural element and the alternation between change and stasis in 'traditional narrative genres', in which a synchronic timelessness is disrupted by a sequentially patterned series of events, a diachronic disordering of stasis.

These observations have a bearing on what might be called the politics of narrative closure. Shoshana Felman argues that Lacan identified with the exiled Oedipus, personally because of his expulsion from the International Psychoanalytic Association, and he identified with *Oedipus at Colonus*, theoretically because of its relation to *Beyond the Pleasure Principle* (the text that orthodoxy could not absorb) and because it tells, not a mythic story but the story of the coming into being of a myth. This has some bearing on the openness of the implicit narration in psychoanalytic practice:

> The psychoanalytic myth derives its theoretical effectiveness not from its truth value, but from its truth-encounter with the other; from its capacity for passing through the other; from its openness that is to an expropriating passage of one insight through another; of one story through another; the passage for example of Oedipus the king through Oedipus at Colonus; of the passage of the myth of 'Instinct' through this later and more troubling myth of 'Death'.[26]

Narrative is outside history but related to it. Terence Turner's emphasis on change through disorder in narrative raises the problem of change in lived political narrative. The potential for change in the disordered middle is in dialectical opposition to the timeless stasis of the beginning and end. There is a similar 'political poetics' inherent in Peter Brooks's return to, 'return of' and 'the end is before the beginning'; and also in Shoshana Felman's perception of the compulsion to repeat and (what she calls) the 'uncertainty principle' as safeguards against new movements, such as psychoanalysis, fossilising into the timeless stasis of institutional authority. For a final word something of this aesthetic of permanent narration is present in François Roustang's observations on the difficulty of maintaining change within the psychoanalytic institution:

> If one wants to be an analyst, one must analyse one's own transference to Freud, one must question his writings, which are not to be taken as the word of the Gospel but as a place where one's fantasies and desires are caught and projected along with Freud's. In this way, the trust we place in advance (*im Voraus*) in his works should become, through deferred action, both the uncertainty and the strength of our discourse.[27]

One strange aspect of the Oedipus story is its lack of clear resolution in the normal narrative sense. The core story contained in Sophocles's *Oedipus Rex* ends with yet another departure, a return to the journey and liminality, threatening the security of every 'and then they lived happily ever after'. *Oedipus at Colonus* ends with the death of the hero and the birth of his Symbolic Order. It is as if the presence of death, the ultimate point of timeless stasis that Peter Brooks has shown to be lying behind the drive to an ending, must be neutralised by the timeless stasis of paternal authority. There is, perhaps, a fundamental tension between the openness of narrative transformation and the censorship imposed by this authority. Of course, both lie within the Symbolic Order. But the father's place in the Lacanian Oedipus complex tips the balance in the paternal direction; the Symbolic Order is born under his aegis. Or so it seems. Just before Oedipus dies, Sophocles introduces an incident that dramatically raises a ghost from the distant past, the compulsion to repeat comes to the fore in a violent return of the repressed.

2   The Beginning: The Son's Inheritance

Just as he had been cursed, just as his father had tried to murder him, Oedipus curses his own sons and condemns them to kill each other.

> Die!
> Die by your own blood brother's hand – die –
> killing the very man who drove you out!
> So I curse your life out!
> I call on the dark depths of Tartarus brimming hate,
> where all our fathers lie, to hale you home!
> I cry to the great goddesses of this grove!
> I cry to the great god War
> who planted that terrible hatred in your hearts!
> Go! – with all my curses thundering in your ears –
> go and herald them out to every man in Thebes
> and all your loyal comrades under arms! Cry out
> that Oedipus has bequeathed these last rights,
> these royal rights of birth to both his sons![28]

Quite apart from the question of the justice of Oedipus's attitude to his sons, or their previous behaviour to him, two elements return here, at the end of the story, that vividly invoke its beginning. First of all, Oedipus continues the curse on his family line and, second, the curse reminds us that he had previously narrowly escaped being killed by his own father, first as a new born infant, and then, in the fateful encounter with Laius at the crossroad. He claims many times that the old man in the carriage would have killed him outright had he not defended himself ('the man I murdered – he'd have murdered me!'). Not only, then, does Oedipus's approaching death bring to mind his father's attempts to kill him, thus evoking Laius's presence in the story, but his father's character returns to haunt Oedipus's relation to his own sons.

Oedipus at Colonus is based on the legend that Sophocles's own birthplace, Colonus, was the place where Oedipus had died. The events and narrative structure are more literary than mythic, so that the play, in being less closely tied to pre-existing myth, can be self-conscious about how myth grows and works. In contrast the pre-history of the Oedipus story remains extremely primitive and has been systematically ignored in both classical tragedy and later tradition. Most commentators, including Freud, leave out the question of why Oedipus and Laius and Jocasta were cursed, and Laius's responsibility for bringing the curse down on them.

Laius's father, Labdakos, died during his son's infancy. The throne was usurped, and later usurped again and Laius was driven into exile. He was given hospitality by King Pelops of Sparta, where he fell in love with the King's beautiful young son Chrysippos. He kidnapped the boy, raped him and caused his death. (It is argued that the outrageousness of this act lay, not in the act of homosexuality, but in the violation of hospitality.) King Pelops then cursed Laius, saying that if he should have a son, the son would kill him. Laius made up his mind never to have children, but one night he got drunk, and slept with his wife Jocasta, who conceived. Later Hera sent the Sphinx to ravage Thebes in retribution for Laius's crime and also, no doubt, to set the scene for Oedipus's victorious arrival in the city.

According to this pre-history of the myth, Laius's aggressive and violent homosexual act is the latent cause of the curse and Oedipus's later suffering. Chrysippos's experience with Laius can act as a displacement on to another young boy from a primal anxiety in son-to-father relations; the repression of this aspect of the myth then becomes a repression of the father's fault in the Oedipal scenario. Marie Balmary explains Freud's oversight in terms of his need to repress the Laius-like qualities of his own father Jacob Freud. She argues that the logical consequence of this (personal) repression was the (theoretical) repression of the father's fault and Freud's decision to 'exonerate' the father of seduction and 'incriminate' the child's fantasy of seduction.[29] It is known that Freud adopted the fantasy theory of seduction during the period of mourning over his own father's death.

This scotomisation of the complementary Oedipus complex is probably rooted in the adult's deep-seated need to place all responsibility for the Oedipus Complex on the child, and to ignore wherever possible those parental attitudes which stimulate the infant's Oedipal tendencies. That this deliberate scotoma is rooted in the charateristic authoritarian atmosphere of the nineteenth-century family is suggested by Freud's own thoughts on the aetiology of hysteria.[30]

Without attempting to solve this problem of primary fault or guilt, the narrative and narrational structures that are basic to the Oedipus myth can recast it so as to avoid a direct choice between fact and fiction or between reality and fantasy. Laius's crime is literally pre-Oedipal; it preexists the life story of his child whose tragic history transmutes the horror generated by the primal father into the father represented by the Symbolic Order in the person of Theseus.

The Oedipus myth, in its transition from the primal father to the father of the Symbolic Order, also shifts the question of fault or guilt out of the mythic terrain of phylogenesis and places it within the psyche, within fantasy and thus also within culture and the possibility of resolution within culture.

The assumption of guilt on the part of the child is essential to the shift in formal and narrational structure in the Oedipus story. Whereas Laius, the guilty father, exists in a sphere of pure action, outside self-consciousness, the Oedipal trajectory gives Oedipus the metaphysical power to reconstitute his own history through the process of narration. This ability to *tell* and transcend is the crucial constitutive aspect of the myth, and is more important a human attribute than unconscious guilt or innocence. It is here that the process of narration in psychoanalysis and the collective compulsion to repeat, that generates narrative in culture, come together in the Oedipus story.

The story of Oedipus's life moves through stages (from victim to royal child, from wanderer to hero-king, from defilement to catharsis, from sanctification to symbolic authority) that span the chasm separating Laius from Theseus. But Laius represents something that returns like a ghostly apparition when his son curses his own sons. In a criss-cross of time and space, from the lower depths of the mind and out of the mists of the past, the primal father erupts like Dennis Hopper's Frank in *Blue Velvet*. Frank is both the sadistic father of the primal scene, and a fearfully erotic father whose homosexual aggression threatens the hero/child with sexual passivity and death. Frank's world comes into its own at night, with the drugs, alcohol, bars and brothels that make up the criminal underbelly concealed by small town America's homely, law-abiding exterior. Jeffrey's descent into the lower depths is like the hero's journey in the folk-tale or *film-noir* that marks a rite of passage; he emerges on the other side as a mature man who has won the right to marry the daughter of the representative of the law. Frank leaves a legacy to the newly mature initiate into the patriarchal order. The end of the movie suggests that he will live on, a point of repression and attraction and fear, within Jeffrey's psyche, waiting for the moment of return. The lower depths of the psyche are condensed with the imagery of the lower depths of the town, inhabited by personifications that are displaced from childhood traumas, the primal fantasies of the Oedipus complex, the castration complex and the primal scene.

Patriarchy is founded on rites and rights of inheritance and exchange of women that neutralise a neurotic, violent father/son rivalry and establish the basis for a symbolic order. But perhaps this symbolic depends shakily on the repression of the primal, pre-Oedipal father so that culture continues to be tinged with violence and institutions that claim to be guardians of the law and defence against chaos are maintained by the violence that lies behind patriarchal authority. The image of the primal *father* confuses the neat polarisation between pre- and post-Oedipal that reproduces a polarisation between mother and father. Julia Kristeva has discussed the phenomenon of horror and disgust as a culture returning under the aegis of a pre-Oedipal mother, a body without boundary, 'an unspeakable'. Perhaps even more 'unspeakable', hardly even achieving symbolisation in the collective fantasy of popular culture, is the threat embodied by the primal father. Perhaps even his lack of cultural recognition is significant, returning rather in symptomatic social and sexual anxieties that afflict our society. Perhaps desire for and fear of a powerful mother and the misogyny it generates conceals something even more disturbing, desire for and fear of a violent father. Perhaps it is the 'unspeakable' ghost of Laius that haunts relations between men, generating homophobic anxieties and an attraction bonded by physical violence represented by Frank's relationship to Jeffrey.

Looking at the Oedipal myth in detail it is remarkable to what extent it is about father/son relations and how marginal the feminine is to the story. Even though the incest theme can suggest a residual memory of ritual and inheritance that pre-date the fully fledged patriarchal order, desire for the mother is more significant as a symptom of father/son rivalry. However, the story's narrative structure and the importance of investigation and telling in the story itself offers a Utopian promise, a pointer towards the transformative power of telling one's own story and the social function of popular culture as the narrativisation of collective fantasy. Recently, feminism through critical and analytical work has been attempting to inflect the way in which our society narrativises itself. In the process, feminist consciousness can affect the discourse of patriarchy and upset the polarisation between masculinity and femininity that keeps its order in place. Shoshana Felman quotes Lacan:

To bring the subject to *recognise* and *name* his desire, this is the nature of the efficacious action of analysis. But it is not a question of recognising something that would have been there already – a given – ready to be captured. In naming it the subject creates, gives rise to something new, makes something new present in the world.[31]

Certainty is the other side of the coin to anxiety. Curiosity and the riddling spirit of the Sphinx activate questions that open up the closures of repression and maintain the force of an 'uncertainty principle'. As Teresa de Lauretis points out at the end of her chapter on Oedipus in *Alice Doesn't*, the story is still in the making. The Sphinx and her riddle are still waiting for a 'beyond'.

Notes

1. This paper has grown out of work initiated and discussed in a graduate seminar in the Department of Cinema Studies, New York University, during the fall semester 1986. I enjoyed and benefited from the seminar enormously. I would like to than the following students who worked with me: Vicky Abrash, Parag Amladi, Catherine Benamou, Sarah Berry, Leo Charney, Manohla Dargis, John Johnson, Alexandra Juhasz, Barbara Kassen-Taranto, Irma Klein, Fay Plant, Doug Riblet, Vince Rocchio, Annabelle Sheehan, Shelley Stamp, Chuck Stephens, Michael Taslitz, Andreas Timmer, Christie Timms, Doug Troyan, Debbie Wulinger.
2. S. Freud, 'The Interpretation of Dreams', *Standard Edition*, vol. iv (London: Hogarth Press) pp. 261–2.
3. S. Freud, 'On Creative Writing and the Ego', *Standard Edition*, vol. ix, p. 148.
4. 'The Interpretation of Dreams', p. 217n.
5. Carl Schorske in his book *Fin de Siècle Vienna* (New York: Alfred A Knopf, 1980) discusses the intricate web of condensation and displacement at work in Freud's dreams about his father, and the political significance they contain: particularly, Freud's reaction to his father's lack of revolutionary spirit in the face of anti-semitism. 'This struck me as unheroic conduct on the part of the big, strong man who was holding the little boy by the hand. I contrasted this scene with one that fitted my feelings better: the scene in which Hannibal's father, Hamilcar Barca, made this boy swear before the household altar to take vengeance on the Romans' ('The Interpretation of Dreams', p. 197). This point brings out the possibility of identification in rebellion between father and son in the face of social, economic and political oppression.
6. Vladimir Propp, 'Oedipus in the Light of Folk-Tale', *Oedipus, a Folk Lore Case-Book* (ed. Lowell Edmunds and Alan Dundas) (New York and London: Garland Publishing Inc., 1984).
7. Teresa de Lauretis: *Alice Doesn't* (Bloomington: Indiana University Press, 1984) p. 116.

8. Sophocles, 'Oedipus the King', *The Three Theban Plays*, trans. Robert Fagles (Harmondsworth: Penguin Classics, 1982) p. 182.
9. Ibid., p. 167.
10. Ibid., p. 183.
11. Tzvetan Todorov, 'Detective Fiction', *Poetics of Prose* (Ithaca: Cornell University Press, 1977).
12. Muriel Gardiner (ed.), *The Wolf-Man and Sigmund Freud* (London: Hogarth Press, 1972) p. 146.
13. Paul Arthur, *Shadows on the Mirror: Film Noir and Cold War America 1945–57* (New York: Praeger, 1989).
14. *The Wolf-Man and Sigmund Freud*, pp. 149–50.
15. S. Freud, 'Two Case Histories', *Standard Edition*, vol. x, pp. 176–7.
16. Jacques Lacan, 'The function and field of speech and language in psychoanalysis', *Ecrits. A Selection* (London: Tavistock Press, 1977) p. 50.
17. Ibid., p. 52.
18. Sophocles, 'Oedipus at Colonus', *The Three Theban Plays*, pp. 295–7 and pp. 314–17.
19. Ibid., p. 300.
20. Anika Lemaire, *Jacques Lacan* (London: Routledge & Kegan Paul, 1970) pp. 91–2.
21. Shoshana Felman, 'Beyond Oedipus. The Specimen Story of Psychoanalysis', *MLN Comparative Literature*, vol. 98, no. 5 (Baltimore: Johns Hopkins University Press, 1983) pp. 1029–30.
22. Peter Brooks, *Reading for the Plot* (New York: Vintage, 1985) pp. 99–100.
23. Ibid., p. 103.
24. Claude Lévi-Strauss, 'The Structural Study of Myth'.
25. Terence Turner, 'Oedipus: Time and Structure in Narrative Form', *Forms of Symbolic Action* (American Ethnological Society, 1969) p. 32.
26. Shoshana Felman, 'Beyond Oedipus', p. 1045.
27. François Ronstang: *Dire Mastery* (Baltimore: Johns Hopkins University Press, 1982) p. 21.
28. 'Oedipus at Colonus', *The Three Theban Plays*, p. 365.
29. Marie Balmary, *Psycho-analysing Psycho-analysis* (Baltimore: Johns Hopkins University Press, 1982).
30. George Devereux, 'Why Oedipus killed Laius', *Oedipus: a Folk Lore Case-Book*, p. 216.
31. Shoshana Felman, 'Beyond Oedipus', p. 1026.